KV-386-314

Ruling Passion

The Erotics of Statecraft in Platonic Political Philosophy

WALLER R. NEWELL

ROWMAN & LITTLEFIELD PUBLISHERS, INC.
Lanham • Boulder • New York • Oxford

ROWMAN & LITTLEFIELD PUBLISHERS, INC.

Published in the United States of America
by Rowman & Littlefield Publishers, Inc.
4720 Boston Way, Lanham, Maryland 20706
http://www.rowmanlittlefield.com

12 Hid's Copse Road
Cumnor Hill, Oxford OX2 9JJ, England

KING ALFRED'S COLLEGE
WINCHESTER

321·07
NEW

Copyright © 2000 by Rowman & Littlefield Publishers, Inc.

All rights reserved. No part of this publication may be reproduced,
stored in a retrieval system, or transmitted in any form or by any
means, electronic, mechanical, photocopying, recording, or otherwise,
without the prior permission of the publisher.

British Library Cataloguing in Publication Information Available

Library of Congress Cataloging-in-Publication Data

Newell, Waller R.
    Ruling passion : the erotics of statecraft in platonic political philosophy / Waller
R. Newell.
        p. cm.
    Includes bibliographical references and index.
    ISBN 0-8476-9726-6 (alk. paper) — ISBN 0-8476-9727-4 (pbk. : alk. paper)
        1. Plato—Contributions in political science.   2. Civil society.   3. Despotism.
    4. Sexual excitement.   5. Sublimation (Psychology).   I. Title.

JC71.P62 N48 2000
321'.07—dc21

                                                                99-058566

Printed in the United States of America

♾ ™The paper used in this publication meets the minimum requirements of American
National Standard for Information Sciences—Permanence of Paper for Printed Library
Materials, ANSI/NISO Z39.48-1992.

Ruling Passion

KA 0260440 X

Contents

Acknowledgments

I thought about and wrote this book over a period of years, and I am deeply grateful for the fellowships and grants that enabled me to do so. Fellowships at the National Humanities Center in Research Triangle Park, North Carolina, and the Woodrow Wilson International Center for Scholars in Washington, D.C., provided me with an ideal balance of solitude and conversation while I wrote the first drafts. I was also generously assisted by a National Endowment for the Humanities Fellowship for University Teachers, and by grants from the Lynde and Harry Bradley Foundation, the Earhart Foundation, and Carleton University.

I am indebted to a number of former teachers and colleagues (happily sometimes the same people) for conversations that stimulated my work on this book. They include my first teachers of political philosophy and friends and colleagues of later years: the late and still missed Allan Bloom, as well as Charles H. Fairbanks, Jr., and Thomas L. Pangle. Special thanks are also due to Stanley Rosen for his encouragement about the central thesis of this book, as well as for much other instructive and pleasant contact, and to Charles Griswold for several excellent Platonic conversations at the Wilson Center.

In addition, I want to thank a number of other colleagues for their useful criticisms and shared enthusiasm, including Henry Higuera (who provided thoughtful advice about an early draft of chapter 1), Leon Craig, Robert Goldberg, Clifford Orwin, Ronald Beiner, Timothy Fuller, Michael Palmer, Peter C. Emberley, Tom Darby, David Halperin, Peter J. Ahrensdorf, and D. Gregory MacIsaac. Above all, I am grateful to my wife and fellow scholar, Jacqueline Etherington Newell, for her constant wise and meticulous advice.

Finally, it is a pleasure to thank my students at Carleton University for the privilege of teaching them Plato over the last twelve years, an experience in which I always received at least as much as I gave. It was a delight to be able to unfold the interpretations that eventually became parts of this book to such gifted and spirited young people.

Introduction

A Platonic Perspective on Eros, Tyranny, and Statesmanship

The purpose of this book is to explore the meaning of *erōs,* tyranny, and statesmanship, and their relationship to one another, in some important works of Platonic political philosophy. My central premise is this. For Plato, tyranny is a misunderstanding of the true meaning of human satisfaction. Its cure is the sublimation of the passions in the pursuit of moral and intellectual virtues grounded in the natural order of the cosmos, solicited by the requirements of a just and moderate statesmanship. Specifically, Plato sees tyranny as a misguided longing for erotic satisfaction that can be corrected by the education of eros toward the proper objects of its passion: civic virtue and philosophy. Philosophically guided statesmanship is thus an irreducible combination of sound policy and sound psychology.

I explore this premise through essays on the *Gorgias,* the *Symposium,* and the *Republic.*[1] Each of these studies stands to a large degree on its own, and each can be read independently of the others. But they are linked by a taxonomy of what I term primordial and transcendental political longing. Primordial political longing is the time-bound, self-conscious, and aggressive dimension of political existence, rooted in the passion of *thumos,* or spirit. Transcendental longing, on the other hand, is the desire to escape the boundaries of selfhood through union with the beautiful and lasting. It is rooted in the passion of eros. As I hope to show, for Plato, honor and love—rooted in thumos and eros respectively—are the two main paths to sound and satisfying statesmanship. These paths overlap to some degree, but they also diverge over crucial issues of morality and character.[2]

Chapters 1 and 2 explore Socrates' encounter with Callicles in the *Gorgias,* and how it illuminates some important aspects of Plato's critique of the Sophists and pre-Socratics. The problem of Callicles forms a kind of leitmotif for the studies in this book. I begin with it, end with it, and keep it in view throughout. As a lover of the boy Demos and the identically named Athenian *dēmos,* or majority, Callicles conflates his expectations from political eminence with the kind of direct erotic pleasure one ordinarily expects from a personal attachment.[3] Because he

1

dreams of possessing the city like a triumphant lover, I see Callicles as Plato's exemplar of the tyrannically inclined personality in its pristine emergence, prior to any redirection by philosophy or a philosophically grounded education. The foreground aim of Platonic statecraft is to enlist ambitious, able, and energetic men like Callicles in the service of the common good, by convincing them that their longings for both honor and pleasure will ultimately better be fulfilled by civic virtue than by tyranny, on the levels of both public and private friendship. I examine the *Symposium* and *Republic* as two extended accounts of statesmanship that might appeal to an ambitious individual like Callicles. The accounts are related in many ways, but they are also very different, perhaps irreconcilable, in others. Each appeals in the main to one of the two paths to transcendence I have sketched. In chapter 3, I discuss the *Symposium* as the erotic path to transcendence. Chapters 4 and 5 examine the *Republic* for the other path, the notion of a civic education rooted in the thumotic part of the soul that makes its appeal to the citizenry primarily through their sense of honor.[4]

Of the two paths to civic and psychic wholeness, I regard the erotic one as fundamental in the sense that eros entails and explains thumos, while the reverse is not the case. Moreover, in my view, the Platonic emphasis on eros as the source of some of the soul's worst depredations and best potentialities for civic virtue and philosophy constitutes an essential difference between Plato's political philosophy and the major schools of modern political thought. In the rest of this introduction, I want to set forth my general grounds for these assertions.

Eros includes, but is not reducible to, sexual desire, for which there are other, more precise terms in ancient Greek. As interpreted by Plato, eros is the longing for union with the beautiful, for which the Greek word means the same as the noble (*to kalon*). Eros is therefore at once the strongest of passions in the individual and so structured as to involve us necessarily with others—friends, family, lovers, and fellow citizens—for its satisfaction. The most famous Platonic depiction of eros is Diotima's Ladder in the *Symposium,* where the longing for wholeness is directed, in ascending order, toward procreation, public life, and philosophy (*Symposium* 201a–212a). The longing for the noble or beautiful is, as Plato interprets it, at once the desire to possess it as one's own and, through possessing what is most perfect, whole, and lasting, to escape the bonds of mortality, of one's "ownness" (what Nietzsche termed one's "cursed ipissimosity") in union with the immortal.

Accordingly, the purpose of the sexual union between man and woman is procreation, because children are a palpable, straightforward effort to perpetuate oneself and one's union with the beloved past a single lifespan. Political eros is more complex and sublime. Here, the "offspring" is some noble project, the service of justice and the common good, in cooperation with one's fellow lovers of virtue. One may gain immortality through the fame of this cooperative enterprise. By joining our beloved in, or educating the beloved toward, the pursuit of a noble public life, we signify that the beauty that attracts us to the beloved is of a higher excellence than mere physical beauty. At the same time, we hope to make ourselves more appealing, more worthy of love in the estimation of the beloved, by engaging in an honorable public life.

The double meaning of *to kalon* as noble and beautiful suggests the immediate unity of what we moderns tend to distinguish, and often wish we could avoid distinguishing—the unity of virtue and happiness.[5] Eros properly directed and fulfilled intertwines the rigor and self-discipline of moral duty with the wholeness and repose of a life well and graciously lived, each restraining and enlivening the other. However, the Platonic understanding of eros adds to this reciprocal unity of duty and satisfaction the fact that, as mortals, we cannot finally escape our "cursed ipissimosity." We long for transcendence. But, like greedy lovers, we want this perfection in the mode of exclusive possession and mastery, which contradicts the longing to transcend our selfhood. Thus, the erotic relationship is not effortless bliss. It always already contains its own implicit conflict between domination and happiness, between analysis and resolution, between self-assertion and self-forgetting. As Diotima sums up this tension between mortality and eternality, "eros wants the good to be one's own forever" (*Symposium* 206a).

This sums up the human dilemma, Platonically speaking. The good cannot be one's own, cannot be owned. It cannot be some individual's property or exclusive possession. But at the same time, we cannot transcend the love of our own without first experiencing the love of our own. As Socrates tells Callicles, we will never know what it means to care for our fellow citizens as a statesman if we have not first learned what it means to care for a single human being (*Gorgias* 515a–d). Accordingly, eros is at once the source of unity and discord in human life, of shared admiration and jealous indignation, of cooperation and competition. This is because eros unites us in the admiration of a good that each person wants to possess exclusively and that no one can permanently possess. In experiencing eros, therefore, we experience the possibility of both political community and tyrannical selfishness, which means to say that the pursuit of erotic satisfaction immediately entails the possibility of injustice and the need for justice. This joint emergence of love and conflict is playfully enacted in the *Symposium* itself, where the philosopher Socrates and the man of action Alcibiades admire, and compete for the affections of, Agathon (whose name means "[the] good"). As I will argue, this playful surface has a lethal undertow that helps explain the open clash of justice and eros in the *Republic,* where eros must be expelled from the education and psychology of the civic-spirited.[6]

When our absorption in the object of longing gives way to a consciousness of our failure to attain it or anxiety about keeping it for ourselves, eros shades into what Plato terms spirit (thumos)—the seat of anger, courage, and zeal in the soul.[7] The spirited man is the revealer of the gods, whom he calls into being to lend his own suffering or frustration the significance of a cosmic opponent, as when Achilles battles the river-god or swears vengeance against Apollo (*Republic* 391a–b).[8] The spirited man can be subversive of civic morality when, like

Leontius in the *Republic,* he is drawn by his taste for conflict to contemplate morbidly and masochistically the crimes and violence on which a lawful society may be distantly founded (439e–440a). Like Polus and Callicles, he may feel he has to aim for political mastery out of a fear that he will otherwise be tyrannized over by a more ruthless competitor (*Gorgias* 468e–469c, 521c). What is common to these manifestations of thumos is that the disjunction between our longings and their goals hurls us back on ourselves, with increased feelings of vulnerability and fear, or anger and belligerence. Spiritedness roars forth when eros is thwarted. Callicles, who has an erotic passion for Demos and the Athenian *dēmos,* loses his temper when Socrates likens his position (politically and personally) to a catamite's. Before that, his mood is one of confidence in his own capacities and of selfless admiration for the even greater "natural master" who soars above all conventional morality (494e–495a). As I will suggest through the case of Callicles, the tension built into eros between the longing for transcendence and the desire for exclusive possession and mastery is, for Plato, the key to understanding the phenomenon of tyrannical ambition—and also the key to the possibility of its cure.

I emphasize *possibility,* for it is no more than that. In all three dialogues, the prospect of such a cure hinges on the harmonious subordination of honor to wisdom. But there is much evidence in the *Gorgias, Symposium,* and *Republic* to make us question whether wisdom and civic virtue are intrinsically related objects of the soul's longing, or at any rate seamlessly related. Much of the time, moreover, eros and thumos appear to be at war with one another for predominance over the soul. In the conclusion, I will examine the cumulative plausibility of the Socratic cure for tyranny based on a considered assessment of the three dialogues. For the moment, however, I want to emphasize Plato's contention that, whatever the difficulties, perhaps the impossibility, of attaining complete union with the noble (and I will examine a number of them), it makes sense at the level of a descriptive phenomenology of politics to characterize human longing in this way. For it is here that the contrast with modern approaches to the phenomenon of civic life, and to political morality generally, is most striking.

Our categories for understanding political actors often require us to choose, or lean toward, one of two equally incomplete notions: that political actors are motivated either by a disinterested devotion to universal justice, or by a desire for personal power, wealth, and status regardless of whatever rhetoric they may employ in public. Two of the chief philosophical sources for these characterizations are (respectively) Kant and Hobbes.[9] But for Plato, political morality is always an interaction of personal motive and public purpose, an interaction that cannot be reduced to either of its poles without dissolving the phenomenon. Hence, political morality cannot be derived either from Kantian altruism or Hobbesian egoism alone.[10] It emerges from a welter of public and private contexts, and is always a mixture of justice and satisfaction. The public goals pursued by citizens will be shaped by the traits of their characters. But the goals themselves will solicit a certain type of personality and shape its traits, in turn modifying the pursuit of the goals. Diotima's

Ladder is a continuum of desires ranked according to the goodness and nobility of their objects in the world—a beauty that mediates civic virtue and public honor. If one can be educated to ascend this ladder from sexual union to the higher unions, tyrannical desires for bodily pleasures and unmerited recognition will be assimilated by the noble, rechanneled into the honor a citizen derives from serving the common good. This understanding of political eros neither cooperates with the desires in the Hobbesian manner, nor represses them in the Kantian manner. Rather, it attempts to satisfy them while—and through—elevating them.

NOTES

1. Unless otherwise indicated, translations of passages from the *Gorgias* and *Symposium* are my own. In the case of the *Republic,* I use the Bloom translation, occasionally amended (New York: Basic Books, 1968).The Greek texts I use are: Plato, *Gorgias,* a revised text with introduction and commentary by E. R. Dodds (Oxford: Oxford University Press, 1979); Plato, *The Symposium of Plato,* edited with introduction, critical notes, and commentary by R. G. Bury (Cambridge: W. Heffer and Sons, 1932); and Plato, *The Republic of Plato,* in two volumes, with critical notes, commentary, and appendices by James Adam (Cambridge: Cambridge University Press, 1920). Citations of Platonic texts are by Stephanus number. Greek terms are italicized upon first appearance, thereafter roman. Greek terms are transliterated unless there is a well known English equivalent (e.g., eros).

2. On interpreting thumos as an existential stance toward the world, consider Paul Ricoeur, *Fallible Man,* trans. Charles Kelbley (Chicago: Henry Regnery, 1965), 161–163, 184–185. On the interrelatedness of thumos and eros, see Thomas Pangle, "The Political Psychology of Religion in Plato's *Laws,"* American Political Science Review 70, no. 4 (December 1976): 1059–1077. For a discussion of Platonic eros, see Stanley Rosen, "The Role of Eros in Plato's Republic," in *The Quarrel between Philosophy and Poetry* (New York: Routledge, 1993, 102–118.

3. On the erotic root of the tyrannical personality, consider Leo Strauss, *On Tyranny* (Ithaca: Cornell University Press, 1968), 90–93. See also W. R. Newell, "Tyranny and the Science of Ruling in Xenophon's *Education of Cyrus,"* Journal of Politics 45 (February 1983): 108–130 and "Machiavelli and Xenophon on Princely Rule: A Double-Edged Encounter," *Journal of Politics* 50 (February 1988): 889–906.

4. On the good and bad potentialities of civic honor, and its connection to the theme of education in the *Republic,* see Hans-Georg Gadamer, *Dialogue and Dialectic,* trans. P. Christopher Smith (New Haven: Yale University Press, 1980), 54–59.

5. On the incompatibility of virtue and happiness, see Immanuel Kant, *The Critique of Practical Reason,* trans. Lewis White Beck (Indianapolis: Bobbs-Merrill, 1956), 42ff. Many contemporary approaches to Plato are grounded in Kantian distinctions between freedom and nature, autonomy and heteronomy, altruism and egoism, and treating others well for their own sake as opposed to for the sake of perfecting oneself. See, for example, the discussion in Richard Kraut, "Egoism, Love and Political Office in Plato," *Philosophical Review* 82, no.3 (1973): 330–334. I share the reservations expressed in some recent works on Plato about this Kantian-inspired approach. See, for example, Charles Griswold, *Self-Knowledge in Plato's "Phaedrus"* (New Haven: Yale University Press, 1986) and Martha

KING ALFRED'S COLLEGE
LIBRARY

Nussbaum, *The Fragility of Goodness,* (Cambridge: Cambridge University Press, 1983), 4–6, 285–287. My general argument is that eros properly understood *entails* what Kant would *distinguish* as moral duty strictly speaking from an inclination such as love.

6. There is a general consensus that the *Gorgias, Symposium,* and *Republic* were composed consecutively, although opinions differ over the intervals between them. Even if the authorial chronology could be unequivocally established, it would in my view yield few if any necessary conclusions about the dialogues' intrinsic philosophical content. My interpretation does not hinge upon the authorial chronology. The dramatic dates are notoriously difficult to establish, but plausible dates (b.c.) are: (1) the *Gorgias,* around 405, although arguably as early as 427, the date of the only attested visit of Gorgias to Athens (E. R. Dodds,ed., *Gorgias,* [Oxford: Oxford University Press,1979] 17); (2) the *Symposium,* around 400 as the recollection of an event that took place in 416 (Alexander Nehemas and Paul Woodruff, eds., *Symposium,* [Indianapolis: Hackett, 1989], xi); (3) the *Republic,* arguably taking place around 410. Thus, the dramatic chronology could conceivably coincide with the authorial chronology. But, again, one should not make too much of it. As Dodds remarks concerning the *Gorgias,* "We must conclude either that Plato did not care how his readers situated his fictions in time or . . . that he deliberately lifted the present fiction" out of its historical circumstances. "In what year are we to imagine the conversation taking place? If Plato ever asked himself this question (which may perhaps be doubted), his answer must have been, 'In no particular year'" (Dodds, *Gorgias,* 17–18). The dialogues are written under the aspect of eternity, showing a recurrent ascent from the here and now toward the sunlight of the truth. That of course does not preclude their revealing an internal biography of Socrates and other recurring characters. In this book I argue that Socrates' account of his initiation into the rites of eros by Diotima in the *Symposium* refers to, or symbolizes, an event that took place relatively far in the past, earlier than the action of the three dialogues I discuss. I argue that this initiation is one of the ways in which Socrates tries to explain his "turn" from natural cosmology to political and ethical philosophy, the symbolization of an experience of philosophic "wonder" that is recounted in other ways in the *Apology* and *Phaedo.*

7. Thumos has been a relatively neglected theme in studies of the history of political thought. A valuable exception is the collection edited by Catherine Zuckert, *Understanding the Political Spirit* (New Haven: Yale University Press, 1988). Of particular interest is the recent study by Leon Craig, *The War Lover: A Study of Plato's "Republic"* (Toronto: University of Toronto Press, 1994). Craig pays special attention to the spirited dimension of the philosopher's soul, arguing that the philosopher's love of wisdom is not explicable apart from a spirited love of victory understood as being directed toward noble objects such as beauty and excellence, and therefore to be distinguished from the vulgar love of honor that confuses the love of the good with the love of one's own. Interesting as I find Craig's approach, I see Plato as deriving the spirited aspect of the philosophic character from the erotic longing for completion, rather than as assigning them equal prominence or deriving the erotic aspect from the thumotic. See the judicious review of Craig by Peter J. Ahrensdorf, *American Political Science Review* 89, no. 2 (June 1995): 482.

8. On the poetic sources of thumos, see Jan Bremmer, *The Early Greek Concept of the Soul* (Princeton: Princeton University Press, 1987). On the continuity between poetic and Platonic thumos, consider Marcus B. Tait, "Spirit, Gentleness and the Philosophic Nature," *TAPA* 80 (1949): 209–211.

9. See the interesting discussion by Stanley Rosen, *Hermeneutics as Politics* (New

York: Oxford University Press, 1987), 40–49. Rosen argues that Kant divorces "theoretical from practical eros." The assimilation of rationality to "mathematical reasoning," severing its connection with political prudence and morality, has the necessary consequence of rendering morality "meaningless." Moreover, political morality, thus severed from transcendence, degenerates into Hobbesian egoism: "If reason is identified with science, then resolve and courage are unreasonable . . . . Kant in effect identifies rationality, in the sense of the instrument of reason, with mathematical thinking, hence with universality and necessity . . . [P]hronēsis is reduced by him to Klugheit, or worldly cleverness, the instrument of self-interest" (45).

10. Zeigler criticizes Santas and Nanikhian for interpreting the Platonic Socrates, particularly in the Gorgias, as a psychological egoist. Gregory Zeigler, "Plato's Gorgias and Psychological Egoism," The Personalist 60 (1979): 123–133; Gerasimos Santas, "Plato on Goodness and Rationality," Revue internationale de philosophie 40 (1986): 97–114; George Nanikhian, "The First Socratic Paradox," Journal of the History of Philosophy (1973). Zeigler's criticism illustrates especially well what I take to be the pitfalls of a Kantian approach to Plato. See the interesting discussion by Kraut, who argues for attributing a much broader conception of self-interest to Plato than is implied by the notion of egoism (Kraut, "Egoism").

Chapter One

The Problem of Callicles

In a famous image in the *Phaedrus,* Plato likens the soul to a flying chariot drawn by two mighty horses. The charioteer is analogous to the intellect, the horses to the two powerful passions of spirit and desire. If the charioteer is in proper control, the wings of eros will guide him toward the empyrean heights of transcendental satisfaction, achieving an approximation in the human soul of the harmonious order that constitutes the cosmos. But if the charioteer loses control, especially to the impetuous steed of desire, they will all plunge downward to their destruction in the primordial depths, a miasma of disorderly happenstance and ungovernable lusts (*Phaedrus* 247–249, 253–254).

This image encapsulates the theme of the following studies. Plato explores an account of human satisfaction whereby the soul is directed away from the tyranny of the passions—an inner disarray that prompts us to tyrannize over others— toward a transcendent satisfaction that imparts an inward economy and harmony to the desires. But this prospect of transcendence is, as Plato presents it, more than a duty or an adjuration to self-repression. Eros itself, properly understood, yearns for this transcendence in order to consummate its own capacity for pleasure. The passions are not simply to be fought down and denied, therefore, but enlisted in the service of a goal that will assimilate their aberrant energies even as it satisfies them, enlisting these energies to move the soul on its ascent and dissipating them as the higher pleasures of civic virtue and philosophy are fulfilled. The tyranni- cally inclined personality will, once his longings have been enlightened as to their purest and most satisfying objects, come to prefer philosophy and statesmanship to exploiting and corrupting others. The horses, left to follow the lead of desire, can plunge the chariot into the primordial abyss. But, properly directed, it is their own energy and natural grace of flight that speed the chariot more surely toward the heights than the charioteer could do on his own.

To hold out such a dazzling prospect is, of course, not the same thing as demon- strating its possibility, or even its plausibility as an initial hypothesis for making sense of our intertwined expectations from public and private life. In the next two chapters, I will set forth some of what I take to be the most compelling grounds on which Plato tries to convince the reader that his account of the soul and its satisfactions does at least provide this initial hypothesis for a better understanding of politics and statesmanship. In elaborating an account of the soul whereby its own erotic satisfaction might be seen to entail the virtues of justice and moderation that sustain a well-governed political community, Plato is at all times aware of a powerful and influential teaching that contradicts it at every point. This was the view, expressed not only in a theoretical manner by the Sophists, but shared by many leading political figures, that the best way of life is not to transcend one's untutored passions in the direction of some alleged ordering of the soul, but, on the contrary, to head willingly for the primordial depths—to unleash one's passions for wealth, sexual pleasure, and glory and to gain enough power to wrest these pleasures from one's competitors. The natural life for individuals or cities, in this view, is to "get the better" (*pleon echein*), whether as tyrant over one's countrymen, by leading them in wars of aggression against other countries, or both. In this understanding of things, no ascent is possible in principle or practice from the primordial to the transcendental. Human happiness consists in descending, as it were, behind the settled conventions and everyday decencies to the subpolitical natural life of the passions, and, energized by these unrestrained impulses for mastery and pleasure, to re-orient oneself to conventional political and moral life determined to take advantage of others by stealth or force. This was the view expressed with such cool effrontery by the Athenian generals on Melos to the small and weak people it suited Athens to annex as a move in its vast geopolitical rivalry with Sparta.

> We hope that you, instead of thinking to influence us by saying . . . that you have done us no wrong, will aim at what is feasible, holding in view the real sentiments of us both, since you know as well as we do that right, as the world goes, is only in question where the necessity is equal, while the strong do what they can and the weak suffer what they must . . . . Of gods we believe, and of men we know, that by a necessary law of nature they rule wherever they can.[1]

Plato brings this view of things to life with special verve and clarity through his depiction of Callicles in the *Gorgias,* with his notorious praise of the "natural master" and the life of victory over others. In chapter 1 we will now examine Socrates' encounter with this complex and intriguing personality.

The special character of the *Gorgias* among Platonic dialogues and, in particular, of Socrates' encounter with Callicles, which takes up its second half, has been widely noted. The *Gorgias* is often held to provide one of the more noteworthy transitions from the early dialogues to such great middle works as the *Republic*. It anticipates the *Republic* in considering the true art of ruling on the analogy of technically skilled craftsmanship, but also in recognizing the need to understand and shape the desires and emotions of citizens. Callicles is the most vivid and formidable of Socrates' opponents yet to appear in a dialogue—one whose praise of the "natural master" has been described as "the most eloquent statement of the immoralist's case in European literature," and who was understandably, therefore, a special favorite of Nietzsche's.[2] Most significant of all, Socrates manifestly fails to win him over, reduced at one point literally to talking to himself. The *Gorgias* thus anticipates the *Republic* in another important sense: By showing the resistance of certain types of personalities to the Socratic elenchus, it supplements what some consider to be the ethical cognitivist position of certain early dialogues—that it is sufficient to know how to live virtuously in order to do so —with the psychological insight that a person may deliberately resist his knowledge of how to live well if the contrary passions are strong enough. Thus, rhetorical and educational persuasion must be backed by rigorous laws if philosophical reforms are to be politically efficacious.

The significance of Socrates' failure to persuade Callicles goes beyond even this. For, while Callicles' character and desires demonstrate some limitations of Socratic persuasion, they also contribute positively to its unfolding. In my view, Socrates deliberately and skillfully encourages and tries to build upon the very passions of erotic longing and belligerence that in a sense defeat him. In other words, Socrates is not merely baffled by a psychological type whose resistance to his arguments he did not foresee and cannot plumb.[3] While hoping to restrain Callicles' passions, Socrates also hopes to enlist them in the service of a more rational and moderate conception of statecraft, and therewith enlist them in a greater appreciation of the philosophic life and its potential contribution to the sound government of Athens. Socrates fails to do so, but that failure yields the positive result of the deeper consideration of the erotic and belligerent passions for which the *Gorgias* prepares the reader in the *Symposium* and *Republic*. Throughout, Socrates' aim remains to channel these passions into the service of the well-ordered political community—neither to repress them nor cooperate with them, but to convert their force, energy, and unclarified longings to public-spirited, and, in the best instance, philosophic aims.

There are two key features of Callicles' arguments and behavior that unlock his character. (1) The trait of Callicles that Plato brings most directly to our attention is that he is erotic, a lover. From the outset, it is the "common feelings" Socrates and Callicles have as lovers (481c) that are supposed to ground the possibility of discussion, refutation, and agreement between them. (2) Unlike the doctrines of the Sophists, whose reasoning in other respects he relies heavily upon, Callicles maintains that it is not only natural for the superior man to rule, but just, and indeed a law of nature. In general for the Sophists, nature and law are terms of distinction. It is sufficient to identify something as conventional in order to demonstrate that it is not natural.[4]

As I will argue, these two features are linked. Socrates and Callicles are united by their search for a natural convention—a natural ordering of the political community—though the conduct of this search simultaneously pulls them apart. Callicles' sense of justice, as well as his aggressiveness, are connected with his erotic feelings. In this way, Plato's portrait of him anticipates and serves as an unforgettable reference point for the more extended considerations of the erotic and spirited dimensions of the soul in the *Symposium* and *Republic*.

SOCRATES AND CALLICLES: TWO KINDS OF EROS (481B–488B)

When Callicles first enters the dialogue to protest that Socrates is turning the real world of self-interest upside down, Socrates does not counter with further arguments of the kind he had previously made to Polus about it being better to suffer injustice than to do it. Instead, he offers an unexpected and rather presumptuous psychoanalysis of Callicles himself. They should be able to understand one another, he says, because they are both lovers and therefore have common feelings. Socrates is the lover of philosophy and Alcibiades, Callicles the lover of the Athenian dēmos (the collective citizenry) and of Demos, son of Pyrilampes. However, Socrates states rather confidently that he knows Callicles' feelings to be in disarray ("out of tune"). For both Demos and the Athenian dēmos have him at their beck and call, making him do one thing and then another depending on their whims (481d–482c).

Bearing in mind Plato's reputation as a philosophical dramatist, for whom theoretical arguments emerge from the context of the lives and experiences of those who make them, we can assume that it is not coincidental that the objects of Callicles' eros have the same name. In this way, Plato suggests that Callicles' quests for political and personal satisfaction are intertwined. It is here, I believe, that we encounter the Platonic understanding of the tyrannically inclined character in its pristine condition, prior to educational or philosophical correction. The problem of Callicles will therefore provide a sort of benchmark for the consideration of tyranny and statesmanship throughout this study. Callicles plans to pursue the Athenian dēmos just as he pursues the boy Demos, in the hope that his beloved will gratify him if he can provide sufficient benefits. Moreover, Callicles' success at winning a more literal kind of gratification from Demos may well depend on his success at wooing the democracy, since it is from the latter that he can win the influence and prestige necessary for wooing the boy.[5] Setting aside the specific conventions of Greek pederasty, most of us have little trouble recognizing this intertwining of public and private ambitions. In order to satisfy our personal longings, whatever they may be, each of us is compelled to seek a measure of wealth and status in society at large. But Callicles' ambition goes much further than this. For as the identical names of the objects of his eros suggest, Callicles hopes to pursue in politics a happiness of the direct intensity and completeness that one ordinarily expects to find only in private life. It is this spontaneous political eros that makes Callicles a kind of revolutionary.

Socrates says he is similarly at the beck and call of Philosophy, but since she— unlike the whimsical Demos and dēmos—always says the same things, Socrates' love life is more stable than that of Callicles. Whereas Callicles is restless and changeable because his beloveds are so fickle, Philosophy is a majestic power speaking through Socrates as if he were her passive medium. She demands consistency from her lover. Philosophy (*hē philosophia*) becomes almost a living being here—a kind of "Madame Philosophy"—as Socrates imparts to this feminine noun a majestic stability as a love object. Socrates' other beloved, Alcibiades, is indeed changeable, but Socrates implies that his higher beloved keeps him from losing himself in longing for the politically ambitious young man. This appears to make him a less craven lover than Callicles, since it is only Alcibiades who is always changing, while Socrates is not at his beck and call. As Socrates depicts himself, then, the objects of his eros are clearly distinguished from one another and clearly ranked, making his feelings more constant and his love life more independent than those of Callicles. Socrates also claims to know that a part of the divided Callicles already believes the words uttered by Philosophy through Socrates that it is better to suffer injustice than to do it (482b). Callicles must refute Philosophy on this score, Socrates claims, or spend the rest of his life in this painful inner division.

Callicles' famous speech in defense of injustice and the natural master is, it should therefore be noted, made in response to Socrates' characterization of Callicles, himself, and their respective erotic conditions.[6] Although he gibes at Socrates for playing to the gallery (482c), he does not actually deny Socrates' depiction of either of their love lives. On the other hand, he is unwilling to submit himself directly to the Socratic elenchus. Instead, like a man familiar with rhetorical contests, Callicles treats Socrates' speech as a challenge to present one of his own. Thus, rather than meeting Socrates' demand that he refute "Madame Philosophy," he presents a competing account of the best way to live. Hence, just as Socrates had personified Philosophy so that she became a kind of goddess whose revelations issue from a transhuman source, Callicles uses language suggestive of a religious revelation to present "nature herself" as manifesting the "shining" truth that it is "just" and a "law of nature" for the better and more powerful to rule over the worse and weaker, and to "get the better" of them.[7] The speech builds up to a kind of epiphany of anti-egalitarianism:

> I think these men are acting in accordance with natural justice when they do such things, and, by God, in accordance with law, too, the law of nature—though not, indeed, the law we frame. For we mold the natures of the best and strongest among us, raising them from infancy by the incantations of a charmed voice, as men do lion cubs. We enslave them by saying that they must be equal, and that only this is noble and justice. Yet I think that if a real man appears of capacity sufficient to shake off and break through our mass of written rules, spells, and charms—all against nature—our erstwhile slave will stand forth revealed as master, and thus natural justice will shine forth! (483e–484a)

Pride and victory are at the heart of Callicles' view of the natural life. He understands the present debate—as, one can assume, he views both his public and private pursuit of erotic fulfilment—as a matter either of winning or being defeated and therefore shamed before the competition. He is ashamed at the idea that conventional morality could shame him into believing that it is better to suffer injustice than to do it. He interprets Polus's and Gorgias's previous poor showings against Socrates as stemming from their shame at being seen to embrace the conventionally disgraceful but naturally correct view that it is better to do injustice than to suffer it (482d–483a). He is determined not to show this weakness to Socrates. Echoing the heroic Achilles, Callicles proclaims that, according to nature, anyone who cannot prevent himself or those dear to him from being harmed is a slave, better off dead than alive. One must either triumph in life or be triumphed over. The many, he claims, are willing to forgo their own chance to triumph rather than risk being oppressed by the victor, and so they lay down laws that prevent everyone from trying to get the better (483b–c). These are the weaker people, not in the sense of being physically weaker—since they can, by banding together, impose their laws on the rare natural "master"—but in the sense of being unimaginative, pusillanimous types with weak passions. Callicles is a firm believer in the natural aristocratic character. His strength of will matched with his sophistication about the status of conventional morality will enable him, he believes, to resist Socrates' trickery in arguing as if the conventionally noble has the same binding force on one's conduct as the naturally noble.

Callicles' speech draws upon certain Sophists' accounts of political society as a contract limiting the pursuit of selfish desires. According to these doctrines, the nature of human beings is complete prior to and apart from the conventions—the laws and morality—of the political community, and natural behavior is the satisfaction of desire. But the rest of Callicles' speech raises doubts about whether the "shining" ideal of the natural master—Callicles' competing version of the true and best life—is possible given the premise that human nature is pre-political. Can human nature so conceived possibly yield a figure so accomplished, or does it not in fact require the conventions of political society to acquire and demonstrate these skills? Certainly the example of Hercules stealing a lone farmer's cattle is far too crude for Callicles' ideal, which may explain why the Pindar quote is not too fresh in his mind (484b.10). In other words, the natural master might well partly—perhaps even entirely—coincide with the conventionally powerful and eminent. Callicles' antinomian love of freedom from the common herd drives him to pose the false antithesis of the natural master who is reduced by the artificial equality of the social compact to being the conventional slave. But, even granting Callicles' idea of natural justice, it does not necessarily follow that the conventional slave deserves in reality to be the natural master, nor that the conventional master deserves in reality to be the natural slave. The three main parts of Callicles' speech spring from this false antithesis: (1) Callicles argues that natural justice stands across a chasm from conventional justice; (2) he argues, on the contrary, that one must immerse oneself in the conventional affairs of the city and serve society so as to advance in life; (3) he tries to strike a compromise between philosophy and the life of political action.[8]

As Callicles himself reveals by turning to historical examples of the master,

Xerxes was heir to a complex cosmopolitan empire, not a wandering marauder (483d.5–7). So nature cannot be so far apart from political society with its rhetorical and other legislative arts, and its customs, as Callicles implies when he wishes to assert the complete freedom of the natural life from conventional restraints. When Callicles turns to philosophy, he forgets his antinomian mood and becomes the defender of getting down to business and getting along with the majority. You need to be a skillful practitioner of everyday political wheeling-dealing, he argues, as against the philosopher's weakness and naivete. Here, the rhetorical usefulness to Callicles of his paradigm of the "natural master" is especially apparent as a way of transcending conventional political morality without renouncing political skill and power. Furthermore, he can use it to pillory Socrates for being both too conventional (with respect to the natural master) and not conventional enough (with respect to the political might that the majority happens to wield here in Athens, and the fact that the natural master's rule would perfect). The "natural master" puts together what Socrates claims must be in contradiction: the true and best life and the life of political ambition. Driving Callicles to make his long and remarkable speech before this audience of connoisseurs of rhetoric is his agonistic keenness to show that he can compete with Socrates in pointing out a natural, unchanging standard for the best life without—as Socrates says he must—having to choose between the best life and a life of political success (513a.7–513b.3).

Callicles ends the speech by attempting a compromise with philosophy that will recognize its merits while subordinating it to the politics of mastery. While Socrates had subordinated Alcibiades to philosophy, Callicles relegates philosophy to being a part of one's youthful preparation for an adult's entry into politics. It is good to philosophize as a boy, but "laughable" when a grown man continues in it. In a boy, it spells good breeding and gentility in contrast with the brashness of a youth of servile origin (485a–c). When Callicles provides here what is obviously an example of his own taste in the young, we realize that the forthrightness of the lower classes is not nearly so appealing to him in real life as it is in his revolutionary fantasy of the hidden master who throws off the chains of a conventional slave. Moreover, to the extent that these remarks shed light on Callicles' pursuit of the boy Demos, we learn from them that he would like Demos to acquire the broad-mindedness that comes from an exposure to philosophy as preparation for a gentleman's sophisticated interest in public affairs. Given the conventions governing Athenian pederasty—that the lover is supposed to help educate the beloved toward "virtue," toward an excellence of achievement in politics and life—the conversation Socrates overheard earlier in which Callicles and his friends discussed the limited benefits of philosophy (487c) may show us how Callicles hoped to convince Demos that the boy will benefit from associating with him.

Philosophy, Callicles goes on, also contributes to a boy's being liberally educated and capable of grand designs in later life. Here we can sense Callicles' appreciation of how a liberal education may be necessary for developing political capacities that might not spring full-blown from nature in the pre-political sense. In this context, Callicles cites with approval "the Poet's" familiar maxim, at the core of traditional

Greek conceptions of gentlemanliness and nobility, that men should seek distinction in the agora (485d). Callicles' attempt at finding a place for philosophy within a life devoted to political action shares the broad-mindedness that Pericles attributed to the Athenians in his famous oration: Capable of both empire and learning, the Athenians do not hide from truth and beauty like the grimly provincial Spartans, but rather spread them with their conquests.[9] The natural master—or, if not that titan, at least Callicles—will, after all, have to be a cultured gentleman in some conventionally recognizable sense. For reasons that emerge more clearly as the dialogue unfolds, Callicles' ambivalent view of philosophizing points to the inability of the Sophists' understanding of human nature to provide Callicles with an image of the completed nobility and beauty that he hopes to find residing in everyday life as he embarks upon his political career.

When it comes to the case of the mature man philosophizing, Callicles reverses every one of these judgments (485a–c, 485e–486c). What was well-bred in the boy becomes laughable in the man. What distinguished the well-bred boy from the slave disgraces a man by allowing him to be treated like a slave. The boy's gracious lisp becomes the man's foolish quibbling. Callicles doubles back and forth between admiration for the "noble soul" that he says nature has given Socrates— his own attempt, perhaps, to psychoanalyze Socrates and try to help him out as Socrates has done with him—and wanting to slap him. The desire to slap is fueled by Callicles' indignation that Socrates does not follow his way, his sense that they are kindred spirits for all that, and his fear that if he fails to *want* to slap such a fool, he will make himself into a fool ready for the slapping. He apologizes for the coarseness of his language here—evincing a certain embarrassment at descending to the brash vulgarity of the masses—but he is unable to renounce the coarse behavior he believes is necessary to survive and prosper in the democratic empire (486c.2–4). In this sequel to the praise of philosophy, we remember that the liberal-minded Pericles was succeeded by the coarse but politically successful plebeian Cleon.[10] Callicles' depiction of the shameful situation awaiting the man who keeps up philosophy for too long reveals his shame at his own attraction to philosophy and his anger at that attraction's pull on him. In this respect, he offers a window into the spirited dimension of the soul prior to any exposure to philosophical moderation. Instead of being ashamed of desire on behalf of wisdom, as Socrates suggests in the *Republic* will be the case when spiritedness is properly educated, Callicles is ashamed of wisdom on behalf of desire. Callicles' ideal of the natural master is also a measure of the distance between his feeling of vulnerability in a rude and tumultuous era and the power he wishes he had to crush his enemies and secure his happiness once and for all. Generous, broad-minded, and urbane when fixed on the beauty and nobility he longs for, Callicles is given to fear, anger, and shame when reminded of the possibility that he will fail in the competition for honor and influence. His eros entails and directs his thumos in the same way that Socrates describes the eros of the tyrant in Book 9 of the *Republic*. When he is successful or contemplating the unimpeded prospect of success, his eros comes to the fore, making him confident and eager. When something or some-one threatens those open vistas, he is thrown back on himself and his potential vul-nerability, which makes him more nakedly combative and defensive.

We must further observe in this connection that Callicles does not necessarily believe himself to be one of the natural masters. He certainly hopes he will prove to be one, but his doubts about his own ultimate merit are conveyed by his claim that "we" enslave the natures of the best to "our" incantations on behalf of equality (483e.1–6). Here he derives his self-respect from despising the part of himself that cannot consistently part ways with conventional morality—if only because he needs to get ahead in the democracy. Callicles genuinely looks up to and admires the nat-ural master as the highest human perfection. He calls such a man's rule "just" and lawful because he is its partisan—partly out of a hope that it might turn out to be his own rule, but also out of a selfless zeal to see a better man than himself trample over the slavish conventions he so despises. Admiration, indignation, and revenge: these comprise an agenda for revolution, not the detached cosmopolitanism of the travel-ing Sophists. By hardening the natural master's triumph from the intermittent upheaval of natural force intimated by some of the pre-Socratics and Sophists into a "law" of nature that ought to shatter the contemptible laws of the majority, Callicles reveals a revolutionary fervor to see the existing morality of equality reversed and the regime reformed—to see the beauty, power, and dignity of nature's rank surge into political life itself, making it truly worthy of love. He wants to be able to feast his eyes on Athens, as Pericles told the Athenians to do at the height of the city's glory. Callicles swears on behalf of the justice of such a man's rule out of anger and frustration at the distance between his own erotic longings and his power to achieve them, but also out of indignation that the pusillanimous majority should ever get in such a man's way, whoever he may turn out to be. The natural master, then, stands not only for Callicles' wish to be a lover powerful enough always to have his way, but is in some measure the *object* of Callicles' own eros, a splendid being who "shines forth revealed as our master."

In response to this remarkable oration, Socrates praises Callicles for his knowl-edge, goodwill, and frankness, and—picking up on Callicles' characterization of himself—stresses repeatedly that Callicles is not ashamed to say what he really thinks, unlike Gorgias and Polus (487a–b). While trying to tame Callicles' feisti-ness toward him personally, Socrates encourages Callicles' desire to shine before their small audience of connoisseurs of rhetoric. As we will see, he also hopes to enlist Callicles' passion and belligerence in the service of an argument about the best life opposite to the one that Callicles professes.

WHO IS "BETTER"? (488B–491D)

Socrates' first argument is that since the many are stronger, they are, on Callicles' own definition of the natural life, better. The laws they lay down—springing from

their core belief in equality and that it is better to suffer injustice than to do it—
are therefore noble and just not only according to convention but according to
nature. The tone of this exchange becomes snappish. Socrates goads Callicles not
to be "ashamed" to admit that the conventional view of justice is in fact the natural one, and to retract his accusation of Socrates for transposing nature and convention to befuddle his interlocutors. Callicles ripostes that Socrates is a shameless trifler to act as if "stronger" meant mere force of numbers rather than a better
type of man (490d–e).

Socrates has for the moment closed the gap Callicles wishes to open between
natural and conventional justice. Callicles is compelled to admit that "better" must
mean better mind or character rather than brute physical strength. Otherwise, the
natural ruler will collapse into the conventional (Athenian majoritarian) one. This
means, however, that nature as understood by Callicles does not alone yield the
characteristics of the "better" man—to some extent at least, he will be shaped by
convention. Callicles both wants and does not want this to be true. Whereas he had
earlier relished the thought of the lowly slave revealing his Herculean force and
smashing the placid conventions of the many, he now castigates Socrates for
equating "a pack of slaves" with nature's ruler (489c). He would like to find a
nobility that transcends convention while reaping all its benefits, but does not see
how to derive it from the Sophists' view of nature. In this unclarified conception
of a conventional superiority sanctioned by and participating in nature, we can see
the germ of the parallel between the city and soul elaborated in the *Republic,* which
hypothesizes a kind of civic authority that is according to nature.

It is because he wishes to reopen the gap between nature and convention that
Callicles responds so eagerly ("Yes, by Zeus!") when Socrates suggests that a
"better" man be defined as an intelligent and prudent man (*phronimos,* 490a). In
order to rescue the natural ruler from assimilation into the majority's conventional
authority, Callicles is driven to accept a definition of superiority that Socrates will
use to move him further and further from the brutal vitality of the Herculean master and closer to the intellectual virtues of soul. Socrates and Callicles agree that
the most knowledgeable man should rule (Socrates apes Callicles' aristocratic
extremism when he says that a prudent man is worth "ten thousand" of the physically strong). But they disagree over the character and motivations of this aristocrat. The psychological disagreement, rooted in their "common feelings" as lovers
whose erotic longings move toward different objects, provides the dramatic undertow for the Socratic elenchus and helps to explain its only very qualified success.

Prudence or practical wisdom (*phronēsis*) generally meant an understanding
earned from a wide experience of human and especially civic affairs. In what will
prove to be a key move in the dialogue, Socrates narrows the meaning of prudence
to the expertise of a craftsman (*technikos*) and defines rule on the analogy of craftsmanship (490b). Callicles lets this narrowing of prudence slip by. His receptive-
ness to the notion of an art of skillful ruling doubtless reflects the fact that a number of professional teachers of rhetoric—including Gorgias—stressed the creative

might of the *technē* of rhetoric that their instruction could impart to those ambitious to take a leading role in politics. But Socrates offers a very different conception of art—art as a reflection of the regularity and form that characterize nature, not the human capacity to mold and shape nature's formless becoming. Because Socrates obtains Callicles' agreement to the assimilation of the prudent ruler to the skilled artisan of ruling, the contradiction between the putative superiority of the natural master and the power of the many that Socrates elicited from Callicles' speech is now redefined as the conflict between intelligence and the power of the many. However, as Socrates proceeds to observe, the kind of skilled intelligence they agree is required in a ruler may be rather weak in comparison with the physical strength of the many, or with the Herculean strength of the natural master to take whatever he desires. For the expert *qua* expert is not entitled to the greatest share of what he produces (for example, cobblers do not get to keep more shoes than anyone else), but only to managerial authority over the stages of production. Like physicians, rulers never take advantage of those on whom they practice their craft insofar as they practice it, but only benefit them (490c).

Several consequences flow from the craft analogy. The example of the physician suggests that the political art would be mainly preventive or curative, healing various moral illnesses. It will not incite to glory as would Homeric poetry (also a kind of making, or *poiēsis*). Moreover, as Dodds notes, the craft analogy anticipates the best regime of the *Republic,* where the Auxiliaries, the class of spirited men, hold the power but none of the property, just as, in the individual soul, spiritedness enforces reason's regulation of desire. Psychologically, therefore, one may say that Socrates would like to unpack Callicles' ambition to rule from what Callicles takes to be the rewards of ambition—a life of unfettered pleasure. Callicles himself provides the opportunity, because his longing for satisfaction encompasses the honor and dignity of success in public life, not merely the private pleasures of hedonism. If Socrates is successful as a kind of therapist of political eros, ambition such as Callicles' might be channeled away from sensual gratification into efficient and disinterested political management. In the *Republic,* the prospects for this reform of political ambition hinge on the doctrine that spiritedness will ally its drive and energy with reason to regulate desire. It also hinges on the reduction of the pleasures obtainable from civic life to the objects of pedestrian desire (*epithumia*)—mere bodily needs for food and drink—while the consummate satisfaction sought by eros is drained out of civic life and approached only through philosophizing. In the encounter between Socrates and Callicles, these premises are prefigured and acted out.

Callicles is beside himself with anger and contempt at Socrates' reduction of the grandeur he hopes to find in politics to a dull and selfless art of management comparable to such plebeian skills as carpentry and shoemaking. (He must be needled in particular by Socrates referring to these crafts and their mundane products as "beautiful" and "good," the traditional Greek evocations of aristocratic morality.) Yet precisely because he objects to the idea that the pedestrian needs served by these arts could be exhaustive of the art of politics, Callicles is driven to elaborate the qualities of soul a ruler needs to distinguish himself from the common run of the technically competent. Refining Socrates' definition of the better as more prudent, he now says that the ruler must be prudent "with respect to the city's affairs"—that is, familiar with the great issues of war, peace, and domestic politics that are debated downtown, as Socrates and cobblers manifestly are not—and "courageous" (491b–c). It is not enough, Callicles is implying, to know the art of politics. One must have the daring to carry out the plans and not be weak-souled. Intelligent, prudent ruling is different in kind from the other arts, requiring the moral supplement of courage. People do not recognize their need for rulers as readily as they do their need for doctors. Rulers have to compete for and win support, and then execute and enforce their plans. Here, too, we see the germ of a view that is elaborated in the *Republic*—the need for wisdom to be supplemented, both within the individual and in well-ordered communities, with the drive and belligerence of the spirited part of the soul. This is one of the ways in which the *Gorgias* could be said to mark a transition from the ethical cognitivism of some of the early dialogues to a greater appreciation of the need to supplement the appeal to knowledge with appeals to honor, zeal, and shame.[11] In a sense, then, Plato concedes that Socrates had something to learn from a man like Callicles, whatever his defects.[12] Moreover, it is not at all clear at this point in the dialogue who possesses the art of ruling or, indeed, what it is. Socrates has provided no content as yet for this art. So far, all he has offered is a hypothetical analogy between something whose scope and methods are self-evident (banausic arts such as cobblery) and something not self-evident at all (who should rule and how).[13]

Worldly, brainy, and courageous men such as these, Callicles argues, deserve more because they are better. Put off by Socrates' reduction of pleasure to the food, drink, and clothing produced by the banausic arts, Callicles does not so much argue here that rulers deserve more of all such commodities as that they *are* more. By reducing hedonism to the bodily needs served by the banausic arts, Socrates is trying again to unpack Callicles' desires from his ambitions, heightening the skill, drive, and self-command required of a ruler and de-emphasizing the enjoyment of pleasure. To the extent that he provokes Callicles' pride into contempt for pleasure defined in a pedestrian way, he enlists Callicles' support. But eros may not be reducible to these pedestrian pleasures—the whole question hangs on this. Callicles thus wants this conclusion and yet does not want it. Socrates teases him by comparing him to Alcibiades for always changing his mind, while he, Socrates (quietly assuming the stability he earlier attributed to his mistress Philosophy), is consistent.

RULE OR SELF-RULE? THE TWO WAYS OF LIFE (491D–494C)

Given the opening by Callicles himself to shift the discussion away from politics understood as a managerial skill comparable to the procurement of mundane necessities to some superior quality of a ruler's character, Socrates suddenly interjects that the true ruler will be the "ruler of his [own] pleasures and desires, moderate and self-controlled" (491d). Rather than be more than others or get more than others, rulers should above all be "more than themselves." But Callicles wants the strength of will needed to rule successfully to be directed toward the fulfilment of erotic longing, not turned inward to restrain those longings. He and Socrates thus snap irritably at one another again, Callicles dismissing the moderate as fools and giving a second speech in which he purports to explain "without reserve" what is naturally noble and just, raising mastery above the low arts and saving it from moderation (491e.5–492c.8).

According to this speech, the "correct" life is the opposite of what Socrates has just argued. We must have the biggest possible and greatest number of desires and never rule over them; on the contrary, they should rule us. Just as Callicles earlier expressed the paradox that the rule of a consummately unjust man is naturally just and lawful, so here he offers it as a kind of categorical imperative of hedonism that we "must" be unrestrained in our longings. Courage and prudence (Callicles now gives courage the priority over the more intellectual virtue) are to serve these desires by procuring their objects. Rather than allow Socrates to reduce rule to management, turning it on the desires themselves, Callicles opens up the floodgates of eros. Desires will unify the soul, not by restraining it, but by summoning its energies toward every beautiful object. The "many" pretend to believe in justice (in the conventional sense) and moderation because they are ashamed of their "incapacity" for such grand desires (492a.5).

Callicles' candor here consists not only in his championing of a life conventionally regarded as indecent, but in making it clear that the natural master, the man of "royal stock," will rule as a tyrant. In Callicles' first speech, the natural master was depicted as being at something of a remove from contemporary Athenian politics—a mythical Herculean figure or a barbarian monarch. Now it is clear that Callicles believes tyrannical power and capacity to be the character of all contemporary rule, not only by individuals but by groups. His phrase "either tyranny or despotism"(492b.3) could well allude, for instance, to the rule of the Thirty at Athens. This was a *dunasteia*—a kind of collective despotism—as opposed to a more law-bound oligarchy, and among its members were a number of Socrates' interlocutors such as Critias.[14] Yet Callicles gives vent to his frustration that even those who do rule today or are authoritative in Athenian affairs are prevented by conventional equality from fulfilling their desires and helping their friends, or are themselves under the spell of this morality. While to Callicles all authority is conventional, it appears that there is something super-conventional about democracy, since it perverts natural might to the furthest possible extreme of leveling all distinctions. One can sense Callicles' anticipatory frustration that he may not achieve as much of the power and reputation he would like in Athenian politics in order to be able to win the gratification of his beloved, or to possess the city itself like a triumphant lover to whom the beloved looks up in admiration. For, as he argues, even though luxury, license, and freedom constitute the true meaning of virtue and happiness and it is naturally noble and just to fulfill all desires and naturally shameful and ugly to thwart them, the pusillanimous majority drags in the "master" of conventional language and censure to define moderation as being noble and just and the natural life as disgraceful. Even those who do in fact rule cannot get their way against this "master." Again, one senses Callicles' double frustration as a lover. He has naturally masterful passions, but must enslave himself to conventional morality in order to get ahead in democratic politics, which precludes from the outset his complete erotic fulfilment as the master of his public and private life. He is shamed by the prospect of being put in the position of having to limit his desires, that is, of having to act as if he were shamed by the morality of equality.

In response to Callicles' second speech, and after once again praising his candor and high breeding (492d), Socrates gives a speech of his own in which he tries to build on their joint shift of emphasis from pedestrian material needs to more complex and grander qualities of soul without asking Callicles to affirm conventional justice as such (492d.6–494a.5). At this point, he aims no further than to persuade Callicles to accept a hedonistic calculus—a scheduling of desires that will serve the desires by minimizing pain.[15] According to a myth he once heard, the desiring part of an immoderate man's soul is like a leaky wine jar that must constantly be refilled. Would it not be better to restrain one's desires so as to enjoy them in peace rather than continually pursuing new ones? In an obvious appeal to Callicles' pride in his independence, Socrates contrasts the credulousness and inconstancy of an immoderate man's desires with the "capacity" (the word just used by Callicles [492a.5] to characterize the superior minority) of a man whose soul is well-ordered (kosmion, 493c–493d.3) The first step to cease being at the beck and call of the Athenian majority and of the son of Pyrilampes, Socrates thus implies, is to cease being at the beck and call of the desires. The way to do this is not to wish to rule everyone in Athens but to rule the desires. In this way Socrates transposes the meaning of "capacity" to the inner strength of character needed for self-rule, while Callicles had just praised it in the sense of the vigor and potency of unrestrained desires. But Callicles is not persuaded.

In his second try, Socrates asks Callicles to compare the lives of a moderate man and an unrestrained man and consider which is happier (493e–494a). In effect, Callicles is being offered for his own judgment what Socrates had psychoanalyzed at the outset as the two contradictory parts of himself. The moderate man need only fill his jars once and enjoy their contents in peace, while the unrestrained man must fill his jars repeatedly. The supplies are meager and the struggle to procure them difficult and painful. Moderating the desires makes one's life less dependent on this struggle, hence less painful, hence more pleasant.

Callicles is still not persuaded. He prefers the *possibility* of limitless pleasures and regards it as worth the risk of pain to try to fulfill them. What truly distresses him is not the fact of his present discontent, but the thought of ever being sufficiently content to give up having to strive, which he compares to being dead. Callicles enjoys the wind in his sails—the feeling of striving and open horizons—as something pleasurable in itself. Since Socrates has tried to dampen the kind of pleasures that would elicit such grand expectations, he is not in a strong position to do anything with this sentiment. While Socrates is doubtless correct that the pursuit of pleasure frequently or perhaps always entails some degree of pain—the pain of lacking the pleasure or of needing to satisfy it again—Socrates gives a very one-sided ontology of the pleasures, one that anticipates and remains unchanged throughout the more formal analysis that follows the myth of the jars. But if there is an overwhelmingly beautiful and desirable object of erotic longing, the pain may well be worth it.

Callicles' eros for the beautiful carries him away on surging desires for honor and delight. In his jars myth, Socrates dams up this erotic stream and sluices it off into a series of separate means toward separate ends. This means-end rationality was prefigured by the distinctions among the banausic arts and their objects, themselves grounded in Socrates' initial identification of a prudent man with a craftsman. Further, by treating the desires strictly as a part of the soul, as he does in this myth, Socrates abstracts from the body's full-blooded enjoyment of even such basic pleasures as food and drink. Thus, the pleasure of drinking wine is likened not to the actual lovely experience of drunkenness, but to storing up wine in a jug. Treating the pleasures as comparable to a row of jugs not only abstracts from the possibility of the unification of desires in the longing for one surpassingly beautiful object; it also abstracts from the heterogeneity and levels of intensity of the pleasures we actually experience. It is hardly surprising that Callicles does not find the argument convincing on hedonistic grounds.[16] On the other hand, Callicles cannot articulate what it is he wants if it is not these sensible jugs of food and drink. His eloquence is stirred more by Socrates' opposition to an inchoate longing than by his ability to explain it. His problem is that when the grandeur of erotic longing is specified, the grandeur seems to reduce down to bodily needs. Callicles, though, is looking for something transcendent, unutterable, "shining" in his love for Demos and the dēmos. He is one of Plato's most vivid exemplars of what we can term political eros, as Aristophanes describes it in the *Symposium:*

> On reaching maturity, these kind alone prove to be real political men. . . . And when the pederast or any other sort of lover happens upon his own half, then they are struck wondrously with friendship, attachment, and love, and are unwilling to be separated even for a small moment . . . though they could not even say what it is they want to get from one another. No one could believe that it was sexual intimacy, or that this alone could be why each rejoices so seriously in being in the other's company, for it is plain that the soul of each wants something else that it is powerless to express—it can only divine what it wants and speak in riddles. (192a–c)

But while Socrates presumably recognizes in Callicles just such an inchoate longing for erotic satisfaction, he does not agree with Aristophanes about the nature of this satisfaction, as we will see at greater length in this chapter and the next.

There are other problems with the myth of the jars that we can summarize briefly. Can anyone rely on his jars staying full? In other words, is a life of moderation existentially possible? Even the orderly man, by Socrates' account, had to fill his jar at one time. In other words, we are not equipped directly by nature with what we need to survive. It may well be that in the real world from which this myth is abstracted, the competition for survival is so ruthless and the means so scarce that we have to strive to the utmost just to break even. If so, Callicles may be right to aim as high as he can in public life so as to gain enough power to escape any possible harm during those awful intervals when the social contract breaks down in crime, war, or revolution.

PLEASURE AND HONOR: SOCRATES' COSTLY DIALECTICAL STRATEGY (494C–495C)

Socrates has failed to convince Callicles of the need for a hedonistic calculus, an approach he thought might be persuasive. He now shifts ground from persuading Callicles to insulting him. Doesn't hedonism, he demands, amount to the happiness of a man who continually itches and scratches? And applying what is true of that bodily pleasure to other kinds, wouldn't the most pleasant life be that of a catamite—a boy who enjoys the passive role in sexual intercourse, or does it for pay, or both? Callicles is aghast at the vulgarity of this comparison: "Aren't you ashamed, Socrates, to lead the argument in this direction?" (494e.7). (As Dodds notes, "the unshockable Callicles is shocked at last.")[17] But Socrates dares Callicles to descend to his level, teasing him for being too well-bred and praising him for his courage and candor. Socrates pointedly reminds Callicles that he was able to defeat Polus and Gorgias by making them ashamed to expose the utter conventionality of justice and nobility.

When Callicles now asks Socrates whether he himself is not ashamed to take the argument in this direction, we sense a cold fury missing from his earlier urbane badinage and rather comic exchanges of insults with Socrates. From this point on, in fact, Callicles becomes markedly more stubborn and suspicious. He no longer tries to compete with Socrates as a candid friend and benefactor trying to save Socrates' "noble soul." Instead, he goes on the defensive. Thus, when Socrates asks him whether there is any pleasure that is not good, Callicles digs in his heels: "So that my argument won't contradict itself if I say they're different, I say they're the same"(495a). In this way, he locks himself into defending a grossly oversimplified definition of hedonism—instead of discriminating, as he has manifestly shown himself capable of doing, between better and worse pleasures. Whereas earlier he had praised the pleasures of the naturally superior man of "royal stock" in contrast with the mundane pleasures of the pusillanimous majority, he now embraces a purblind defense of hedonism according to which all pleasures are good without qualification. Though his friendliness all along had a prickly side,

Socrates has drained the goodwill away, leaving Callicles feeling threatened and open to insult. Psychologically, the dialogue is over at this point.

Callicles is so offended because Socrates' rather juvenile-sounding insult in fact cuts to the heart of his intertwined public and private longings. The insult implies that either Callicles is like a prostitute who enjoys sex for pay or that Demos is, in which case Callicles is shamed by his choice of a beloved. If we extend the comparison to the Athenian dēmos, it would mean that Callicles' pursuit of its favors and its reward of his public accomplishments would compare in each case to a prostitute giving sexual service for pay. Callicles' anger, therefore, reveals something about him that his arguments do not. He does not really seek unlimited and indiscriminate pleasure, but pleasure mediated by honor. A life of pure hedonism, after all, might more easily be achieved by a man of means who lives in private luxury and avoids the toils and danger of a political career. Callicles wants Demos and the dēmos to honor him, and not merely to like what he does for them. And, in turn, he wants to be able to respect them so that their esteem is worth having.

Why, then, does Socrates provoke a reaction that makes conversation with Callicles all but fruitless? Callicles is an unprecedented kind of interlocutor for Socrates. Socrates may not yet know all the ways in which a man like this will react, and so may be trying out a dialectical strategy. This is the first time in the dialogue that Callicles has been manifestly shamed by anything Socrates has said. Before now, Callicles had argued as if he were untouched by conventional sources of dishonor—the dishonor of yielding to one's desires at the sacrifice of all decency and all respect for others' loved ones, families, and property. The marauding Hercules was his professed model of manliness. He was ashamed only at the thought that he could be shamed into repressing his eros; ironically, the only activity he thought should be practiced with moderation was philosophy. Now, however, it is apparent that Callicles *can* experience shame at certain implications about the character of his own public and private longings.[18] He is indignant that he or his beloved should be thought of as wanton and incapable of restraint. Throughout their encounter, Socrates has encouraged Callicles' shamelessness so as to push their argument beyond the bounds of conventional justice toward a natural standard of justice, and played upon his belligerence so as to disentangle his sense of honor from his passions. Now Callicles has been rudely brought up against the possibility in his own life of a natural basis *for* conventional justice.

That natural basis may be eros itself, not in the sense of the unrestrained gratification of desire, but because eros seems to be directed, in the very structure of its longing, toward an honorable object of consummation. Our eros for another individual or for the fame and sense of achievement to be won in public life wants the object of longing to be honorable so that the beloved will be loyal to us and so that their affection will reflect honor on ourselves. We want to be admired by admirable people. This means that we become angry not only at threats to our exclusive possession of the beloved, but at slights to the beloved's honor, since we derive our own self-esteem from it. We demand justice, therefore, in order to

secure what we possess and to protect its dignity. Callicles, then, reveals something of the same inconsistency as Strepsiades, the student of Socrates in Aristophanes' parody, the *Clouds*. Both men are drawn by their love of their own (in
Strepsiades' case, his aristocratic wastrel of a son) to repudiate conventional justice and seek to get the better, turning to sophists for help. Both men find that turning to nature in the pre-Socratic sense, while liberating them from their obligations
to their fellow citizens, removes in turn any basis for their beloveds' obligations
to them, and any ground on which they or their beloveds could be considered worthy of love and esteem.[19]

Socrates evidently hoped that by goading Callicles to recognize that even he
regarded some pleasures as shameful, and that a certain degree of shame was necessary for his own capacity to honor what he loves, Socrates could persuade him
of the need to distinguish between good and bad pleasures and redirect Callicles'
ambition toward the inner self-mastery required to rank these desires. In this way,
as in the *Republic,* the cosmology of the good might be shown to be indispensable
for the ordered happiness of the individual soul. This is the formal turn the argument now takes. Callicles ought to do this—to distinguish good from bad and
noble from base pleasures—in order to preserve his honor, and especially since
Socrates has not yet insisted that pleasures be assessed according to their justice.
In fact, nothing in the dialogue so far requires Callicles to accept the morality of
equality he despises. At this point, he could elaborate a life of political eminence
and intense, if not unbridled, pleasure. But the price Socrates pays dialectically for
provoking Callicles' shame rooted in his eros is that Callicles becomes even more
deeply ashamed of *being* ashamed than he is ashamed. Rather than admit that he
needs to think more carefully about whether some pleasures are better than others,
he digs in his heels and resolves not to be budged from the narrowest, most purblind version of his argument: all pleasures are always good. He feels abused. Socrates is not only threatening to curtail his eros, but to disgrace him as well. His
flash of shame at the implications of hedonism for his own life rebounds into anger
at the enemy who would, as it were, slap his face in front of their audience.
Whereas before he was at least open to considering Socrates' perspective, hopeful that he could perhaps even persuade Socrates and so resolve his own "doubleness," he now prefers maintaining an untenable position to admitting the contra-
dictoriness of his way of life. Socrates needs to engage Callicles' pride so as to
turn him away from pleasures toward orderliness of soul. But Callicles' pride triumphs over his openness to argument.[20]

SOCRATES' REFUTATION OF NARROW HEDONISM (495C–503D)

Socrates offers two proofs against Callicles' purblind defense of hedonism and
invites him to "come and attack" them. (1) Good and evil, well-being and misfor-
tune, happiness and unhappiness are opposites. But pleasure and pain are mixed

and can cease together. A life of pleasure therefore cannot be a good and happy life. (2) If a pleasant life is the same as a good life, there is no difference between good (prudent and brave) men and bad men (cowards and fools). This is because fools and cowards feel pleasures to the same degree as good men, or even more keenly (for instance, a coward will feel the pleasure of escaping from battle more keenly than a brave man). Thus, on Callicles' argument, bad men are as "good" as or even "better" than good men with respect to living pleasurably.

Callicles' distrust of Socrates, revealed by his grudging, short answers, prevents him from exploring the weaknesses in these proofs. Two are especially pertinent. (1) Socrates simply asserts the identity of bodily pleasures such as eating that are accompanied by and cease together with pain (in this case, hunger) with pleasures of soul, slipping this by Callicles' refusal to be drawn beyond his narrow position. But there may well be pleasures that do not cease or that even increase, and that contain little or no admixture of pain. Among these are the desires for knowledge of the whole and for the noble or beautiful that Plato presents Socrates exploring in the *Symposium* and expresses himself in the Seventh Letter. Moreover, as we noted with Socrates' "jars" speech, there may be pleasures so intense—and whose attainment confers such honor and satisfaction—that they are worth undergoing great pain, toil, and danger to aim for. The longing for satisfaction through political eminence that Callicles feels but cannot articulate may be one of these. (2) It was Callicles himself who, early on in their dialogue, characterized the better men as prudent and brave (491c). Thus, in driving Callicles' argument here to render good men indistinguishable from bad men, Socrates is goading him to object, trying to enlist Callicles' own preference for rank—for honor, brains, and courage— over a witless self-indulgence requiring no degree of character. At the same time, however, Socrates has abstracted pleasure from grand ambition and political preeminence by identifying pleasure with the most mundane bodily desires. Were Callicles not so alienated at this point, he might argue that better men enjoy pleasures of a dignity and intensity unavailable to fools and cowards. Socrates consistently tries to make Callicles choose between a dry managerial politics or a base hedonism.

Thus, when Callicles now oils out of his purblind defense of hedonism and blandly claims to have distinguished between better and worse pleasures all along (499b), he is not simply performing a shameless *volte-face*. This really is his considered view. His love of Demos and the Athenian dēmos evinces his longing for ranked pleasures, for a noble hedonism uniting public fame with personal fulfilment. As an admirer of brains, moreover, he has no difficulty agreeing with Socrates that one must be an expert (technikos) in order to distinguish correctly between better and worse pleasures. Further, because he is ambitious, he takes it as a matter of course that it is occasionally useful to undergo pain and risk.[21] At bottom, freedom is more important to Callicles than hedonism. "How can a man be happy," he asks Socrates, "if he's a slave to anything?" (491e.5–6). Callicles professes an argument on behalf of maximum hedonism because he does not want his freedom restricted by moderation or conventional justice. He will not renounce the scope of his longings, and so retreats again into sullen short answers when he senses how Socrates is attempting to alter his own sense of hierarchy. For Callicles has no idea of going beyond the need to pursue grand (hence "better") pleasures as opposed to pedestrian ones, and to choose intelligently the means of attaining them. But Socrates wants Callicles' agreement to the very different proposition that all actions, including pleasures, are pursued for the *sake* of the good (500a.2–3).

By introducing the principle of the good, Socrates now has an explicit criterion for assessing the two ways of life with which his dialogue with Callicles began.[22] Recalling the schema he had established earlier with Polus, Socrates distinguishes between an art like medicine that aims at the good and a mere knack like cooking that aims at pleasure. Art knows the nature of what it treats and can give its account (*logos*) and cause (*aitia*), whereas the practitioners of knacks are unskilled panderers (501a–b). Callicles' professed way of life, which, as Socrates depicts it, appears to parallel a knack, is "to fare like a man"—to practice rhetoric and politics "as we practice them now" so as to win over the dēmos (500c). Socrates' way of life corresponds by implication to the skillful pursuit of the good—a way of life, we recall, that he has all along claimed to know holds an attraction for Callicles as well. As he told Callicles at the outset, until Callicles can reconcile his pursuit of political mastery with his attraction to the words that Philosophy utters through Socrates—that it is better to suffer injustice than do it—he will live in a frustrating division of soul.

But, whereas earlier Socrates seemed to be saying that Callicles must choose between the clarity and moderation of philosophy, on the one hand, and the shallow knack of the rhetorician on the other, now he holds out the prospect of a "correct" (*orthos*) rhetoric. Rhetoricians, he claims, generally flatter and pander to the dēmos in a heedless way (a way lacking phronēsis, the virtue of prudence that he and Callicles have agreed characterizes the best rulers). But, he adds, there might be a "noble" art of rhetoric that produces pleasures or pains according to the good (503a.5–9). It is an intriguing question, and one that will be important in the remaining chapters of this study, to consider with which of the two ways of life—philosophy or political action—this correct art of statesmanship resides. Or is there a third term? Does Socrates mean that he would make the best rhetorician, providing guidance for Callicles and other citizens, because his eros is primarily directed toward philosophy? Socrates' claim to possess a well-ordered eros in comparison with Callicles' disorderly longings may be seen as the germ of the claim elaborated in Book 6 of the *Republic,* according to which the philosopher's immoderate passion for knowledge absorbs the erotic longings that ordinarily result in tyranny and injustice, as well as the claim attributed by Socrates to Diotima in the *Symposium* that a properly directed eros is the true ground of phronēsis—issues we will deal with at length in the next two chapters. Toward the end of the *Gorgias,* Socrates claims explicitly that, inasmuch as he looks for clear knowledge about the proper aims of rhetoric and statecraft, he is more truly a ruler in Athens than those who actually exercise power but lack reflection: "I think I am one of the few Athenians, not to say the only one, attempting the true art of statesmanship (*politikē technē*); nowadays, I alone am handling political affairs (*prattein ta politika,* 521d). On the other hand, Socrates might be suggesting that Callicles could qualify as a practitioner of the true art of rhetoric—that a reformed version of Callicles' way of life might provide a third alternative between philosophy and untutored political commitment. Here we encounter the germ of a problem that looms large in the *Republic.* The ambitious men do not primarily want to philosophize, and the philosophers do not primarily want to rule. Is the very prospect of political life governed according to prudence and reason therefore hopeless in principle? Or might some kind of education provided by philosophers for the civically ambitious provide a third way?

Although Callicles again withdraws from the argument, he shows no indignation at Socrates' equation of poetry with the knack of gratification rather than with the art of improvement (501e–503a). When Socrates argues that poetry flatters the crowd and reduces free citizens to the level of women and children, we sense an appeal to Callicles that runs throughout the dialogue: Treat your two beloveds, Demos and Athens, not as spoiled children whose every whim is to be indulged, but as free men who need to be and will submit to being improved. When it comes to posing the same question about orators, Callicles becomes actively interested in the argument for a moment. He shows that he really is concerned about the public good, about his country, and is not the craven hedonist he defends in his most truculent moments. For he admits that there are indeed some orators who merely gratify the city while others really benefit it. He candidly admits that he cannot name a single living politician who practices the beneficial variety of rhetoric (503b). At this point, Socrates moves as close to Callicles' position as at any time in their discussion. Whereas up to now Socrates has identified the political art with a dry managerial skill that seemed to leave no room for Callicles' erotic expectations from public life, he now describes it somewhat more feelingly as a "noble" rhetoric striving to achieve the best. More explicitly than before, in other words, he tries to enlist Callicles' love of nobility and honor in the distinguished service of a well ordered common good, rather than simply exhorting him to moderate his desires. For just a moment, the beautiful offers an object for their "common feelings" as lovers.

But the revival of the dialogue is brief. While Callicles is only too willing to concede the decline of contemporary Athens, he is shocked that Socrates will not concede the greatness of her past leaders, Themistocles, Pericles, and the other builders of empire (503c). After almost touching, Socrates and Callicles part once again, and the prospect of a third way between philosophy and political action subsists only in argument, if at all. Socrates has not yet demonstrated—certainly not to Callicles—that the art of beneficial rule is not wholly compatible with the intelligence and discipline required by imperialism itself:

with the short-term self-control needed for the long-term achievement of power, wealth, and glory. Pericles, after all, had adjured the Athenians to be moderate — not in Socrates' sense of refraining from the pursuit of these pleasures, but in the sense of scheduling conquests in order to consolidate and enjoy the fruits of victory.[23] Clearly it is only in this instrumental sense that Callicles can accede to Socrates' use of the good as a criterion for the art of government. Moreover, it is clear that Socrates' kind of conservatism is far from being synonymous with a patriotic loyalty to Athens. As one who has feasted his eyes on the empire and loves her, Callicles cannot bear to hear her glorious achievements treated so slightingly.

THE PROPER AIMS OF RHETORIC, FRIENDSHIP, AND GOVERNMENT (503D–523A)

As Socrates drives his argument forward, Callicles retreats again into short and sullen answers. Precisely because they go largely unopposed, Socrates' points reveal what he would like to achieve with Callicles and the measure of his failure. A good rhetorician, Socrates says, should always have an end in view. Like a well-constructed house, rhetoric should possess order and harmony (*kosmion,* the term used in the "jars" speech to describe a soul whose desires are distinct and restrained). Just as the body is made orderly by such arts as medicine, the soul is ordered by the lawful and law, including justice and moderation. Just as a sick man must moderate his pleasures until he recovers, so must a bad soul be punished — denied pleasures — until it is good. Callicles flares up at Socrates' relentless parsing of terms, calling him a "slave driver" and refusing now even to speak. Socrates reproaches him: they should be rivals in seeking the truth about these matters through discussion, because it concerns the common good (505e). This sums up the recurrent dilemma of Socrates' and Callicles' dialogue. As we recall from the beginning, the psychological basis for the common good that their discussion is supposed to be illuminating is the "common feelings" Socrates says he and Callicles share as lovers. But it is precisely these common feelings that drive them apart as they attempt to clarify them, since the objects of these feelings are so different for each of them. Socrates hoped to engage Callicles' love of victory, but this is just what makes Callicles unreachable by dialectic. Socrates' refutation triumphs as its psychological hold drains away, leaving Socrates reduced to continuing both parts of the dialogue himself. Socrates' clarity about his own eros compared with Callicles' inchoate longing, however, lends this often fractious encounter a tone that is considerably more comedic than tragic.

Callicles' speech on behalf of the natural master had viewed the superior man in terms of an ontology derived from certain Sophists and pre-Socratics, as we shall consider in detail in the next chapter. The master emerges from nature as a spontaneous, Herculean force, complete prior to and apart from convention, education, and art. This upsurge of natural might corresponds to the view of some pre-

Socratics that the "first" and "noblest" things come into being through chance (*tuchē*) rather than by art and law (*Laws* 889a–890b). Socrates is attempting to reverse this ontology by appealing to Callicles' sense of rank and his search for completed objects of longing within conventional political and private life. Socrates wants to convince him that the "excellence" of soul he admires so much is "present" and "most nobly" effected by an arrangement of art, not through chance becoming (506d–e): "Surely the virtue of each thing, whether of an implement or a body or a soul or any living being, does not come about in the noblest way through a mere accident, but by an order, a correctness, and an art that is apportioned to each one specifically. Is this so?" Since Callicles by this time will not even answer, Socrates replies for him: "I certainly agree" (506d.5–8). In other words, the objects of erotic longing can only be articulated through a cosmology of levels of the good comparable in their clarity and orderliness to the stages of skilled production. As we will consider more thematically in the next chapter, nature, virtue, and art emerge together in the erotic longing for completion.[24]

Socrates, of course, never presents the analogy of virtue to technē as more than a hypothesis, a useful starting point for clarifying the passions. This is evident in the passage just quoted. Although Socrates is emphatic that the stability and integrity of a thing are present in it due to art and order (*taxis*) rather than chance, and that an orderly soul is "necessarily" better than a disorderly one (506e.5–7), when it comes to deriving the "good" in each thing exclusively from its technē and taxis, his responses to his own questions are more tentative—"so it seems so to me" (506e.1–4). He is certain the good is not like chance. He is not so sure it is exactly like art. There are problems with the analogy that Callicles, in his unwillingness to participate in the dialogue, again lets slip by. It is not clear that the fully rounded excellence of an orderly soul is analogous to the virtue produced in bodily matter by art. When the art of medicine has made a sick man well, he gets pleasure, or at least the absence of pain and the pleasant sensation of health, back again. But what does the soul get when it is "cured" by the orderliness of justice, moderation, and law besides this very orderliness? Are justice, moderation, and law the cause of the soul's orderliness or its outcome? If they are the cause of the soul's orderliness, in what specific good (pleasure or benefit) do they result comparable to a tangible good like health? If they are the outcome of the soul's orderliness, what is good about them apart from this orderliness?

Callicles' silence also obscures a significant radicalization of Socrates' argument here. Socrates is no longer merely distinguishing between better and worse desires and urging Callicles to think about pursuing the former rather than the latter. Increasingly, he is hardening the distinction between body and soul into a fixed division, and relegating desire entirely to the body. Instead, therefore, of recommending a hedonistic calculus, as he did earlier, Socrates is now subordinating the pleasures altogether to the formal, contentless good of a well-ordered cosmos. Eventually, he will abandon the distinction between better and worse pleasures and declare, in a kind of reverse parody of Callicles' own purblind position, that pleasure is worth nothing compared to the good. Much as Callicles may benefit from a measure of this kind of austerity, Socrates has by this point obviated any way of showing how orderliness of soul makes us happy as well as orderly. The *Gorgias* shows Socratic reasoning attempting to work with the erotic longing for transcendence so vividly exemplified by Callicles. But it does not succeed in fleshing out the middle range of an articulated hierarchy of erotic completions to fill the chasm between indiscriminate pleasures and contentless virtue.

Socrates' provisional search to articulate this middle range is evident, however, when he goes on to try to make his cosmic hypothesis specifically support friendship (*philia,* 507d–508a). All along he has tried to unpack Callicles' sense of honor from his desires, to convince Callicles of what he already senses, that his relationship with Demos and with the city of Athens cannot be one of unrestrained longing on both sides, but must be one in which each can honor the other. The new cosmology he sketches to support philia is as follows: (1) Friendship is based on sharing and the whole cosmos is held together by sharing, moderation, and justice. (2) The orderliness is one of geometrical proportionality, embracing both physical and human nature. Thus, human virtue mirrors the order of the whole. Geometrical proportionality is the opposite of pleonexia, of getting the better—a life devoted to domination that is grounded in the mistaken view of the whole as a purposeless flux of impulse and force. Socrates expresses his regret that Callicles has not been inculcated earlier with the temper of proportionality: "You hold that getting the better of others is what one must do, because you neglect geometry."

At this point, Socrates integrates several strands of the dialogue in a rather gravely beautiful summation of how the true art of rhetoric will operate. He treats justice and moderation as the equivalents of geometrical proportionality in the soul. Every citizen should aim to cultivate this harmoniousness in his own soul and in the souls of his friends, whether in their private relationships or in their relationships as citizens, or both:

> We must strive so far as possible never to stand in need of punishment; but if we or any one of our associates, either an individual or a city, needs chastisement, then they and we must submit to justice and be punished, if we are going to be happy. To me, at least, this seems to be the end and aim which a man must keep in mind throughout his life. He must turn all his own efforts and those of his country to bring it about that justice and moderation shall effect a happy life. He must not allow his desires to run riot, nor, by striving to fulfill the endless torment of satisfying them, live the life of a brigand. Such a man could not be on friendly terms with any other man, nor with God, for he would be incapable of sharing; and where there is no sharing, there can be no friendship. (507d–e)

If Callicles cannot refute these arguments, there will follow

> all those consequences that preceded your question as to whether I was in earnest when I maintained that if a wrong is done, one will have to accuse oneself or one's son or comrade, and it is for this purpose that we must use rhetoric; also the point that

you thought Polus conceded to me through shame is, after all, quite true: namely, that to do injustice is worse in proportion as it is a baser act. . . . Surely this must be the sort of aid that it is shameful not to be able to give to oneself and one's friends and intimates. (508b)[25]

By weaving the benefits of proportionality into his characterization of the right kind of friendship between citizens of a city governed by the correct art of rhetoric, Socrates is appealing directly to Callicles' frustrations as a lover—in the dual sense we noted at the outset of being a lover of Demos and the dēmos. Callicles experiences eros as a series of extremes. The lover pursues his beloved with complete abandon and, if successful, woos the beloved into submission. If unsuccessful, the lover is frustrated, jealous, and led around helplessly by his quarry. Callicles cannot see either politics or private life in any but these stark terms of victory or failure, mastery or slavery. Socrates, however, is arguing that there is an element of equality in eros—of mutuality, honor for the beloved, and therefore self-restraint—as well as rank (the longing to possess something beautiful and admirable, the longing to rise to heights of honor and pleasure). Geometrical order gives both rank and equality their due by means of proportion. In this way, Socrates attempts, in a provisional manner, to bridge or at least narrow the chasm Callicles sees between nature and convention. This chasm is between, on the one hand, the longing for consummate satisfaction whose outcome will prove the pursuer to be either a victor or a failure, and whose pursuit Callicles sees as the only manly way to live, and, on the other hand, an equality that is artificially imposed on the superior by the pusillanimous. Socrates hopes his sketch of an orderly friendship will help Callicles find the basis in his own character for narrowing this chasm. If he does, he will approach Demos and the dēmos as a potential benefactor, not as a potential ravisher. They will respect one another because the good will mediate objectively between them as that for the sake of which they love. Moreover, Socrates leaves Callicles with something of an upper hand in this reformed relationship, in some measure salvaging his ambition by redirecting it. For although he argues formally that both parties in a friendship may need to be punished in order to restrain their desires and keep their souls in order, most of the wording places one partner in the position of authority, dispensing punishments as needed to a city, "son, or comrade" (508b). If Callicles were to follow this advice, his eros would perhaps be less wretchedly consuming. Respecting his beloved and respected in turn, he would be a moderate leader of the common good. Still, Socrates is frank that Callicles' "love of [the] Dēmos" is likely to make him unable to accept his own salvation. Moreover, another question suggests itself. If Demos and the city of Athens were so moderate, what pleasure would motivate Callicles to want to benefit them? Can a deep, even if restrained, love of a friend or of one's country be based on justice of the Socratic sort?

In attempting to tame Callicles' eros, Socrates appeals not only to his generous side, but, finally, to his fearful and combative side. Callicles comes briefly to life again when Socrates observes that we want an art that will enable us not only to avoid doing injustice but also to avoid suffering it (510b). This sounds to Callicles like a sensible emendation of Socrates' original bizarre maxim. Callicles even praises Socrates for finally making some sense when he suggests that the best way to avoid being harmed might be to become a ruler or the friend of a ruler. But Socrates strikes at the heart of Callicles' insecurity when he goes on to observe that Callicles will have to imitate and flatter the dēmos in every way, that he will become indistinguishable from the many whom he affects to look down on. The dēmos will be the "master," not him. Callicles responds that whoever imitates this master, thereby gaining power and influence, can do whatever he wants—kill and rob—and become the master himself (511a). Callicles is somewhat diminished by this exchange. Until now, he has tried to argue as if conventional morality prevented the superior from rising above the impotent majority. Now he is constrained to admit that this majority calls the shots for people like himself, setting the terms for success in politics. Callicles really cannot be certain whether he will be the master or the slave, even—indeed, especially—if he succeeds in a political career. Socrates is telling him that, at bottom, he simply cannot have the synthesis he wants between natural independence and conventional success, not as he understands those things:

> If you believe that there is anyone in the world who can give you an art of such a kind as will make you powerful in the city but unlike it in constitution [*politeia*], whether for better or for worse, it seems to me, Callicles, that you are wrongly advised. For you cannot just be an imitator, but must be like them in your nature, if you wish to achieve a bond of friendship with the Athenian dēmos and, by God, with the son of Pyrilampes too. (513a–b)

The Sophists are deluded, in other words, when they advise their clients that they teach an art of rhetoric that enables a solitary selfish individual to pursue his ambitions and pleasures perfectly camouflaged and immunized from the larger community. As the *Republic* argues at length, the soul of the individual cannot be explored apart from its relationship to the politeia, and each will shape the other. Callicles is correct, Socrates implies, to long for true natural independence and fulfilment. But natural independence will have to come on terms other than political mastery—otherwise it will unavoidably collapse into the vulgar conventions that Callicles claims so vehemently to despise. Callicles is correct to believe in a natural aristocrat. But because of the influence of the Sophists, he is wrong about the aims and content of a naturally superior character—although the *Gorgias* itself, inasmuch as Socrates' appeal to Callicles' pride has backfired and simply made Callicles unwilling to converse, can offer no more than a sketch of what that character might be and how it might influence statesmanship. Callicles more than suspects that he cannot be the master of the dēmos without becoming its slave. But he wants above all not to be a failure, not to be vulnerable to insult and injury. Confessing to the impasse between the two sides of his soul that Socrates diagnosed right at the outset, he finally replies: "I don't know how, but somehow it seems to me that you speak well, Socrates. And yet I share the feeling of many—I'm not persuaded" (513c). Socrates had evidently hoped that his and Callicles' "common feelings" as lovers of the noble would enable him to move Callicles to a rigorous reflection on what it would really mean to live according to nature rather than convention. But perhaps because he lacks the taste for geometry that might specify and temper the richness of his eros, Callicles proves at length to be not as strong a character as Socrates. He confesses now that whatever feelings he may share in common with Socrates are outweighed by the feeling common to "the many" that one's own safety and pleasure must take priority over everything else. Socrates comes to the heart of the matter when he replies: "It's because an eros for [the] dēmos dwells in your soul, Callicles, and resists me."

Socrates makes one more attempt to redirect Callicles' eros from the extremes of natural and conventional mastery and slavery to friendship guided by the good. A man who is ambitious for political success, he says, should prove his competence to care for the common good by first showing that he can care for a single person in private life (515a–b). In another clear gibe at the character of Callicles' love life, Socrates asks Callicles if anyone has ever been improved by "intercourse" with him. Callicles accuses Socrates of picking another fight with him and of saying anything, however base, to triumph in an argument. As before, with Socrates' coarser comparison of his love life to that of a catamite, Callicles seems open to a sense of shame about his personal relations that he denies feeling about his public ambitions—in this case, the implication that the boy Demos is in no way improved by associating with his lover, but is pursued only to give gratification and be indulged. Socrates attempts to extend Callicles' prickliness over the questionable honor of his love life to a recognition of the questionable honor of imperial politics. Earlier rulers, he says, have flattered and indulged the Athenian people. Now that its greedy hopes have been dashed, the dēmos revenges itself on the new generation of leaders who cannot continue to deliver the expected levels of glory and plunder (518c–519b). Socrates is implying that the all-consuming character of Callicles' erotic life is emblematic of the imperial city in the fever of its decline and disillusionment. Continuing hopes of pleasure and power alternate with waves of frustration and anger. If Callicles enters politics bent on continuing to flatter the democracy's imperial passions, he will be in as much danger from the backlash of disappointment as Socrates, maybe more. As much for his own safety as for the common good, therefore, Callicles should be a new type of politician— masterful on behalf of moderation. He should persuade and drive the Athenians to be better.

Socrates ties this critique of Athenian politics to a more general point about rhetoric. A real art, he observes, achieves real control. A herdsman's animals, for instance, do not rebel because the herdsman knows their real, very simple needs and how to meet them (511c–512d, 516a–d). But rhetoric of the kind Callicles presently admires is not, Socrates contends, effective in controlling the multitude nor a substitute for their power. It cannot be relied upon to shield one from the multitude's spasms of anger. In one of the fragments attributed to him, Gorgias claims that logos has the power totally to transform its hearers' perceptions, beliefs, and actions. But according to Socrates, any statesman who fails to see that the persuasive power of rhetoric must be undergirded and enforced by laws and punishments to cow the passions is in for a rude awakening. In the *Clouds,* Aristophanes depicts Socrates as ruefully learning that the natural passions do not stand across a gulf from logos and nomos, to be externally manipulated by the rhetorician. Rather, the passions recurrently erupt in the midst of convention and speech, both demanding justice and undermining it. Socrates certainly knows this in the *Gorgias,* and as we will see in chapters 4 and 5, it forms a basic premise of the constitution ordered on the pattern of the good.

CONCLUSION

Callicles' erotic longing for public and private fulfilment reveals his intimation of a natural hierarchy of completed beings. The intimation that nature transcends politics by pointing toward the completion of the nobility and happiness at which politics aims is incompatible with the Sophists' understanding of nature as the generative substratum of conventional phenomena. The generative view of nature complements Callicles' attraction toward the means to political power and success. The successful "master" will, in his ruthlessness and daring, imitate the primordial impulses out of which, according to the Sophists, the settled appearances of physical reality and conventional existence originally and arbitrarily issued. But nothing in this ontology of primordialism can supply Callicles with knowledge of the substantive satisfactions that political power should be used to attain.

Let us review the main arguments with which Socrates attempts to articulate this substantive satisfaction, since they will continue to be important for the Socratic understanding of statesmanship discussed in the chapters to come. By narrowing phronēsis to technē, Socrates reduces the exhilarating, unspecifiable adventure Callicles expects from a career in politics to a benevolent, moderate, calmly managerial art of rule. The orderliness and clarity of technē and its objects are held, in turn, to intimate the orderliness and clarity that constitute the good of the cosmos. Unlike the accidental motions that the Sophists mistakenly see at the core of the world, the good governing the cosmos and human life is objectively real, permanent, and self-subsistent, while pleasure and pain are the human equivalent of transience and instability. Callicles, however, cannot bring himself to agree. Whenever Socrates uses phronēsis to imply the skill and discrimination a successful ruler needs, he concurs. But whenever Socrates begins to elevate prudence from a means for the efficient pursuit of pleasure and honor to the regulator of pleasure and honor, he digs in his heels. Callicles would rather resist clarifying eros than rob it of its grandeur.

The most durable common ground between Socrates and Callicles is their concern for Athens. Because he loves Athens—even as a would-be ravisher—Callicles wants Athens to be honorable, to be worthy of love, and wants her love to be worth having in return. He wants Athens not only to be powerful but admirable, so that he can feast his eyes on her. Here, at least, he will admit the possibility of a good more important than his own. Socrates tries to persuade him that he will be happier in his private love life, and will better serve Athens, by restraining his private and public eros in favor of a friendship that mirrors the philia ordering the whole. The feverish quality of Callicles' love life, Socrates means him to see, is emblematic of Athenian imperialism, alternating between victory and defeat, generosity and rage. Just as Callicles should not indulge the boy Demos but improve him, so should he not pander to the expansionistic desires of the dēmos. Otherwise, he will be caught in the backlash of disappointment when the empire declines. A city where friendship devoted to the good moderates eros with appropriate rhetoric, laws, and punishments will have to curtail its eros for the possessions of others. It will avoid war and conquest, and turn away as much as possible from foreign affairs to the responsibilities of domestic self-government. But Callicles, much as he senses the soundness of these warnings, cannot give up the erotic splendor of Athenian imperialism. He is not sure he could love so prim a beloved. His interest in the art of ruling is for the sake of a more efficient imperialism. He is shocked at Socrates' slight regard for Pericles and longs for the heady beginnings of Athen's climb to preeminence.

Friendship appears to be the most promising outcome of Socrates' attempt to resolve the confusion produced in Callicles' soul by his eros, since friendship moderates eros without denying it. But in the *Gorgias,* Socrates has yet to fill the gap between, on the one hand, the life of indiscriminate hedonism that Callicles avers and, on the other, the art of ruling as a kind of arid managerial expertise. As yet, the good is rather contentless, its connection with the pleasures of friendship more asserted than demonstrated. As we observed, one of Socrates' analogies points to this difficulty. Just as the physician's art cures the body, Socrates argues, the true art of rule would cure the soul. The soul properly tended by this art would be orderly in the manner of a well-built house (503e–504a). The problem is that the physician's art brings a palpable benefit and satisfaction to the body—if not pleasure, at least the absence of pain and the refreshing feeling of health restored. But what does the orderliness of the art of ruling bring the soul except orderliness? It seems as if the reward of being orderly is being orderly. What the *Gorgias* does not fully elaborate is a kind of pleasure that would not entail pain, tyranny, and chaos in the soul. If the art of ruling is to be joined with an art of noble rhetoric, as Socrates says it should, then the life of a statesman must not only be good but beautiful and satisfying.

The failure of the *Gorgias* to elaborate a kind of pleasure that does not entail pain or tyranny is connected with its failure to elaborate the philosophic life in its own right, as distinguished from a reformed rhetoric and statecraft. From the outset of his dialogue with Callicles, as we have seen, Socrates identifies the good life with philosophy. But the structure and premises of the dialogue as a whole severely limit the grounds on which Socrates can attempt to persuade Callicles of this identification, thereby resolving his "doubleness." In the *Gorgias* as a whole, philosophy first emerges in the guise of the legislative art. At its most basic level of plausibility, Socrates' claim to "practice politics" in Athens is grounded in the assumption that ordinary citizens can understand that laws should be intelligent and not arbitrary, governed by technē and phronēsis (as Socrates argues to Callicles) rather than chance. In the conversation with Callicles, it transpires that mathematical cosmology provides the basis for this prudent and reasonable art of ruling, just as in the analogy of the ship of state in the *Republic* the pilot's guidance of the ship derives from his knowledge of the stars (*Republic* 488d–489c).

Socrates derives the orderliness and harmony of the soul from this mathematical cosmology. Reformed rhetoric will encourage the soul's development of these qualities, summed up by the virtue of moderation. But this means that statecraft in the *Gorgias* is, according to the schema for a philosophic education presented in the *Republic,* limited to the third level of the Divided Line. According to that schema, the Ideas are higher than mathematical reasoning (*Republic* 510b–511e), and, for reasons I will discuss in chapters 4 and 5, they are intuited erotically, a hallmark of the philosophic character. The virtual absence of the Ideas from the *Gorgias* is evident not only from the absence of eros in Socrates' initial discussions with Gorgias and Polus, but from the failure of the participants to ask the question, "What is justice?" Until Callicles joins in, they equate the meaning of justice with whatever laws and mores prevail according to convention, and merely ask whether justice so conceived is good, pleasant, or teachable.

Hence, from the outset, the *Gorgias* does not thematically connect good citizenship and reformed rhetoric with the highest happiness or satisfaction. Callicles and Socrates do try to remedy this deficiency halfway through the proceedings. When Callicles distinguishes between what is just and noble according to convention and according to nature, he is the first participant in the dialogue to apply an explicit philosophical standard to assessing politics and morality. Socrates responds to this theoretical widening of the dialogue by widening his own psychological approach through a diagnosis of Callicles' erotic doubleness. In so doing, he outlines for the first time a full portrait of the nascent tyrannical personality based on misguided eros, as opposed to the cruder and psychologically narrower version of tyranny based on fear and punitiveness that had emerged from the earlier discussion with Polus (eg., 471a–d, 473c). But the attempt at this late stage to widen the discussion of rhetoric to include the full erotic parameters of natural happiness and wisdom is, so to speak, stillborn, owing to the mathematical quality of the analysis of rhetoric with which Socrates refuted Gorgias and Polus. Socrates used the epistēmē of mathematical reasoning to grab Gorgias's attention early on with the hypothesis of a grid for distinguishing sham from real arts. By setting up the dialogue in this way, Socrates limits the grounds on which he can address the issue of Callicles' happiness. Callicles is attracted in some measure by philosophy, and even by Socrates' link of statesmanship to wisdom, at least the practical wisdom of a successful ruler. But because philosophy in the *Gorgias* aims no higher than mathematical cosmology, Socrates cannot reveal its full erotic splendors to him in the way that he can in the *Republic,* when he dazzles Glaucon with the Images of the Sun, the Line, and the Cave. Whereas in the *Republic* philosophy emerges in the Image of the Cave as a splendid, superior alternative to political virtue, in the *Gorgias* it is conflated with moderation as the rather prim guardian of political virtue.

The peaks are missing from the *Gorgias.* While Socrates asks Callicles to rule himself rather than be ruled by eros, and to be a friend of (the) Demos rather than a predator, he never directly asks Callicles to philosophize, because philosophy is never fully disentangled from the reformed art of rhetoric parsed out by the grid. The most he can ask Callicles to do is to reform statesmanship and limit his intake of pleasures. Glaucon, in contrast with Callicles, is well versed in mathematics before the *Republic* begins. Already as a boy he has been disciplined by mathematics in the way that Socrates laments has never happened to Callicles, a root disorder in Callicles' soul that prevents him from resisting (the) Demos. Whereas Socrates cannot ultimately raise Callicles even to the level of mathematical reasoning, Glaucon starts the *Republic* having already absorbed it. Hence, as we will see in detail in chapter 4, the stakes in the *Republic* are higher: not just a reformed art of rhetoric allying itself with moderation, but a full-blown civic *paideia* that is philosophically grounded within a harmonious soul and a unified city, according to nature and according to logos, crowned by an explicit account of the transpolitical pleasures of philosophizing. Whereas in the *Gorgias,* philosophy is to some extent conflated with politikē, in the *Republic,* the superiority of philosophy to political virtues of even the highest order is made manifest, hence the superiority of its erotic satisfactions to those of tyranny. At the same time, and for this very reason, the city is more clearly transcended by philosophy in the *Republic* than is the case in the *Gorgias.* Thus, as we will see, the city is also more openly and radically undermined in the *Republic,* and philosophy more clearly exposed to the charges of sedition and impiety.

NOTES

1. Thucydides *The Peloponnesian War* 5. 87– 91.
2. Paul Shorey quoted in Dodds, *Gorgias,* 266. See also 387–391.
3. Consider George Klosko, "The Insufficiency of Reason in Plato's *Gorgias,*" *Western Political Quarterly* 36 (1983): 579, 586.
4. Dodds, *Gorgias,* 268.
5. See Michel Foucault, *The Use of Pleasure,* trans. Robert Hurley (New York: Vintage Books, 1986), 46–47, 85, and David Halperin, *One Hundred Years of Homosexuality* (New York: Routledge, 1990), 30–37. They are especially helpful for an understanding of

how, for the Greeks of the classical age, the experience of eros was inseparable from the experience of civic virtue, status, and prestige.

6. As Shorey aptly describes him, Callicles is the "embodiment of all the immoralist tendencies of the age." Paul Shorey, *What Plato Said* (Chicago: University of Chicago Press, 1968), 141, 146–147.

7. On this language, see Dodds, *Gorgias,* 267.

8. Consider Seth Benardete, *The Rhetoric of Morality and Philosophy* (Chicago: University of Chicago Press, 1991), 64–67.

9. Thucydides *The Peloponnesian War* 2.37–42. As Friedlander observes, in the debate between the two ways of life, three issues converge and intertwine: justice versus injustice, philosophy versus politics, and Socrates versus Athens. Paul Friedlander, *Plato: An Introduction* (Princeton: Princeton University Press, 1973), 261.

10. Thucydides *The Peloponnesian War* 3.35–40.

11. As Cooper observes, though, one can push this distinction too far. Socrates always presented virtue as entailing the goal or activity of living. He never depicted it simply as a nonaffective and instrumental means to an end outside of itself (that is, pleasure). John Cooper, "The *Gorgias* and Irwin's Socrates," *Review of Metaphysics* 35 (March 1982): 587.

12. Callicles' contention that knowledge must be supplemented with bravery and capacity explicitly contradicts the idea that knowledge is sufficient for living virtuously. As Cooper observes ("The *Gorgias,*" 581), it is Plato the philosophical dramatist who is responsible for depicting the views of Callicles, and he lets this one go unchallenged. Virtue does not assimilate courage and capacity to knowledge. Instead, virtue is at least partly affective.

13. As Irwin notes, hedonism seems to be the best experiential defense for the craft analogy. Terrence Irwin, *Plato's Moral Theory* (Oxford: Clarendon Press, 1977), 116.

14. Dodds, *Gorgias,* 295.

15. See Irwin, *Plato's Moral Theory,* 122–125: Socrates' argument on behalf of an orderly soul does not necessarily lead to justice conceived of as preferring another's good to one's own, or to preferring to suffer injustice rather than do it.

16. As Irwin observes, in the "jars" story no specific desires are identified and no inherent limits are set on any of them (*Plato's Moral Theory,* 123–124). In a way, this makes Socrates' argument unfair, since it precludes a ranking of substantive pleasures that itself entails moderation. But Callicles is not this Lucretian kind of philosophical hedonist. He sets himself up for the "jars" story and its dialectical aftermath by denying qualitative distinctions and rankings among the various pleasures.

17. Dodds, *Gorgias,* 307. It is impossible for Callicles to see either himself or Demos in the situation of a prostitue who enjoys the passive "feminine" role of wanton submission to desire. See Foucault, *Use of Pleasure,* 85.

18. According to Cooper, Callicles argues that: (1) We should never prevent our desires from growing, and (2) We should never be ashamed of fulfilling them (Cooper, "The *Gorgias,*" 584). Cooper claims that Socrates cannot argue against hedonism on the basis of shame because shame is not a proper motive; only the good is. But far from being "silent" about shame, it seems to me that Socrates tries rather blatantly to shame Callicles by comparing his love life to that of a catamite. Socrates is trying to enlist Callicles' loyalty to the good not only on the basis of reason, but also on the basis of pride. And pride, like shame, is connected to the place of eros in human life.

19. Consider the discussion of the *Clouds* in Mary P. Nicholls, *Socrates and the Politi-*

cal Community: An Ancient Debate (Albany: State University of New York Press, 1983), 35.

20. Consider Irwin, *Plato's Moral Theory,* 130–131: "The Socratic defense against Callicles shows the incoherence in Callicles' defense of an unjust way of life, but does not vindicate justice; and that whole argument is plausible partly because Socrates recognizes non-rational desires, and so undermines his basic doctrine." The elenchus does not elicit agreement because there is no underlying agreement based on "common feelings" about the proper object of eros, the good. This disjunction between discourse and passion explains Callicles' wordless stubbornness after the catamite insult. Precisely by recognizing "non-rational" desires (to use Irwin's term), Socrates vitiates his own defense of philosophical hedonism. The latter, while it might not lead to public justice, might arguably forestall injustice and tyranny of the kind that Callicles extols. But to term these desires as "non-rational" prejudges the question of whether a more adequate account of eros might be given that entails both hedonistic fulfillment and moral duty. As I argue in chapter 3, the *Symposium* presents such an account of erotic passion as a structured longing that entails the goodness that Socrates here radically distinguishes from the pleasant.

21. As Irwin puts it, "Callicles cannot both reject all restraint and advocate a way of life which requires courage" (*Plato's Moral Theory,* 121).

22. Friedlander, *Plato,* 268.

23. Thucydides *The Peloponnesian War* 2.65–67.

24. As Zeigler observes, we need a technikos (skilled craftsman) in order to pursue the good because it is not a matter of subjective preference, but instead is grounded in the objective ordering of the whole (Zeigler, "Plato's *Gorgias,*" 124–125). In order to craft our souls to be in greater conformity with this cosmological ordering principle, we may well have to undergo pain and the sacrifice of baser, more pedestrian pleasures. As Socrates presents it, one's true "advantage" might well require one to undergo punishment. Thus, as Zeigler puts it, it is "bizarre" to characterize Socrates as a psychological egoist, since this view is usually associated with the individual's minimization of pain and maximization of the pleasures of sense.

25. The two quotations are from the translation by Helmbold, which has a certain Victorian gravity suitable to the context. Plato, *Gorgias,* trans. W. C. Helmbold (New York: Bobbs-Merill, 1952).

Chapter 2

The Ontology of Primordialism and the Platonic Critique of the Sophists

Near the beginning of Book 10 of the *Laws,* the Athenian Stranger criticizes Kleinias for believing that the only reason people are attracted to a life of godlessness is because they cannot resist their desires (*Laws* 884a–890d). Living off the beaten track, the Athenian tells the old Cretan, Kleinias does not realize that the gravest threat to the just city whose founding they are setting forth is a kind of ignorance that passes for wisdom in sophisticated centers of learning like Athens. These theoretical doctrines greatly exacerbate any natural leaning toward immoderation. In trying to bring Kleinias up to date on these new doctrines, the Athenian Stranger telescopes the views of a number of unidentified pre-Socratic thinkers, Sophists, and poets,[1] showing how the corrupt political teachings are grounded in a certain kind of cosmological speculation. Because Kleinias is a neophyte in this sort of speculation, the account Plato has the Athenian Stranger give here of the connection between bad cosmology and bad politics is trenchant and extensive to a degree rarely found elsewhere in the dialogues.

In this chapter, I will interpret what Plato takes to be the main principles of this "modern" wisdom, drawing mainly on the discussion in the *Laws.* These principles yield a view of nature and being that I designate the ontology of primordialism. I will try to show how this ontology grounds a number of the key premises we identify with the political teachings of the Sophists. Specifically, I argue that the ontology of primordialism leads to several paradoxes in the Sophists' account of politics: (1) the view that art is, on the whole, "paltry" (*Laws* 889d), and yet can possess enormous power in political affairs, and (2) a stance toward the political status quo that is at once conservative and subversive. I will then return to the discussion of Callicles, showing how these paradoxes come to light in a number of the key issues that Socrates attempts to debate with him in the *Gorgias.* In particular, I think it can be shown how the ontology of primordialism helps trap Callicles into a position of affirming the conventional status quo on precisely the grounds that he hopes will give him a sense of radical independence from it. This

43

is the contradiction that Socrates bores in on when he sums up their disagreement by telling Callicles straight out that he cannot, given his understanding of the good life, be the city's master without for that very reason being its slave (*Gorgias* 513a–b). At the same time, as we observed in the last chapter, it is Callicles' own frustration as a lover that provides Socrates' point of departure for exposing the deficiencies of the Sophists' understanding of statesmanship. As this more detailed consideration of Sophistry will reveal, the ontological arguments of the Platonic Socrates' predecessors and contemporaries fail to yield a coherent account of civic and erotic satisfaction in the experience of a prospective Athenian statesman like Callicles.

Scholars have long debated exactly whom the Athenian Stranger has in mind when he argues that these cosmological speculations lead to the view that the natural life is one of getting the better of others. We should bear in mind that Plato's purpose in rehearsing these arguments is more rhetorical than theoretical. When I use the term "rhetorical," I do not mean in the ordinary contemporary sense of deception or stretching the truth, but in the sense intended by Platonic and Aristotelian political thought: the shaping of theoretical arguments to the passions, interests, and psychology of a specific audience, notably the citizenry of a political community. The Athenian Stranger is letting Kleinias know as much as he thinks the old Cretan needs to know and can absorb in order to frame sound laws. As Aristotle was to remark in the *Nicomachean Ethics,* a legislator needs to know just so much about the soul, and with just such precision, as is useful for shedding light on the practical problems of prudent statecraft.[2]

Accordingly, we should not expect Plato's presentation of rival philosophical doctrines to be either exhaustive or fair in the modern scholarly sense. Plainly certain pre-Socratics are excluded, especially those like Parmenides, who stressed the stable and absolute reality that perdured through all apparent change. The pre-Socratic teachings Plato has in mind are those of the "motion men," as he terms them in the *Theaetetus*—the belief that instability and impermanence are the reality of nature (*Theaetetus* 181a). In the *Theaetetus,* too, Plato presents this as the single most influential outcome of the speculations of other philosophers and Sophists, as well as of the poets. "All the wise in succession," Socrates claims, including Heracleitus, Empedocles, and Protagoras, as well as the tragic and comic poets, believe things are the "offspring" of "flow and motion," so that nothing "ever is but is always becoming" (*Theaetetus* 152d–e, 180d). Heracleitus comes particularly to mind when we examine the discussion in *Laws* 10, and I will suggest some other parallels to specific Sophists and pre-Socratics.

The other thing to bear in mind is that the presentation of the Sophists is not entirely fair to them in the sense of being a neutral description of their teachings. For, whereas some of the Sophists (Antiphon and Protagoras, for example) did not, or at least claimed not, teach that tyranny and pleonexia were the necessary outcome of their views about human nature and the cosmos, this is the general conclusion that the Athenian Stranger derives from the cosmology of motion.[3] As I shall suggest, however, there are reasons for Plato's implication that, whatever reservations some of the Sophists may have entertained about tyranny, their teachings did in truth support "getting the better" more consistently than any other outcome. In sum, my interest in discussing these passages is not to offer a comprehensive interpretation of pre-Socratic philosophy or Sophistry, even from Plato's viewpoint, but rather to focus on what Plato, in those of his writings most directly concerned with statesmanship and the political community, believed to be the most direct and palpable moral outcome of the frame of mind arising from a generally Heracleitean view of the world when applied to politics.

Finally, we should note that Book 10 of the *Laws* does not accept the clear distinction made by some modern scholars between pre-Socratics and Sophists. This is the notion that the Sophists, in their concern with the real world of politics and profit, were reacting against the purely theoretical, detached speculations of the pre-Socratic thinkers. More recent scholarship has, indeed, made this dividing line fuzzy if not evanescent. The relationship between pre-Socratics and Sophists should be viewed not so much as a dichotomy as dialectical. In other words, although the Sophists were indeed reacting to some of the pre-Socratics' detachment from political and other practical matters, it is the pre-Socratics' own principles that they brought to bear on the study of human nature.[4] Although they developed and transformed these ontological speculations in applying them to concrete issues, the practical teachings they derived were deeply affected by those speculations, as the following discussion will confirm. Apart from the considerable internal textual evidence of the dependence of many Sophistical teachings on principles derived from the pre-Socratics, the relationship is also confirmed by what little we know about the intellectual pedigree of some of these figures. Gorgias, for instance, was the pupil of Empedocles. Along with Anaxagoras and Democritus, Empedocles asserted the plurality and variability of everyday experience as against the monistic essentialism of Parmenides. Although Empedocles tried to lend greater phenomenological content to the Heracleitean theory of motion by introducing intermediate distinctions through the combinations of earth, water, air, and fire governed by an overall alternation between love and strife, the basic categories of his thought are manifestly dependent on Heracleitus and the "motion men."[5]

THE PRIMORDIALIST UNDERSTANDING OF NATURE

As it is presented in the *Laws,* the fundamental premise of the ontology of primordialism is that nature (*phusis*) is genesis. The "first" things are generated out of random motions. They come into being "according to chance" (*kata tuchē*) and "out of necessity" (*ex anangkē*). The first beings, such as the heavenly bodies, are first both in the sense of temporal priority and in the sense of being the "greatest" and "noblest" beings generated out of "nature and chance." These primordial movements in turn generate smaller combinations of "chance powers," including plants and animals, down to the settled appearance of the world as we observe it in everyday life. All of these mixtures come into being by happenstance, bereft of intelligence (*nous*), art (technē), or divine governance. Nature, then, is to be understood primarily in terms of the invisible origins out of which visible reality has issued and is issuing: the roots rather than the visible form and completion (*Laws* 888e–889c).[6]

Whatever does not spring out of nature exists by art, which came "later" than the first works of nature. The arts are "mortal," both in the sense of being possessed by humans alone among living creatures and in the sense of being short-lived and paltry in comparison with the primordial might and grandeur of nature's motions. Arts such as "music" (tragic and lyric poetry) are altogether paltry because they are sheer fabrications, with no roots in nature's generative might. There are, however, arts like medicine, farming, and gymnastic that "generate" something "serious" because they share their power "in common" with nature's power. Medicine, farming, and gymnastic serve our natural bodily needs. In this sense, the serious arts, although they are not on a level with the "first" and "noblest" beings, are grounded in nature (*Laws* 889d–890a). The primordialist conception of art as rehearsed by Plato enables us to see a crucial foil for the craft analogy that is a hallmark of the Socratic elenchus. For whereas art, in the primordialist ontology, is a way of tracing and tapping the vital rhythms of nature's disorder, in the Socratic conception of technē, artistic fabrication intimates by analogy the orderliness of the world as a whole. As the examples of serious arts in the primordialist ontology suggest, they do not so much imitate the form and structure of the world as stimulate and guide forth the healthy vigor of the earth and the bodily vigor of human beings. This carries the further implication that the bodily aspect of human life, the aspect that most manifestly "grows," is the part of human life closest to nature altogether.

Accordingly, the human counterparts of nature's spontaneous motions are the desires. The chance motions and unstructured energies of phusis well up in us as the drive to maintain our lives and gratify our passions. Law and convention (nomos) forbid us to gratify these desires, but these prohibitions are rootless constructions imposed against nature. A sign of the flimsiness of the laws in comparison with nature is that they change from place to place and time to time, while natural selfishness is a universal constant. The "correct" life "according to nature" is to "dominate the rest" so as to gratify these desires to the utmost (*Laws* 889e–890a). The best life, in other words, is the life of getting the better. In the *Gorgias,* this is the stance toward life that Socrates diagnoses as being symptomatic of Callicles' erotic disorder. Stemming from Callicles' disordered erotic longings and exacerbating them, Socrates implies, is the view Callicles derives from the Sophists that the world as a whole is a tumult of impulse and accident.

According to the primordialist ontology, nomos commands us to believe that the gods enjoin us to seek peace and respect the lives, families, and property of our fellow citizens (890a). But the natural condition of man is the murderous civil strife and crime that erupt when the fabric of everyday law-abidingness breaks down under the shock of foreign aggression and partisan hatred. In contrast to the artificial dictates of nomos, nature drives us through the passions spontaneously to strive for "victory" over others "by force." The laws say that we must not believe this, that it is unjust and wicked. But to accept such conventional restraints on human nature is to live like "a slave." The terminology reminds us of Callicles' contention to Socrates that understanding nature makes it impossible for a real man to be reconciled to the shackles of conventional morality and authority (*Gorgias* 483a.8–b.4). The tension and spiritedness of Callicles' famous speech issue from this determination to become, or at least serve the cause of, the natural master, so that he will not have to be the slave of conventional morality and its censorious strictures against pleasure and glory. In Plato's presentation, then, the most consistent implication of the primordialist ontology is that tyranny is the best way of life. The "force" displayed by the successful victor in taking maximum advantage of others is the eruption into the settled horizon of everyday morality of the primordial motions of phusis itself. Nature's formless potency erupts in the untutored, spontaneous passion to rule, requiring the violation of the laws and even the overthrow of the established order.

A further sign of this tyrannical implication is that, while the primordialist ontology as presented in the *Laws* denies that justice exists by nature at all, it does aver—as does Callicles in his speech—that there is a "noble" life according to nature that differs from conventional nobility (*Laws* 889e. Cf. *Gorgias* 482e.4–7). While conventional nobility includes the moderation and self-restraint that Callicles considers too restrictive of his prospects for happiness, the naturally noble presumably partakes, on a human level, of those great motions said to generate the "noblest" beings out of "nature and chance." A spontaneous passion for mastery over others and unrestrained pleasures enjoyed at the expense of others constitute the human counterpart of those grand natural motions bereft of nous. In this ontology, human nature is seen as pre-political, self-interested, and complete prior to and apart from any shaping by law, statecraft, or education. The primordialist ontology thus helps us to see why Callicles, when he is trying to illustrate his paradigm of the "natural master" in the first part of his opening speech, chooses men who stand outside of convention altogether—a prehistoric wandering marauder like Hercules or a Persian king like Xerxes, whose individual power is so absolute that he is beyond all legal restraint. And yet, Callicles' own longings for a career of political preeminence, his admiration for a naturally masterful ruler whose passions would flower in the possession of absolute power, are in revealing ways frustrated by the very ontology he invokes. The primordialist ontology contains a number of paradoxes and ambiguities that help not only to explain Callicles' attraction to it, but also why he departs from it in significant respects in facing the problems of his own life as a prospective Athenian leader. Callicles' dissatisfactions help us to see the point of departure for Socrates' own account of the soul, whereby the passions, properly understood, aim to transcend their own primordial impulses.

SOME PARADOXES OF PRIMORDIALISM

One of the paradoxes of the primordialist ontology concerns the question of art. As we have seen, while the arts are generally held to be unnatural in the primordialist ontology, some of them are held to be grounded in nature to a degree. The status of the political art is especially ambiguous. Legislation is held to be purely by art, hence purely unnatural. But a small part of the art of ruling is, like the "serious" arts, in "partnership with nature" (*Laws* 889d–e). The Athenian Stranger does not identify this small quasi-natural aspect of the political art, but I would conjecture that it is the part, chiefly represented by rhetoric, that enables one to take advantage of others while camouflaging one's intentions behind a carapace of plausible arguments couched in terms of conventional belief, or by making oneself appear virtuous in conventional terms. To the extent that logos is aimed at the creation of such rhetorical effects, logos may be said to tap the generative power of phusis itself, making new phenomena come into being and pass away whenever it is advantageous to the rhetorician.

This sense of a natural grounding for logos must accordingly be understood in sharp contrast to the Socratic sense. For Socrates, the structure and clarity of logos demonstrate its privileged access to the structure and clarity of the cosmos. Hence, for Socrates, reasoned discourse is capable of transcending convention through the clarification of conversation. Dialectic helps us to sift through the shortcomings of conventional understandings of virtue by exposing them to the light of those stable forms in which nature's development is consummated. But for the primordialist ontology, nature is a formless, unstructured genesis.[7] Such structure as logos is capable of achieving, therefore, is a human fabrication, the imposition of a temporary form on the shifting currents of nature. As Socrates has Protagoras put it in the *Theaetetus,* when we say that a thing "is," implying that the distinction between being and not-being is grounded in the structure of the world, we do not "speak correctly" (*Theaetetus* 152d). For what seems to "be" is only the temporary concatenation of clashing motions. Nothing ever is "one," but emerges out of and passes back into becoming. Such stability as nature can achieve comes from the vital flow of energy coursing through phenomena, not from the husk of its current outward structure. Hence, nothing "ever is but is always becoming" (*Theaetetus* 152d–e). To the extent that a thing comes to rest and remains "one," this is not, as Parmenides thought, its participation in true being, but, on the contrary, its atrophy and loss of natural sustenance. Rest is "non-being and perishing," while the real is synonymous with the concatenated motions of whatever appears to be (*Theaetetus* 153a). Thus, "becoming both seems to be and is," and the seeming is all that we can say about what really is. Being, in other words, is phenomenon without noumenon.[8] Identity and contradiction are principles of discourse, not of the world. For Socrates, by contrast, they are principles of discourse because they are principles of the world.

As a consequence of the primordialist understanding of nature and being, then, the art of rhetoric turns out in a sense to be anything but paltry. Indeed, to the extent that it can tap into the profound underlying power of nature to generate and recombine phenomena, it promises a kind of demiurgic power to find a purchase in the midst of becoming and create new combinations of beings.[9] The praise of technē understood in the primordialist sense can be found in many teachings of the Sophists or in the beliefs of those influenced by them. For example, in his speech in Book 2 of the *Republic,* Glaucon sets forth one version of the Sophists' critique of conventional justice. In so doing, he evinces his enthusiasm for a technē of selfishness, an art so efficacious in manipulating and recombining the motions that generate appearances that it would enable a perfectly unjust man, even a tyrant, to seem to others to be perfectly just even as he exploits them (*Republic* 360e–361a). The omnipotence of the rhetorician's art is well conveyed by the fragments attributed to Gorgias:

> Speech is a great power, which achieves the most divine works by means of the smallest and least visible form; for it can even put a stop to fear, remove grief, and increase pity. . . . The power of the incantations [of words] uniting with the feeling in the soul, soothes and persuades and transports by means of its wizardry. That Persuasion, when added to speech, can also make any impression it wishes on the soul, can be shown firstly from the arguments of the cosmologists, who by removing one opinion and implanting another, cause what is incredible and invisible to appear before the eyes of the mind; secondly, from legal contests, in which a speech can sway and persuade a crowd by the skill of its composition, not by the truth of its statements.[10]

Empedocles, the teacher of Gorgias, claimed that someone who learned from him could harness the very powers of nature and make them serve human purposes: "You shall check the force of the unwearying winds which rush upon the earth and lay waste the cultivated fields. And again, if you wish, you shall conduct the breezes back again. And you shall bring out of Hades a dead man restored to strength."[11]

The ambivalent status of art within the primordialist ontology helps us to understand Callicles' qualified tolerance of the analogy proposed by Socrates between the naturally superior and prudent man and a skilled craftsman (technikos) of ruling (*Gorgias* 490a). Moreover, having perhaps absorbed the view that "music" is an altogether paltry art in comparison with the serious crafts that serve bodily needs, Callicles offers no opposition to Socrates' disparaging assessment of the contribution made by tragic poetry to the correct art of rhetoric (*Gorgias* 502). He probably shares Gorgias's confidence that rhetoric is the only art worth knowing. Indeed, when Gorgias claims that rhetoric can produce any belief the rhetorician wishes to in its audience, he includes the effects produced by tragic poetry.

This echoes a claim made, according to Plato, by many of the pre-Socratics and Sophists to have displaced the authority of the poets in shaping the beliefs of the Greeks, so that, as Socrates wryly remarks, today even the shoemakers know that everything is in motion and nothing "is" (*Theaetetus* 180d). And in this connection, we should note a complication that will prove to be important when we examine Socrates' proposals for the reform of poetry and other sources of belief about the cosmos. For, as Socrates depicts them in the *Theaetetus,* the pre-Socratics and Sophists displaced the authority of the poets not in the sense of contravening their teachings, but in the sense of teaching openly what the poets themselves, as far back as Homer, had believed but had hidden in the allusiveness of their verse: that the world was indeed based on motion, flow, and chance (152e, 179e, 180d, cf. *Protagoras* 316d). As I will argue in chapters 3, 4, and 5, for Socrates the pre-Socratics and Sophists on the one hand and the poets on the other constitute two variants of the primordialist ontology. The poets react to the terrible truth that "nothing is" by praising virtue as a way of life that is unnatural and painful but nevertheless necessary if the polis is to stave off the Dionysian chaos that impinges on its settled conventions through war, selfish passion, and hubristic ambition. The Sophists' teachings react by arguing that one can embrace the truth that "nothing is" and live according to one's desires without suffering the tragic consequences visited upon a figure like Oedipus the tyrant—so long as one is able to camouflage this pursuit of the natural life with a rhetoric of moral decency. In Socrates' critique, as we will see, both views corrode the possibilities of civic and moral virtue: the Sophists openly and shamelessly, the tragedians in a more complicated, unintended way.

It is precisely Callicles' respect for a political technē that leads him into a dialectical noose from which he can extricate himself only by refusing to converse. As we saw in the last chapter, one of Socrates' first responses to the paradigm of natural mastery that Callicles sets forth in his long speech is to get Callicles to agree that a man with the capacity to rule will be prudent (phronimos). Callicles readily grants that the natural master will possess a superior endowment of brains, courage, and experience in political affairs. Otherwise, his strength of character could not be distinguished from the mere bodily strength that a "pack of slaves" might achieve when they pool forces. He is further amenable when Socrates takes the argument a crucial step further, narrowing the meaning of phronēsis by identifying it with an expert craftsman of ruling (*Gorgias* 488b–491d). This sets up a quandary for the rest of the dialogue. Whenever Callicles thinks that Socrates is elaborating a technē of rule that would enable a statesman to aggrandize himself and his city, he agrees to the craft analogy. But he bridles and backtracks whenever Socrates attempts to turn technē—and by implication the art of ruling—from the servant of bodily pleasures into the regulator of bodily pleasures by taking the rigor and clarity of the arts to be reflective of the cosmos as it is instantiated in the housekeeping of the soul (*Gorgias* 504). Again and again throughout their encounter, Socrates' apparent progress toward agreement is disrupted by Callicles' refusal to follow the logos of the craft analogy from a means for producing greater power, wealth, and honor for the artisan to the self-forgetting orderliness of soul prescribed by Socrates.

The primordialist ontology helps to explain another ambivalent feature of the conventionalist position that causes Callicles a good deal of perplexity in his dialogue with Socrates. This is the fact that the teachings of the Sophists derived from the ontological priority of tuchē could apparently support, on the one hand, a conservative, positivistic defense of the status quo, or, on the other hand, its subversion and overthrow.[12] This ambivalent stance toward established political authority is rooted in the paradoxicality of the primordialist interpretation of nature—the issuing forth of beings "according to chance" and "by necessity." Whatever comes into being does so by accident—"according to chance." Therefore, whatever it happens to turn out to be, this is what it must be—"by necessity." Each being is a destiny. It springs unpredictably out of genesis, and so must be the shape into which it happens to have settled until it passes back into the matrix of subphenomenal motion.

This paradox extends to political life as well. Conventional standards of justice are constantly changing, coming into being and passing away. Despite what they claim, none of them possesses permanent validity. They are therefore "authoritative" (*kurios*) only for as long as they last "in time" (*Laws* 889e–890a).[13] This is the subversive implication of the conventionalist view of justice. What is known to be a temporary phenomenon thrown up by chance cannot be morally binding on a serious person. But this means, on the other hand, that for so long as these appearances do last, they are absolutely authoritative in a positivistic sense. This is the conservative implication. They must be obeyed by those who live under them. They are authoritative for as long as they appear. In this context, the moral or juridical "must" of such an obligation collapses into the brute fact that the rulers will enforce obedience to their dictates.[14] Convention must be whatever it currently is, because convention is the only stability of which phusis is capable in political and moral terms. There is nothing truly stable and universal toward which nature directs us that can be said to transcend convention and provide a substantive standard for determining whether or to what degree a given, particular nomos is deserving of obedience or not. As one of Heracleitus's fragments puts it, nature is war or strife (*polemos*): "War is both king of all and father of all, and it has revealed some as gods, others as men; some it has made slaves, others free." Master and slave, ruler and ruled, issue forth from this matrix of conflict, the all-consuming fire at the heart of life. Whoever prevails, prevails—until they are overcome by another upsurge of unfathomable force. As long as they last, they are obeyed. One cannot ask if their authority is just or unjust, because no supersensible and eternal standards exist for making such a judgment.[15]

Thus, political life is both all that it can be and capable of radical reshaping. This ambiguity is evident, for instance, in Thrasymachus's famous definition of justice as "the advantage of the stronger" (*Republic* 338c). On one level, and as he initially presents it, this is a doctrine of strict legal positivism: the ruling party, be it one person, a group, or a majority, sets forth laws that serve its interests, calls them just, and enforces their obedience. The ruled must obey them because they must, although the rulers' task of staying in power will be easier to the extent that the ruled are deluded into thinking these conventions are true in themselves or upheld by the gods. The rulers have the power, and there is no other source of authority in politics, whatever claims to divine or eternal validity established authorities may make. But, Thrasymachus goes on to argue, one who knows the technē of rule possesses a skilled efficiency in pursuing his advantage that sets him apart from the feckless and inconsistent selfishness that we often observe in conventional political authorities, especially when they actually believe in their own conventions preaching justice, moderation, and piety. The ruler may indeed benefit the ruled, but only in the sense, Thrasymachus claims, that a shepherd fattens his flock prior to the slaughter (*Republic* 343b–344d). The metaphor implies that only the tyrant can really be said to realize the fullest possibilities of natural selfishness. This titan can, and therefore should, trample over the conventions of less vigorously and efficiently selfish authorities. As in the Athenian generals' speech on Melos, it is necessary to rule where one has the chance to do so, and the chance and necessity both establish the rightness of doing so.[16]

THE CONSERVATIVE AND REVOLUTIONARY IMPLICATIONS OF CONVENTIONALISM

Of course, some Sophists argued that the safe and efficient pursuit of self-interest made it in one's best interest to obey the social compact and not step out of line in the dangerous pursuit of a superlative degree of pleasure or honor.[17] In this variation of conventionalism, while convention is not exactly natural, nature supplies a solid motive for abiding by it. Protagoras was perhaps the most thoughtful of those Sophists who tried to reconcile the primordialist ontology of nature with a responsible stance toward government and statecraft.[18] Protagoras argued that, precisely because man's natural condition is so crudely rapacious and unrestrained, one is led to prize the order and civility that conventional political authority has managed to achieve more keenly than if one thought order and civility were spontaneous traits. As Socrates presents him in the *Theaetetus,* Protagoras claims to use rhetoric to help a society be "better," although he does not claim to be making its ways more "true" (166d, 172a–b, 177d–e, 180a–c). This is because, for Protagoras, everything is both true and not true, and appearance is all the reality there is. We can plausibly reconstruct his position as presented in the *Theaetetus* as follows: Each society, rooted in a spontaneous original generation of nature, has developed along its own unique path and settled down into its present appearance and conventions. To be "better" would mean to be attuned to, to tap the vital rhythms, of that "way"—to help the city better (more efficiently, prudently) achieve what it holds to be best for itself. This is the sense in which Thucydides notes the moderation of Pericles. He was not moderate in the Socratic sense of avoiding empire, but in the sense that he cautioned the city to protect its empire by avoiding new adventures that did not square with its resources and vulnerability to domestic turmoil.[19]

Thus, in a certain sense, the Sophist could be seen as a conservative, someone who supports the powers that be and helps the city achieve its agenda. Thrasymachus and Gorgias both depict themselves in this light, and by some accounts Gorgias had extensive experience in real-life diplomacy and politics. Indeed, this may help explain a puzzling remark of Callicles—his contemptuous dismissal of "Sophists" without seeming to understand that Gorgias fits into this category (*Gorgias* 529a). A source of the respect of men like Polus and Callicles for Gorgias must have been that he did not appear to be a mere intellectual trifler, but a man whose sagacity gave him a role in the great affairs of state. The sense in which Socrates is, by contrast, a subversive is well illustrated in the *Gorgias* when Callicles bridles at Socrates' low regard for Pericles and the glories of empire. But the conservatism of the Sophists is, at bottom, a shifting and dubious proposition, particularly if the conservation of the political community means primarily the education of citizens to treat each other decently and to place the common interest above the private. Nothing in principle prevents the Sophist from trying to reshape convention for his own profit or for the profit of whoever pays for the Sophist's services. Since the basis of the current permanence is the more primordial impermanence, no existing order of things can be truly permanent or binding on human conduct, or even a partial approximation of eternal standards. If, as Protagoras (like all the Sophists) argued, self-interest is at bottom the natural life, it is hard to reconcile this basic premise with the good of the community in any but an instrumental sense that arguably must give way when an individual can preserve himself or increase his pleasures by abrogating the social contract openly or by stealth.

In my view this is why Plato, in telescoping the Sophistical teachings and their primordialist ontology in the *Laws* for critical scrutiny from the viewpoint of a well-founded politeia, emphasizes that the most prevalent and consistent moral-political outcome of these teachings is that tyranny is the best way of life.[20] The pre-Socratics sometimes intimated that violent disorder was at the very core of all life—hence, Heracleitus's maxims that "war is the father of all" and "strife is justice." Even if, as is likely, these maxims were not meant literally, or exclusively, in a political sense, but were meditations on the Being of beings, it is hardly surprising that they might have been taken to imply a tyrannical and imperialistic political outcome. According to another of the Gorgias fragments, "our struggle in life requires two virtues, courage and wisdom—readiness to endure a danger and skilful knowledge of how to manage it."[21] This lends added force to our observation in chapter 1 that, of the virtues discussed in the *Gorgias,* Callicles will agree with Socrates on the worth of courage and wisdom, but not of moderation and justice.

The insufficiency of the Sophists' understanding of nature and politics for enabling Callicles to articulate his expectations from public life becomes manifest when Socrates asks whether it is the Athenian majority or Callicles' natural master that is really "stronger," hence "better" (*Gorgias* 488b–491d). What Callicles wants from this dialogue is to find a standard for distinguishing the superior qualities of mind and character that entitle the natural master to rule (were he to emerge on the scene) from the combined physical strength of the Athenian dēmos that does in fact rule. But if bodily strength and desires are indeed the truly natural aspect of human life, mirroring the fact that nature itself is a cycle of vital movements without form or purpose, and if a large mass of people can combine their strength and desires so as to set up a political authority that will serve their interests as they perceive them, then Callicles really has no standard for protesting the assimilation of natural superiority to the brute might of that mass of people and their authoritative conventions. The Sophists' claim to possess an art of politics that only the enlightened few can master is their way of attempting to introduce an aristocratic distinction between those truly deserving to rule and the unimaginative authorities that usually do rule.[22] Hence, Thrasymachus's initial endorsement of all existing conventional authority acts as a kind of protective carapace for his more considered but potentially offensive view that only the individual of strong ambition and the skill to achieve it is living naturally in the full sense (*Republic* 340e–341a, 343b–344b). But since that art of politics provides no universal discursive structure for substantively distinguishing between a naturally superior statesman and the brute power of the status quo, and since that art always reduces to maximizing the bodily interests that the unimaginative masses share with the outstanding people, then again it would seem that this art provides no consistent standard for claiming that the dullards who do in fact have power and authority should somehow give way to anyone else. Professional teachers of rhetoric like Thrasymachus blustered their way through this ambiguity, adding it to their bag of tricks to make themselves pleasing to different kinds of audience. Hence, Thrasymachus could pose at one time as the bluff pragmatist, the legal positivist for whom any attempt to distinguish between who in fact has power and who should have power is just a pack of intellectual nonsense, and, at other times, as the purveyor of an exclusive intellectual skill that only the finest people are capable of grasping.

Callicles is faced with this ambiguity in his own life, in his own expectations from the political career on which he is just embarking. The Sophists' teachings force him to concede, on the one hand, the logic of positivistic conservatism. He cannot gainsay Socrates' conclusion that, on his own definition of "better" as unqualified political might, the Athenian dēmos whose egalitarianism he volubly disdains has every bit as good a title to rule as does his "natural master." Indeed, the dēmos *is* the natural master in Athens. Because Callicles hates this conclusion with every fiber of his being, he clings to the notion of an aristocratic art of statecraft. But since he is equally unwilling to follow Socrates along the logic of the craft analogy, which leads to the forgetting of one's self-interest and the subordination of pleasure to the managerial orderliness of moderate statesmanship, Callicles ends up back in the same dilemma. For although the Sophists' understanding of the art of rule is meant to provide this aristocratic distinction between the uninformed conventional authorities and the gifted few meant for greatness, at bottom it is in the service of a crude political domination that unavoidably collapses back into the domination exercised in fact by whatever unimaginative and vulgar political authorities actually exist. Callicles veers constantly back and forth between the unreconcilable conservative and revolutionary dimensions of Sophistry. He switches between the bluff man of affairs who warns Socrates that his naivete and inexperience will get him in trouble with the Big Boys, and the aristocratic radical who looks down on the powers that be on behalf of a standard of superiority that, at least in his rich imagination, would blast the democratic polis apart. These switches reveal his inability, given the teachings he has absorbed, to articulate the naturally independent life toward which his eros draws him in inchoate longing and admiration. He wants neither to be the prehistoric marauder Hercules nor the weakling Socrates, but he does not know where to find the third alternative. This is the "doubleness" of soul that Socrates, with his usual finesse in erotic matters, has sensed in Callicles now and in the past (*Gorgias* 481a–483a). His point of departure for attempting to wean Callicles of his love of the dēmos is to spark Callicles' reflection on the "common feelings" they share as lovers: feelings that make Callicles a frustrated and confused lover, but that in Socrates' case are, he claims, directed toward a series of distinct and ranked objects of longing— "my Alcibiades" and Philosophy.

The paradoxes of primordialism, and the sharp contrast between Socratic cosmology and that of the Sophists, weave in and out of the arguments about the meaning of statecraft (politikē) in the *Gorgias*. On the face of it, the encounter between Socrates and Callicles can be viewed as an encounter between theory and practice—the man of affairs upbraiding the detached and retiring thinker for his naivete. Indeed, there is a good deal of badinage to this effect. But this first impression does not hold up. Although somewhat closer to political realities than the *Republic,* whose chief interlocutor Glaucon is younger and politically less experienced than Callicles, the *Gorgias* is, like the *Republic,* primarily an exploration of how to think about political phenomena, including how to think about ruling, rather than what to do about them. Socrates' contention in the *Gorgias* that he alone "practices politics" in Athens today is only relatively less utopian-sounding than his contention in the *Republic* that the ills of the city will not be healed unless philosophers rule. By the same token, of course, as the Athenian Stranger tries to tell Kleinias, practical issues of governance are now closely intertwined with differing philosophical speculations about the cosmos. Pure practice is not possible in a world where philosophy has made its appearance.

In Socrates' dialogue with Callicles, then, it is not so much a matter of theory versus practice as theory versus theory.[23] Callicles' argument on behalf of natural mastery, and his dismissal of equality as a pusillanimous convention, are for obvious reasons not things he could say in public to the Athenians. Even the upper classes of Athenian society might take offense at the implication that their entitlement to honor and wealth rests on convention only, and would deserve to be swept

away by someone who is noble by nature. It is quite conceivable that, if his public career takes off, Callicles will present himself as a friend of the democracy
(*Gorgias* 515a, 521a–b). In so doing, he would carry out in deed the contradiction
with which Socrates embarrasses Gorgias and Thrasymachus in discussion. The
Sophists can teach rhetorical techniques for coloring oneself to blend in with the
justice of any given regime, but at bottom they do not believe the justice of any
given regime to have a basis in nature.

Despite its ontological paradoxes, Sophistry does possess a certain kind of inner
coherence between speech and deed if we grant its main premise that human
beings are by nature individualistic and compelled to get the better. For there is a
natural link between what the Sophists, and sophisticated politicians like Callicles,
actually believe to be true by nature, and the conventionally acceptable things they
may say in public. According to Callicles, the pusillanimous majority of human
beings do actually believe, by nature or in their heart of hearts, that mastery is the
best life, although they profess to believe in equality (483b–d). In contradistinc-
tion to what they profess in speech, the many silently want what Callicles says only
the naturally noble have the guts to try to do: rule without constraint and maximize
their pleasure and honor. Thus, by professing to believe in conventional morality
in his public speeches, Callicles may conceivably plan to protect himself with a
carapace of respectability, while through his political actions he can lead the Athenians in such a way as to gratify their unspoken longings for tyranny, perhaps
through restoring the city's Themistoclean and Periclean greatness in foreign
affairs. In this way, as he hopes, Callicles can serve and rule the many at the same
time.

Still, in the *Gorgias* itself, Socrates and Callicles are not so much debating the
comparative merits of philosophical contemplation and political action as the
comparative merits of two different kinds of philosophical speech for understanding politics and its relationship with philosophy. In the wider sphere of the everyday political hurly-burly that Callicles is embarked upon, Callicles may prove to
be too clever by half. The elaborate combination of egalitarian public speech with
a private belief in inegalitarian natural right that is required by Callicles' absorption of Sophistical teachings may prove to be less effective in a political career
than the blunt, crude, but effective grasp of the realities of power displayed by a
man like Cleon in Thucydides, who despised rhetoricians and decried their influence over Athenian public life.[24]

In this respect, the *Gorgias* may also be said to explore the question of whether
and to what degree philosophical friendships (the "common feelings" that Socrates and Callicles at least initially share as lovers of the beautiful) are the same as
political friendships or alliances—or, to put it more bluntly, whether discussing
statesmanship is necessarily of much use in practicing it. Although Callicles may
be more attuned to the rough and tumble of politics than, say, Glaucon in the
Republic, he is only just about to launch a political career. His experience is limited. His speech about the natural master is rather fanciful in comparison with the

often tedious requirements of political success. While the older Gorgias is happy to talk about the usefulness of rhetoric in gaining public support for such sober municipal projects as harbors and walls (445d–e), Callicles is bored to death by any discussion of the banausic arts (491a). Although he presents it as a way of showing his hard-nosed familiarity with the real world in contrast with Socrates' childish moralism, Callicles' speech is perhaps more revealing of a young man's as yet untested longings for political life, more connected with that philosophical side of life in which Callicles says noble and broad-minded youths should indulge for a period, than with what actually awaits him in politics (484c, 485a). Socrates, having overheard this side of Callicles on an earlier occasion, begins by believing he can win Callicles over as his philosophical friend.

In this way, then, Socrates' encounter with Callicles has more to do with political philosophy than with actual politics, notwithstanding my observation in chapter 1 that the premises of the dialogue prevent a full and open discussion of the independent pleasures of philosophy as distinct from politikē. Its purpose is not so much to provide a plan for reforming Athenian politics as to reflect on how one should think about virtue and statesmanship—although, as I will discuss at length in chapter 3, this would not preclude such reflections reaching out to affect wider circles of active citizens and politicians. As Callicles himself lectures Socrates, when you enter the real world of political factions and alliances—as opposed to philosophical friendships based on reflecting on the phenomena of political life— you must be prepared to slap or be slapped. You need power both to reward your friends and harm your enemies (485c, 486c). Like all the Platonic dialogues, the *Gorgias* is a temporary island of discourse at rest within the stormy seas of the city in motion. There are no slaps, only verbal refutations. As we have observed, Callicles is afraid of the side of himself that may be attracted to philosophizing because it will corrode his resolve to slap rather than be slapped. But his very ability to articulate this dilemma suggests that, at bottom, he may already be too reflective a person to do the harsh things that a Cleon or a Meletus would do without much reflection at all.

SOUL CAME FIRST: THE PLATONIC REVERSAL.

In a nutshell, the response of the Athenian Stranger to the pernicious influence of the primordialist ontology is to reverse its main premise: "When they use the term nature, they mean the process by which the primary substances were created. But if it can be shown that soul came first, it will be quite correct to say that soul is preeminently natural" (*Laws* 892). In the following chapters, I will examine some of the ways in which Plato attempts this grand reversal: the transposition of soul constituted by nous for the unfathomable motions of tuchē. But we must always bear in mind that, in Platonic political philosophy, cosmologies grow out of, and respond to, the psychological traits and needs of the type of people to whom they are addressed—in the main, good citizens with a friendship for philosophy. Plato places these cosmological teachings in a dialogical context in order to show the noble rhetoric of statecraft in action. For it is precisely these conversations about virtue that constitute the core of Socrates' claim to be one of the few men in Athens who attempts the true art of ruling and the only one who is actually "practicing politics."

Although, as I have just suggested, Callicles and Socrates are not so much debating the comparative merits of political theory and practice as they are offering different theories of politics, in Platonic political philosophy, theories always emerge from character, each shaping the other. Callicles' absorption of Sophistical teachings is shaped by the kind of man he is, and his character modifies his selection and understanding of those teachings. Callicles does not admire tyranny because he first came to believe in Heracleitean metaphysics. Rather, because of his root erotic disorder, he is attracted to teachings that support and exacerbate his underlying ambitions for political mastery. Accordingly, the refutation of the doctrines must be grounded in a therapy for the eros. Another of the Gorgias fragments sheds some possible light on how the Socratic therapy tries to treat the disorders of the soul that underlie the attraction to unsound doctrines. The fragment reads: "The glory (kosmos) of a city is courage; of a body, beauty; of a soul, wisdom; of action, virtue; of speech, truth."[25] The fragment states that the "cosmos" of a city—its wholeness and substance—resides in its exercise of the active, aggressive virtue of courage. The "cosmos" of a body is another active, generative, and living quality—its physical beauty. Extending the implied analogy to the rest of the list, we can surmise that, for Gorgias, the wholeness and beauty of the soul reside in an active, engaged kind of wisdom (perhaps exemplified by Gorgias's own career), while the "cosmos" of speech is "truth" in the primordialist sense— the infusion into logos of the seeming/being of phusis, according to which nothing "is." If Callicles has absorbed these kinds of speculations, it is little wonder that, as Socrates implies, he jumbles up his private erotic longing (his love of the boy Demos) with his expectations from a career in politics (his love of the Athenian dēmos). In other words, he expects to find a "cosmos"—a sense of repose and satisfaction—in the consummation of his eros for the Athenian dēmos as gratifying to his passions as the consummation of his longing for the beautiful body of the son of Pyrilampes. What is common to the attributions of "cosmos" to different phenomena in the Gorgias fragment is the identification of the full, hale being of a thing with some active and somatic quality. This helps us to understand why Socrates, by contrast, is so bent on convincing Callicles to view a well-ordered (kosmion) soul as being analogous, not to some such pulse of energy and passion, but to the stable order (taxis) of a well-constructed house or any structure informed by nous.

I have tried to show in the last two chapters how the inadequacy of the Sophists' teachings for articulating Callicles' longing for true natural independence is revealed by his own behavior and arguments. To the extent that Callicles accepts

Socrates' psychoanalysis of his erotic doubleness—and this is the one claim of Socrates he never challenges directly—Socrates' diagnosis of Callicles' character is already a part of the Platonic critique of Sophistry. Why? Because only Socrates and not the Sophists can account for the interesting truth about Callicles' eros — that it is a *structured* longing that seeks not merely to overthrow nomos but to embody its satisfaction *in* a nomos "according to nature." Callicles needs "political science" in what I will argue is the Socratic meaning of the term—not a teaching about nature that exposes the political community as artificial, but the search for a set of political conventions that are according to nature rather than against it. In what follows, therefore, the doctrinal assertions about the orderliness of the cosmos and the soul will be effective, on Plato's own ground rules, only to the extent that they successfully address the fundamental erotic "doubleness" that motivates the tyrannically inclined personality to reject the common good and pursue pleonexia. And to the extent that they fail to do this, we will have an indication from Plato both of how these doctrinal assertions fail to stand up on purely metaphysical grounds and of the limitations on reason's power to reform politics. As I will argue in chapter 4, the test case for this marriage of metaphysics and morals is the "correct opinion" of the Auxiliaries' education in the *Republic*—an education that, as I interpret it, attempts to impart certain Socratic traits to the civic-spirited.

As we will see in the chapters to come, Socrates wishes to persuade his listeners that moderation and justice in civic life are not only compatible with, but necessary for, friendships and erotic relationships that are truly satisfying. Reason should rule, but in the sense of persuading citizens that they will be happiest if their passions are educated to fulfill their best potential.

This does not mean constraint and force can be excluded from statecraft. One of the most important differences between Socrates and the Sophists is over this. For, despite their tough-minded identification of ruling with self-interest, Sophists like Gorgias seemed to believe that speech could achieve anything—that, as in Glaucon's model of the perfectly unjust man, it could disguise you from retribution in the way that Gyges' ring made that usurper invisible (*Republic* 360b–361a). Precisely because Socrates believes, by contrast, that speeches will be persuasive only to the extent that they provide therapy for directing the passions away from their aberrant aims toward their fullest satisfaction, he does not believe that rhetoric can provide a kind of insulation from the anger and resentment that one's actions might produce in other people. As the image of the chariot from the *Phaedrus* implies, reason and speech cooperate with the passions, controlling them by redirecting and fulfilling their own energies—not by casting a kind of spell over them as if words alone could produce changes in behavior, as the Gorgias fragment about the power of rhetoric suggests. For this reason, Socrates is more keenly aware than the Sophists of the extent to which the passions can elude or resist this appeal from reasoned speech, and the need therefore to supplement persuasion with, as it were, the bridles and harness of legislation, castigation, and punishment (*Gorgias* 480a.6–480d). A well-arranged politeia rules primarily by persuasion, not compulsion. But through its laws and habituation it shapes the passions, and it reserves punishments for the intractable.

Since the tyrant is the paradigm of the man in whom passion rules, he is the limit test case for elaborating the prospects of such a civic paideia. If a well-ordered constitution does not find a place for this kind of person, if it does not find a way of redirecting his passions for honor and pleasure to the service of the common good, then one of the most potent threats to political order and stability will stand outside of the constitutional arrangement. This is one of the reasons why a work like the *Republic* begins with and returns to the temptations of tyranny (Books 2 and 9). It makes no sense, from the Platonic viewpoint, to discuss the characteristics of the best constitution unless from the outset it can account for, contain, and tame, through civic education, this most subversive and destructive of challenges to the whole notion of the common good. The guide to this education is a philosopher who is himself motivated by the desire to know, and who, as I will argue in chapter 3, stimulates his friends to question their own conceptions of the good life out of an eros for their neediness. Socrates' philanthropy is a direct consequence of his own gratification through philosophical conversation—a model for the union of pleasure and duty that constitutes his claim to be the only Athenian who "practices politics."

The novelty of the Platonic reversal is revealed in its basics by the *Alcibiades* I, a dialogue that prefigures many of the issues we will explore in later chapters. As Socrates describes the young Alcibiades, he displays the supreme self-confidence that was a constant trait throughout his life. In presenting himself to the young man as a prospective teacher, Socrates not only does not criticize his ambitions, but begins by enflaming them. For, in telling Alcibiades what he has observed about him from a distance, he stresses how much Alcibiades wants everyone to love him and longs for a fame that will carry him beyond Athens and "fill all mankind with his name and power" (105c). Enflaming Alcibiades' ambition for world fame is the first step in expanding Alcibiades' horizons beyond the Athenian polis to the universality of philosophical reflection. In order to compensate for the poverty of Athens' own concern with a proper civic education, Socrates must transport Alcibiades in his imagination to a world where a lifelong concern with virtue breeds rulers who experience the heights of prestige and pleasure while ruling benevolently (121–124). He then brings Alcibiades back to his real city, hoping to have sparked in him an awareness of his need for further reflection on what it would mean to be a good statesman.

Furthermore, by so ably articulating Alcibiades' own ambitions, perhaps even enflaming them beyond the young man's own conscious awareness, Socrates makes himself intriguing. For, although he can manifestly understand Alcibiades' ambitions, his own life appears to share nothing in common with them. If Socrates thinks it is natural for a talented young man to aim for such honor, why hasn't he? What does he do that is so much preferable? We see in this first encounter a germ of Alcibiades' enduring fascination with the older man. Despite his plain looks and evident lack of wealth and influence, Socrates recognizes Alcibiades' own vaunting ambition and in so doing demonstrates that, in some peculiar way beyond

Alcibiades' experience of life, Socrates is also self-confident and in need of no one—with the crucial and mystifying difference that the source of his independence is something other than political success. Beginning his approach to Alcibiades by confessing his erotic passion for the younger man, Socrates predicts that it is Alcibiades himself who will become attached to Socrates—he will "long to know" what Socrates has divined about his character and prospects (104c–d). In this early encounter, as I will argue at length in the next chapter, we already see the basis for Alcibiades' accusation in the *Symposium* (some fifteen years later within the dramatic universe of the dialogues) that Socrates always ends up as the beloved rather than the lover, drawing all longing toward himself.

In this first encounter, Socrates criticizes Alcibiades for "rushing toward politics before you have been educated" (118b). His claim here is extreme. Powerful, wealthy, and cultured Athens, which prided itself on being the "school of Hellas," in truth has no education worthy of the name. Socrates claims that neither Alcibiades nor anyone else has been properly educated about the meaning of virtue, as is evidenced by Alcibiades' befuddlement over the relation of justice to nobility. Alcibiades concedes that this is so. Even though his guardian is the illustrious and influential Pericles, his only education was at the hands of an old servant (122b). Pericles himself, Alcibiades points out, was educated by the natural philosopher Anaxagoras and the poet Damon. But Socrates tellingly replies that this was no real education because Pericles did not in turn teach or improve anyone else, including (implicitly) his own nephew, who is ambitious to equal and even surpass his achievements (119a). In Athens, Socrates claims, an education in virtue is left to private speculation or to the advice on success with which private individuals woo their beloveds. The Sophists teach one how to pursue one's own advantage and how to disguise this from the credulous. But the barrenness of their concern with the common good—with the constitution (politeia) as a source of education that shapes citizens' characters instead of just a convention to be manipulated—is exposed by its contrast with the elaborate stages of the Persian paideia.

The dialogue thus gives us a particularly vivid impression of how the traditional sources of Greek paideia—the Homeric heroism still alive at Marathon—have declined during Athens' rise to empire.[26] It is the same state of affairs lamented in the *Clouds* when Aristophanes presents the Unjust Logos defending self-interest and injustice while mercilessly ridiculing the rather tired defense of traditional virtues offered by the Just Logos (*Clouds* 890–955, 1035–1105). Socrates' praise of Persia and Sparta with their care for education fills the erotic opening in Alcibiades' soul created by his confusion with the completed image of a well-ordered constitution that does not merely coerce obedience, or buy it through the protection of interests, but shapes the characters of its statesmen so that they can fulfill their own moral and intellectual capacities. In a sense, Socrates' royal myth of an idealized Persian monarchy is a rehearsal for the "city in speech" elaborated by the *Republic,* taking the soul out of itself so as to clarify and specify the stages of its education in association with others, then returning it to the actual community able to "found" this "pattern" in itself, equipped with a standard for effecting whatever partial reforms real circumstances permit (*Republic* 592a–b). In so doing, Socrates again enflames Alcibiades' eros to rule, especially in detailing the might and splendor of the Persian king. But he enflames it in order to enlist it in a more careful reflection on the requirements of the common good whose leader he might become: Eros grounds and stimulates analysis. He hopes Alcibiades will fulfill his ambitions for public honor by improving his own city in similar ways. He takes him beyond Athens to lead him to the universality of thought about the best constitution, so as to return him to his own world better equipped to see its shortcomings. In this sense, the heuristic embellishment of Sparta and Persia as paradigmatic constitutions prefigures the cycle of the *Republic* as it is crystallized in the Image of the Cave: reflecting on the shortcomings of the politics practiced around us leads us in search of a clarifying "form" of noncontradictory virtue, a glimpse of the light of true being that enables us to return to our own community with a critical insight into its deficiencies. Socrates' dialogue with Alcibiades is a good illustration of what Socrates says everyone needs in the Image of the Cave: someone to "turn them around" to gaze at the light of universal truth, and then to turn back to their own community able to see it clearly for the first time.

The *Alcibiades* I thus illustrates the political implications of the general ontological transposition of soul for tuchē that the Athenian Stranger offers as the metaphysical remedy for the harmful effects of the primordialist ontology. The turning effected by Alcibiades' confusion and Socrates' fashioning of an image of a good constitution to fill that openness in the young man's soul helps explain the shift that occurs in the last part of the dialogue from the art of ruling *per se* to the duty of self-examination that Socrates derives from the old saying, "know thyself." The art of ruling must begin with learning the art of caring for one's own soul and those of one's fellow citizens. Before one can know how to rule others, one must prove that one knows how to benefit them. And this first requires putting one's own soul in the right condition. More important than the dialogue's concluding exchanges is the royal myth itself. In laying out the virtues of the Persian king, showing how a good education can bring the rewards of political success without involving vice, Socrates has at least expanded Alcibiades' sense of what care for the soul involves. It remains to be seen how the primary human passions of love and honor can be educated in a community of citizens—not an empire or monarchy—so that the individual citizen might find the satisfaction of his nature in the performance of his duty.

LOVE AND HONOR: THE TWO PATHS TO THE ART OF STATESMANSHIP

Before turning to the *Symposium* and *Republic*, it will be useful to give the reader a brief overview of how I will proceed. Unless properly directed, eros is incompatible either with true pleasure or with honor. The treatment is an education that will encourage the soul to be orderly (kosmion) in a way that reflects the harmonious proportionality characteristic of true being. Chance, accident, and motion are characteristic of the least real dimension of being—the falling away of a thing from its *eidos*. To believe in the primordialist ontology is to exacerbate the power of the passions over oneself. This places one under the sway of fortune, both in the sense that one abandons one's self-control to the irrational forces that act on human nature through the passions, summoning us to frenzy and disarray, and in the sense that, to the extent that we gratify these passions by pursuing their perishable correlates in the world, we are dependent for our happiness on external goods that do not last and can easily be destroyed or impeded by our enemies. As a monster of erotic dissipation, the tyrant is the very slave of fortune.

I will emphasize two different paths that Socrates sets forth as a therapy for the tyrannical character. One path, explored in the *Symposium*, educates eros in such a way as to direct it toward its best hope for satisfaction through philosophizing, an ascent that entails as one of its stages noble service to the political community. The other path is a harder one—as the Image of the Cave puts it, a steep and rocky ascent (*Republic* 515e). Instead of being educated, political eros is extirpated from the optimal community. For the erotic satisfaction of civic fame in Diotima's Ladder, the *Republic* substitutes a dignified self-control reinforced by an education in the harmony of the cosmos. This inculcation of the taste for orderliness provides a certain graciousness of character but not the prospect of direct erotic fulfilment through serving the city.

These paths represent different aspects of the problematic proposition that human longing, even when properly educated, could be permanently and completely fulfilled by any particular ordering of the political community. That question remains an open one in the Platonic corpus because, for reasons I will enlarge upon below, the debate over whether duty to the common good should be the primary aim of the good life as opposed to the pleasure and happiness of the individual is coeval with the human condition. As Diotima puts it, eros wants the good to be its own forever (*Symposium* 206a). To be human is to long for transcendence of the limitations of the human condition, but to long for it in a way that makes the good a possession—a paradox that introduces the possibility of mastery and tyranny in the very moment of awakening love. Can this passion be sublimated by a redirection that involves both philosophic and civic virtue? Or must it be repressed on the political level while a fortunate few are able to gratify it through philosophy and philosophic friendship? Plato does not offer a definitive resolution of this question, only perspectives for continuing reflection.

One of the constants of the Platonic approach, however, is the use of technē as an analogy for the orderliness that the cosmos might impart to a soul properly educated to receive it. As we have seen in this chapter, in some of the writings attributed to the Sophists and pre-Socratics we encounter the view that technē can provide an instrument for human mastery. The supposition that what "is" is in truth a concatenation of transient becomings led some—as evidenced by the Gorgias fragment—to postulate an art of rhetoric that could rearrange these appearances so as to convince the audience of anything the orator wished. As one of the sayings attributed to Empedocles implies, some even entertained the Faustian notion that the wise man who understood the roots of phusis in tuchē could refashion the world, calling the great chaotic forces underlying the superficial stability into his service like a magician. But whenever Socrates uses the analogy of virtue to art, tyranny and pleonexia are shown to be senseless. The Sophists and pre-Socratics offered a view of the world in which being is indistinguishable from seeming; in which law, custom, and adjurations to restraint are mere transient concatenations of motion that a person wise in the ways of nature can prudently ignore or even manipulate to his advantage in the minds of the gullible "many." But the Platonic Socrates says, in effect: Look around you. Is it really the case that nothing "is," as Heracleitus, Protagoras, and others maintain? Are there not some solid factual limitations on what we can say is or is not the case? Some of the Sophists had a view of technē akin to modern utilitarianism and instrumental reasoning. That is to say, they viewed it as a tool whereby the individual can maximize his power. But whereas the utilitarian interpretation of technē is self-assertive, the Socratic view of technē is self-forgetting. Instead of seeing art primarily in terms of fabrication and effectuation, Socrates invites us to trace the patterns of the total ensemble linking artisan, art, and product, an ensemble that points in turn to the cosmic orderliness grounding all intelligible activity. The arts offer themselves as a rudimentary beginning point, a hypothesis, for thinking through the possible stability of the world in the vacuum left by the pre-Socratics and the Sophists. The arts, as Socrates presents them, are reliably, objectively connected to the world. They achieve what they set out to do, they can be repeated over and over again, and they are valid in any place regardless of whatever conventions reign locally. No Sophist can convince anyone that he can make a shoe if he does not in fact possess the art of cobblery. The flimsiness of the rhetorician's claims when tested against the achievements of the banausic arts invites us to think through the likelihood that there is an equally solid art for the governing of human beings against which the claims of the Sophists would be likewise exposed as a mere knack or cajolery. In other words, Socrates asks, might the clarity and structure characteristic of the arts extend to more complex, controversial phenomena like justice? Might their relatively straightforward clarity be an intimation of an orderliness that more elusively, but just as surely, perdures through the changeability of the most important political and moral phenomena?

Socrates begins the search for justice in the *Republic* with a maxim from Simonides. But he disposes of Simonides in a few sentences, proposing instead that they look for justice as if it were an art: just as medicine distributes treatment to sickness, so would the art of justice distribute a good to its beneficiaries (*Republic* 332c–d). In this way, he attempts to give his listeners a foothold in a world where every traditional authority has been rendered dubious. As Socrates employs the analogy of technē to virtue and statecraft, it always leads to a forgetting of self and a distancing from one's own passions, never to the domination and exploitation of others whether through guile or force (*Republic* 335c–e, 346d–e). Time and again in the dialogues, we encounter Socrates making an argument like the following: You want to be the master of Athens. Rulers must possess the art of governance to a superlative degree. But in the case of every art that we can readily specify—humbler arts like carpentry, hence more easily identifiable in a way that will gain wide agreement for the purposes of discussion—the practice of that art diminishes one's profit from it rather than increases it. It can never be the task of medicine or horse-training to harm bodies or horses for the gain of the expert in those fields. The skilled ruler, insofar as he is expert, could therefore never rule in such a way as to exploit his subjects.[27]

NOTES

1. The poets were commonly included among the "wise." As Jaeger observes: "[The Sophists] were the heirs of the educational tradition of the poets: they were the successors of Homer and Hesiod, Solon and Theognis, Simonides and Pindar." Werner Jaeger, *Paideia*, vol. 1, trans. Gilbert Highet (New York: Oxford University Press, 1965), 289–296.
2. Aristotle *Nicomachean Ethics* 1102a.25.
3. See W. K. C. Guthrie, *The Sophists* (Cambridge: Cambridge University Press, 1983), 60–68, 107–108.
4. Guthrie characterizes Sophistry as "the reaction towards humanism." W. K. C. Guthrie, *The Greek Philosophers* (New York: Harper Torchbooks, 1975), 63 ff. I am arguing instead that it should be seen as an extension of pre-Socratic ontology to practical affairs, especially as Athens became more powerful during the fifth century B.C. The very distinction between "Sophists" and "pre-Socratics" is to a large extent a convention of interpretation: all such figures were called, or claimed to be, "wise." Moreover, Guthrie's thesis is qualified by his own meticulous scholarship in reconstructing the known or plausible teacher-student relationships among the various "Sophists" and "pre-Socratics." In his later work, Guthrie relaxes the dichotomy (see, e.g., *The Sophists,* 4). Dodds states the alternative thesis as follows: "[T]he Greek Enlightenment was not initiated by the Sophists. The Enlightenment is of course much older; its roots are in sixth-century Ionia." Dodds goes on to maintain that, just as the assaults on tradition associated with Sophists such as Gorgias, Protagoras, and their followers like Callicles were grounded in philosophical speculations about nature and being, so had seemingly purely philosophical figures like Heracleitus been equally engaged in "a whole series of direct assaults" on the tradition ("the conglomerate," as Dodds renders the word *nomos* in an attempt to convey its meaning as a whole complex of interlocking social, religious, and legal prohibitions against vice and impiety). "Had Heracleitus been an Athenian, he would pretty certainly have been had up for blasphemy," as were later "Sophists" like Socrates. E. R. Dodds, *The Greeks and the Irrational* (Berkeley: University of California Press, 1984), 50–55.
5. See Guthrie, *The Sophists,* 269–272 and *The Greek Philosophers,* 50–55.
6. One of the unnamed sources would appear to be Anaximander. See Guthrie, *The Greek Philosophers,* 27–29 and note 13 below.
7. The primordialist ontology is conveyed by a number of the fragments attributed to

Heracleitus: "This ordered universe [*kosmos*], which is the same for all, was not created by any one of the gods or of mankind, but it was ever and is and ever shall be ever-living Fire, kindled in measure and quenched in measure." "One should know that war is general [universal] and jurisdiction is strife, and everything comes about by way of strife and necessity." Heracleitus 30, 80. *In Ancilla to the Pre-Socratic Philosophers,* trans. Kathleen Freeman (Oxford: Basil Blackwell, 1948), 26, 30.

8. As an intriguingly Heideggerian fragment attributed to Gorgias puts it, "Being is unrecognizable unless it succeeds in seeming, and seeming is weak unless it succeeds in being." Gorgias 26. In Freeman, *Ancilla, 139*. By contrast, it would be closer to the Platonic understanding to say that being is weaker and less recognizable to the extent that it merely seems.

9. Cf. Xenophon *Memorabilia* 1.1.8–16 and W. K. C. Guthrie, *History of Greek Philosophy,* vol. 1 (Cambridge: Cambridge University Press, 1969), 50.

10. Gorgias 13, 14. In Freeman, *Ancilla.*

11. Empedocles 111. In Freeman, *Ancilla,* 64.

12. Those who were for *nomos* and those who were against it, as Guthrie has it (Guthrie, *The Sophists,* 60, 101).

13. In this connection, the wording of the Anaximander fragment is pertinent: "Whence things have their origin, there they must also pass away according to necessity; for they must pay penalty and be judged for their injustice, according to the ordinance of time." Quoted in Martin Heidegger, *Early Greek Thinking,* trans. David F. Krell (Chicago: Harper and Row, 1984), 13. In Heidegger's interpretation of pre-Socratic ontology, "justice" is grounded in the acceptance of a return to the origins whence all things issue, an acceptance of the passing of one's time. Injustice and tyranny spring from the wish to remain in being past one's destined time.

14. Thrasymachus: "Each ruling group sets down laws for its own advantage; a democracy sets down democratic laws, a tyranny, tyrannic laws, and the others do the same. And they declare that what they have set down—their own advantage—is just for the ruled, and the man who departs from it they punish as a breaker of the law and a doer of unjust deeds." Plato *Republic* 338e–339a.

15. Heracleitus 53. In Freeman, *Ancilla,* 28.

16. Thucydides *The Peloponnesian War* 5. 84–116.

17. Antiphon: "Nothing is worse for mankind than anarchy. Hence our forefathers instilled obedience into their children, so that when they grow up they might not be overcome by any great change of fortune." Antiphon 61. In Freeman, *Ancilla,* 152.

18. As Nussbaum shrewdly observes, because Protagoras's conception of art is so close to *phusis* in the primordialist sense, it offers only a limited prospect for real control, and in this sense parallels from a philosophical perspective the conservatism of the tragic wise man Teresias, whose recipe for avoiding the reverses of fortune is to understand in the first place that human contrivance cannot do much to alter the unfathomable necessities of life: "We could say, then, that Protagoras' *technē* follows Teresias' advice. It leaves our original problems more or less where it found them, making small advances in clarity and self-understanding, but remaining close to current beliefs and practices. He can claim to teach a *technē* that increases our control over *tuchē;* but the internality and plurality of its ends, and the absence of any qualitative measure, seem to leave his art lacking in precision and therefore in potential for decisive progress." Nussbaum, *The Fragility of Goodness,* 105. See also Dodds, *The Greeks,* 184 and Thomas A. Cole, "The Relativism of Protagoras," in

Yale Classical Studies, vol. 22, ed. Adam Parry (Cambridge: Cambridge University Press, 1972).

19. Thucydides *Peloponnesian War* 2.65–67.

20. Dodds sums up the relationship judiciously: "it would be dishonest not to recognize that the new rationalism carried with it real as well as imaginary dangers for the social order. In discarding the Inherited Conglomerate, many people discarded with it the religious restraints that had held human egotism on the leash. To men of strong moral principle . . . a Protagoras or a Democritus—that did not matter; their conscience was adult enough to stand up without props. It was otherwise with most of their pupils. To them, the liberation of the individual meant an unlimited freedom of self-assertion. . . . The new rationalism did not *enable* men to behave like beasts—men have always been able to do that. But it enabled them to justify their brutality to themselves, and that at a time when the external temptations to brutal conduct were particularly strong." Dodds, *The Greeks,* 191.

21. Gorgias 8. In Freeman, *Ancilla,* 130.

22. As Jaeger observes, "From its first appearance . . . the aim of the educational movement led by the Sophists was not to educate the people, but to educate the leaders of the people. At bottom, it was only the old problem of the aristocracy in a new form." Jaeger, *Paideia,* 296.

23. Consider the discussion in Stanley Rosen, *The Quarrel,* 47–55.

24. Thucydides *Peloponnesian War* 3.37–41.

25. Gorgias 11.1. In Freeman, *Ancilla,* 131.

26. On ancient Greek perceptions of the connection between the Sophists and the decline of traditional virtue, see Guthrie, *The Sophists,* 19–50. See also the discussion in Richard Kraut, *Socrates and the State* (Princeton: Princeton University Press, 1984), 224–227.

27. This is the primary reason why it is mistaken to identify Socratic technē with utilitarianism or "technical" reasoning in the modern sense, as does Irwin. See the critique of Irwin's position by Nussbaum, *The Fragility of Goodness,* 97–98. The craft analogy points to the objective rationality that structures the cosmos. It leads to the forgetting of one's own interests and passions, and to a reflection on how the world is well-ordered apart from one's passions.

Chapter Three

The Erotics of Statecraft

In the *Gorgias,* Socrates ties the cosmology of geometrical proportionality to a sketch of orderly, moderate friendship. His aim is to restrain Callicles' eros and convince him of the need to replace his all-or-nothing approach to his love life with a more mutual, two-sided relationship mediated by an objective good at which both partners aim. I suggested that, owing to the dichotomous distinction Socrates makes between, on the one hand, pedestrian hedonism and, on the other, a rather passionless statecraft, Socrates is unable to fill in the promised therapy of friendship within a well-ordered politeia. We turn to the *Symposium* because it is there that the question of eros is addressed at length and in the sense that we saw emerge from Socrates' psychoanalysis of Callicles. For although it is not, on the face of it, an especially "political" dialogue, the *Symposium* has important implications for the question of what kind of political community and public career might conceivably satisfy the erotic longing for transcendence. As in the *Gorgias,* the varieties of personal eros explored in the dialogue are intertwined with different perceptions of, and expectations from, public life.[1]

There is another reason for turning to the *Symposium.* A longstanding controversy surrounds the interpretation of what the Platonic Socrates means by the good life. Is it primarily to be understood in terms of one's duties toward others—especially as these are manifested by the virtues of a good citizen? Or is it primarily to be understood in terms of one's own pleasure—not, to be sure, in a crude or carnal way, but the pleasure of cultivating the harmonious ordering of one's own soul? The debate reaches back to classical antiquity, when both Stoics and Epicureans claimed Socrates as a founder. And clearly one can extract many passages from the dialogues in which Socrates appears to urge, on the one hand, a Stoic position of self-abnegation and devotion to the common good or, on the other hand, a devotion to the pleasures of philosophizing that can at best be said to entail just behavior toward others in one's external conduct.[2] As Socrates puts it in Book 6 of the *Republic,* the philosopher's passions are so focused on the pleasures of learning that he has no energy left to compete with or harm others over the usual objects of desire (485d–e).

Now to some extent, this way of posing the interpretive question stems from the enormous influence of Kant on modern philosophical terminology. For the conflict between perfectionism (and other varieties of egoism) and moral duty is, at bottom, grounded in the Kantian distinction between nature and freedom. This is a distinction between nature understood as those inclinations whose gratification we are compelled to seek, and moral freedom as the degree of success we achieve in willing ourselves not to allow our conduct to be determined by the satisfaction of those inclinations. For Plato, by contrast, it is precisely in fulfilling our nature to the fullest degree that we cultivate the moral virtues, since for Plato nature is most informatively defined in terms of stability and order. Moreover, as the life of the Platonic Socrates shows, philosophical knowledge itself is directed by erotic longing. Strictly speaking, then, for Plato there is no conflict between duty and inclination. As in Diotima's Ladder, when eros is properly clarified as to its potential for satisfaction, passion achieves fulfilment through civic virtue and philosophy. Put another way, for Kant, the criterion for virtue is our willing a will undetermined to the degree humanly possible by any substantive object from the realm of natural determinations. For Plato, however, the question is not how we can in general avoid the choice of a particular object of the natural inclinations, but rather, *which* particular object is naturally most worth choosing, most conducive to a happy life?[3] Granting that Plato does not recognize the Kantian distinction between egoistic/heteronomous actions and altruistic/autonomous actions, it does not necessarily follow, of course, that the Platonic account of satisfaction and duty is therefore consistent or convincing. Even if we dispose of the distorting influence of Kantian problematics in stating the issues, it may still be the case that Plato is wrong, or insufficiently convincing, in arguing that pleasure and duty can coincide in a common object of natural longing. But to see where a possible resolution might lie, we do have to examine Socrates' statements on their own terms, free of Kantian encrustation.

In this chapter, I propose to shed some light on the debate by examining the teaching about Eros unfolded by Socrates in the *Symposium*. It is here, especially in the presentation of Diotima's Ladder, that we find what may be the paradigmatic statement of anti-Kantianism. For it is precisely in the passions—the "pathological" realm that Kant banished from the subject matter of the metaphysics of morals—that Diotima finds the surest human proclivity toward civic and contemplative virtue. My focus, however, is not only the positive doctrine itself—which has been well discussed in other places—but how it is illuminated and modified by the speeches and actions that take place in the dialogue after the arrival of Alcibiades. My specific aim is to show how this part of the *Symposium* rather unexpectedly helps us to make sense of a puzzling, and on the face of it absurd, contention that Socrates makes in the *Gorgias:* that he is one of the few men in Athens to properly undertake the art of ruling and the only one to "practice politics"(521d). I will try to show that the core of this claim, and the best way to make sense of it, resides in what I term the philosophical erotics that Socrates practices both in speech and in deed in the *Symposium*. It is in the midst of this seemingly most personal of Socratic conversations, in my view, that we are offered one of the most vivid examples of what Socrates means by "ruling" and "practicing politics." Philosophical erotics comprise a kind of pleasure that is at one and the same time egoistic or self-perfecting and philanthropic. Moreover, the benefit to others is not a mere second-order consequence of Socrates' pleasure, nor the mere outward appearance of moderation with respect to common pleasures in a man who is inwardly immoderately devoted to the pleasures of philosophy. Instead, Socrates' philanthropy is bound up with the very essence of his pleasure in the most intimate way. At the same time, I argue, Socrates' philosophical erotics are at the core of the "Stoic" position that he argues most consistently in the *Apology,* where he depicts himself as so devoted to the discussion of virtue that he serves the common good of Athens better than anyone else, and at the sacrifice of his personal interests.

Because a certain kind of "Epicureanism" is at the core of Socratic "Stoicism," the interpretation I present here also helps to soften what some take to be the politically pessimistic conclusion of the *Republic* that one cannot hope for the "noble city" (*kallipolis*) to really exist, but must be content with founding its pattern in one's own soul. Considered in conjunction with the *Symposium,* this is not a pessimistic practical outcome. For, as I interpret it, Socrates "practices politics" primarily by cultivating friendships. Although the *Republic* culminates in the lesson that one cannot impose the pattern of the good *tout court* on a city, one can begin to cultivate friends in one's actual city—friendships guided by the pattern of the good that one founds in the soul through philosophical investigations of politics and virtue of the kind that Socrates conducts with his partners. Beginning with these friendships mediated by the good, one can move outward gradually to effect larger reforms in the direction of the optimal politiea. The *Republic* can arguably be taken to result in the elevation of the philosophic life over the life of civic virtue, to the detriment of the latter's natural grounding. There are serious bases for this view, a theme I will pursue at length in chapters 4 and 5. But if we consider the extra light that the *Symposium* sheds on the content of the philosophic life, we find that the philosophic life itself always leads us back to the erotics of statecraft and friendship as the propaedeutic for whatever partial political reforms can be carried out under the conditions at hand. Philosophizing in the Socratic sense, I will argue, needs civic virtue, or, to put it another way, Socratic philosophy is indivisibly political philosophy. Founding the city in one's own soul means a devotion to the good that will guide one's personal and civic friendships. The core of this mission on behalf of the good is erotic satisfaction rightly understood. This is how Socrates can claim to be actually "practicing politics" here and now.

FIVE ACCOUNTS OF EROS

Each of the five speakers prior to Socrates in the *Symposium* elaborates a different aspect of the phenomenon of eros, leaving Socrates to propound a new

synthesis that draws together some of their tenets while excluding others. Phaedrus understands eros mainly as a longing for the physical beauty of another
(178c–179b). Pausanias expands the meaning of erotic attraction to include not
only physical beauty but nobility of character. He criticizes Phaedrus's argument
for failing to distinguish between good and bad eros. Bad eros is the love for
another based on physical beauty alone. A good erotic relationship, by contrast, is
one in which the lover is attracted to the beloved mainly because of the beloved's
pursuit of virtue. The lover can therefore become the younger man's teacher in
their joint pursuit of noble action. He believes Phaedrus's view of eros gives pederasty a bad name, since it is indistinguishable from wanton lust: "The one who is
wicked is the one more in love with the body than with the soul. For he is not a
lasting lover, because he loves something that is not lasting" (183e). His own argument may thus be seen as an effort to make such relationships respectable. He
believes that virtuous pederastic friendships might be openly regulated by law —
as are other erotic ties like those among family members — since they contribute
to the overall virtuousness of relations among citizens (182c, 184c). Like Callicles, Pausanias is sensitive to possible imputations about his public character as a
citizen and gentleman based on the character of his private love life. He would like
to forestall any such embarrassment by having his love life publicly sanctioned as
a manly association that contributes to a proud civic-spiritedness:

> For the barbarians, because of their tyrannies, this [pederasty] as well as philosophy
> and the love of gymnastics is shameful. For, I suspect, it is not to the advantage of the
> rulers that great and lofty thoughts emerge among their subjects, nor strong friend-
> ships and associations. . . . [Good eros] is very worthwhile for both city and private
> men, for it compels both the lover himself and the beloved . . . to act vigorously on
> behalf of virtue. (182b, 185b–c)

In the next speech, the philosophical physician Eryximachos retains the distinction made by Pausanias between good and bad eros, but takes the meaning of
eros beyond human affairs, seeing it as the main element in a cosmology of harmony among contraries that characterizes the entire world. According to him, all
of human and nonhuman existence is made up of contraries, as Heracleitus had
maintained. However, whereas Heracleitus believed that the dynamic equilibrium
of the cosmos is maintained by the total ensemble of tensions among these like and
unlike parts, Eryximachos argues that an art (technē) guided by knowledge (epistēmē) of eros enables us to "heal" the contraries in our lives (186c–e, 188e). If we
match up our needs in a balanced manner, we will live in an orderly, pious, moderate, and just way, healed by the therapeutic power of good eros. But if one need
overwhelms the rest, we will be enslaved by bad eros, just as the harmony of the
world at large is upset by plagues and storms (188a–b).

The comic poet Aristophanes also regards eros as a healer. But he returns from
the lofty cosmological level of Eryximachos's speech to an emphasis on human
experience, treating eros as the longing for wholeness that people feel when they

love each other. He transposes this wholeness to a golden age in the past, when, he claims, man was whole in the literal, physical sense: a circular being made up of what the gods subsequently split into the different genders (190a). Now, each genus seeks reunification with the genus to which its antecedents were fused in the golden age, whether male or female (192c–d). In Aristophanes' speech, then, eros is not the good life itself, nor the highest principle of unity for the entire cosmos. Instead, it is the specifically human longing for the good life — for wholeness through loving another human being: "From this source, then, eros is mutually ingrained among human beings, bringing together the halves of their original nature, trying to make one out of two and healing the wound of human nature. The cause of this is that our original nature was one and we were wholes; this desire and pursuit of the whole is called eros" (191d, 193a). At the same time, however, in Aristophanes' presentation no single, transcendental object of eros fulfills all human longings. Instead, he sees the objects of eros as a plurality of distinct, bodily universals: the circular fusions of each possible pairing of genders. Aristophanes' interest in love is not restricted to the "manly" pederastic kind: he describes heterosexual and lesbian pairings. But like Pausanias, he does regard pederastic relationships as the special characteristic of men suited for political careers: "Those who are slices of the male pursue the masculine; those are the best of boys and lads, because they are naturally the most manly. On reaching maturity, this sort alone go into politics, real men" (191e–192b).

For reasons I will explore shortly, Aristophanes' account of eros provides the most significant theoretical contrast with the account that Socrates subsequently attributes to Diotima. It also has far-reaching implications for how we understand the satisfactions available from political life. In Aristophanes' account of the golden age, the circle men build a tower to storm the heavens, and are consequently cut in half by Zeus to limit their hubris (190b–d). Thus, while in Diotima's account eros leads to a self-forgetting absorption in the object of desire, for Aristophanes, eros in its anthropological origins was preceded and stimulated by a more fundamental hubris, a self-assertive desire to rival or dispossess the gods. While eros in the present springs from a longing for reconciliation that may be touching given the current fragmented condition of human life, the achievement of this reconciliation might well lead back to the overweening hubris of mankind's primordial origins — back down to strife (polemos), not "on up" to Diotima's perfect, motionless, unchanging good. Indeed, Aristophanes warns, if human beings today fail to behave in an orderly fashion, the gods may well split them again into even thinner slices. For Aristophanes, the tendency to engage in aggressive violence is the primordial nature of human beings.

Although Aristophanes adds a human touch to the purely cosmological speculations of Eryximachos, his account of the origins of the whole is largely in keeping with our consideration in chapter 2 of the primordialist ontology. Distinctions, including the distinctions we make through logos, stem from our neediness and fragmentation, and these in turn signify the loss of our primordial wholeness and circularity. But we cannot return to those vital origins without undermining all political and social order. Hence, Aristophanes stands for a certain kind of regretful and resigned conservatism. The polis has built up a bulwark of order and security based on the necessity of split, fragmented human beings to cooperate. Insofar as civilization is good, it would not be good for humans to return to their primordial, hubristic wholeness. From a civilizational standpoint, the golden age—when we get what we want—is bad. As Aristophanes says, echoing Eryximachos's medicinal language, the city's health comes from its constraint by piety and duty (193d). Convention, law, and custom save us from nature understood as primordial genesis.

These considerations also help us to understand why pederastic unions may be closer to the primordial origins of phusis than other erotic unions. Sexual union aims most fundamentally to recover the androgynous unity of the circle-beings, not to replicate the existing halves. Children are no more than such replicated halves, necessary for the propagation of the species, but perpetuating humans' alienated modern existence. Pederasty is more clearly rooted in the primordial origins in the sense that it aims for unity between lover and beloved without the superfluous by-product and distraction of children and family. Its consummation does not generate more splits. Moreover, pederasty is also closer to the origins of phusis because of its connection with political ambition, the most palpable residue in the present of the original hubris of the circle men.

This points to the fundamental absurdity of the polis from Aristophanes' perspective, a source of his comedic conservatism, or conservatism lightened by a sense of the ludicrousness of human pretensions to civic virtue. The type of person most likely to serve the city with distinction—the politically ambitious pederast—is also the one most likely to usurp its stability and throw off the constraints of nomos. Eros is indeed the key to understanding humans. In this Aristophanes agrees with his fellow dinner partners and obeys the ground rule to praise eros. But the possession of what eros yearns for leads to arrogant, warlike ambition and the overturning of all order and moderation. The pursuit of the good by eros undermines civic virtue. Whereas, for Diotima, the eternal good solicits eros toward itself, for Aristophanes, eros does not even arise until the primordial wholeness for which it retrospectively yearns has been ruthlessly cut away by the gods. In this respect, eros for Aristophanes is basically tragic and nostalgic; far from being drawn toward an object that will remove the pain of its neediness, eros cannot exist apart from the pain of its irredeemable deprival. Love is a wound.

Last among the speakers before Socrates, the tragic poet Agathon treats eros as a pulse of beauty that knits together both human life and the larger order of the cosmos. His understanding of eros is more hierarchical than that of the earlier speakers. He does not regard eros as the healer of all contraries in the cosmos, as had Eryximachos. For him, its harmony is found only among "blooming" and "beautiful" beings, not ugly and discordant forces (196a). Contrary to Eryximachos and Aristophanes, he does not believe that eros is present in all beings and people, but only in "soft," gracious gods and men (195e). In his view, eros is not so much the longing for the beautiful as it is itself a kind of beautiful power that graces the best parts of the cosmos.

Despite their differing perspectives on love, there is no disagreement among the five speakers on two important points. Like Callicles, they all appear to agree that the experience of eros links the pleasures and satisfactions of private life with the larger concerns of public life and citizen virtue. As Phaedrus and Pausanius depict it, the affection between lovers and beloveds will make the citizen body as a whole friendlier and more loyal to the common good, especially in battle. All agree that lover and beloved can be united by a regard for virtue as the common motive for their friendship. But, again like Callicles, they understand civic virtue largely as the demonstration of prowess in the contest among the best, most manly men for power, status, and wealth. For them, virtue has a competitive, agonistic edge that seems to be best expressed by martial prowess or by victory over competing factions for a lion's share of political influence. Manliness, war, and public prominence are thus closely intertwined in the notions of eros discussed by the five speakers, as they are for Callicles. Thus, although their speeches show convincingly enough that eros can provide a powerful motive for bringing people together in both private and civic friendships, as with Callicles it is not clear that this agonistic kind of virtue is compatible with the moderate harmoniousness that Socrates tries to convince his interlocutors is best for the health of the soul and of the political community.

The other striking point on which all agree is that no one has praised or understood eros sufficiently, or recognized its preeminent place in life before now (189c–d). Phaedrus claims that eros is the oldest force in the world, having issued directly out of the primordial chaos along with the earth (178c–179d).[4] When Pausanias distinguishes between good and bad eros, he depicts the lustful, indiscriminate kind of eros as a newer god, while good eros—the more vigorous, serious pederasty guided by nous that he would like to see sanctioned and codified by law—he identifies with an older god, thus lending it the venerability of tradition (181). Agathon reverses this genealogy when he claims that eros is the youngest, newest god and is the special patron of whatever is young and fresh. For Agathon, the rise of this new god of love illustrates the superiority of the modern age to the grim traditions of the archaic Greeks. The old gods of Hesiod and Parmenides, he says, were gods of the primordial "necessity" out of which the world originally issued—comparable to the "first" motions that arise "out of necessity" according to the primordialist ontology (195c, 197b; *Laws* 888e–889c). They were gods of clashing forces and titanic struggle. As these primordial forces gave way over time to stability and civilization, Eros came into his own as the god of the peace and happiness achieved in the modern era (197b–c). New poets, accordingly, are needed to replace the old poets and their superseded gods.

On the face of it, Phaedrus's and Pausanias's contention that eros has not been properly recognized as the oldest god contradicts Agathon's proclamation of this new god's supersession of the old gods. But both genealogies stem from the same root concern. Whether the speakers in this eulogy to Eros place the god in a past so ancient that it has been forgotten, or in events so recent that few as yet grasp them, they have in common a dissatisfaction with the received wisdom about who and what governs the cosmos. Altogether we have the impression of the diminution of the old Homeric morality and Hesiodic theogony, and the search for something to fill the vacuum of departed tradition.[5] In a similar way, Callicles waxes eloquent over his "shining" vision of the prospective "natural master," a figure who seems to unite the sophisticated amorality of the modern age at its cutting edge with the titanic, Herculean qualities of the most distant past, now that the qualities of gentlemanly virtue and nobility (*kalokagathia*) are no longer authoritatively defined by the older poets. Whether we see eros here as a brand-new god, or as a god so old that it has escaped notice before now and is therefore in another sense new, clearly these men believe a new god is needed to replace the old gods of Marathon and the simple, unsophisticated probity evoked by Aristophanes' Just Speech in the *Clouds*.

Moreover, these five speakers—clearly urbane and knowledgeable men—make little mention of the pre-Socratics or Sophists except to criticize them. Like Callicles, they are attracted in some measure to the primordialist ontology and the freedom from conventional morality embodied in its teachings. But clearly they do not find any one of these cosmological doctrines satisfactory for articulating their own longings or their perceptions of politics, morality, and justice. As with Callicles, we may surmise that the insufficiency of the primordialist teaching has left a chasm for some way of articulating and ranking the completed ends at which private and public eros should aim, as opposed to positing that human nature is characterized by sub-political desires in abstraction from any substantive elaboration of friendship and statesmanship.[6] As Agathon's praise of Eros as the new, as yet insufficiently recognized deity of modern civilization and its achievements reveals (196b–c, 197b–c), these thoughtful Athenians are looking for a new anchor, a new standard for how to live. Eros would seem to provide a natural explanation of the longing for transcendence that had once been directed by the traditional Homeric conventions of heroic virtue. There is no going back to the Just Argument. Eros is especially suitable as a new god because Athens has become so much richer, expansive, and broad-minded with the rise of empire—a "feverish city," to use Socrates' phrase in the *Republic*, whose expanded longings for every kind of pleasure make it impossible to return to the archaic huts and bean pots of the "city of pigs" (*Republic* 372e). The tendency of the speakers to see civic virtue and preeminence as akin to an erotic satisfaction shows how political ambition is losing its mooring in the austerity and piety of ancestral tradition.

DIOTIMAN EROS

Socrates' own endorsement of eros is both sweeping and sober. Responding to the concerns of the earlier speakers, Socrates' presentation of eros combines three dimensions: (1) the emphasis of Phaedrus, Pausanias, and Aristophanes on human love; (2) Eryximachos's approach to eros as a cosmological healing force; and (3)

Agathon's insistence on a hierarchy of beautiful beings. But, in synthesizing these anthropological, cosmological, and hierarchical approaches, Socrates' own depiction of eros is not quite like any one of them. The previous speakers, especially Agathon, tended to argue that eros is the longing for the beautiful, and that the beautiful things are good chiefly because they are beautiful. In the teaching about eros that Socrates attributes to Diotima, however, it is primarily the good that is the object of eros, and it is to the extent that the objects of eros are good that they may be said to be beautiful (201b–c, 204e). As he tries to do with Callicles, then, Socrates attempts to interpret eros as the proper ordering of the desires for the sake of the good. It follows from this that the erotic experience itself—the potency and richness of longing—is not the beautiful and good life, as the previous speakers (with the exception of Aristophanes) had tended to maintain, but the means to something higher and better than itself. Thus, whereas Agathon had enthused about the beauty and grace of a life suffused by eros, Socrates depicts eros as something needy, wily, and impoverished.

We do not experience eros as pleasurable in itself, he claims, but as a "necessity"—a drive to obtain something we lack (200a–200c). In this respect, Socrates is closer to the pathos of Aristophanes' erotic anthropology of incompleteness than he is to Agathon's celebration of Eros as the new god of civilization whose peace and beauty transcend the grim necessities of the past. On the other hand, Socrates agrees with Agathon that the titanic "necessity" of the primordialist ontology and the old theogony is too crude and violent to explain the complexities of erotic longing in the human soul. But whereas Agathon proclaims the supersession of necessity by love, Socrates depicts them as two recurrent aspects of the same natural experience. He reduces necessity from the awesome invisible origin of all beings to a recurrent everyday longing to be fulfilled within the civic association. Rather than attempt to replace the ontology of motion and becoming with an ontology of triumphant beauty and form, Socrates shows how the consideration of phusis within the erotic and political complexities of conventional human experience yields an understanding of how stability emerges recurrently from motion, fortune, and impermanence.

We can detect in Agathon's account of love's victory over necessity another variation of the position advanced by Protagoras, according to which civilization has gradually advanced out of the barbaric early ages when human life was directly assailed and threatened by the motions of the natural world. Socrates' position is a middle ground between the view of some Sophists that nature's great motions still determine human nature directly and the view of others that convention, art, and law have built up artificial protections from nature's direct incursions. Necessity was not regnant in the origins, Socrates implies—neither is love regnant now. "Since you yourself agree," he says Diotima told him, "that Eros is not good or beautiful, do not suppose, rather, that he must be ugly and bad, but something between the two" (202b). Phusis is the coming to presence of form within the limitations of necessity, chance, and motion. Eros is itself necessitous, but the necessity is "marvelous" rather than grim, because it constantly reawakens our most revealingly human longings and directs them toward a stable object of fruition (200b.1). In love as in metaphysics, chance has its place—but not a sovereign place.

If, as Alcibiades later drunkenly charges, Socrates is bent on wooing Agathon—on wooing, as it were, (the) good at this dinner party devoted to praising love—then we might say that while Socrates is attracted to the cosmos of beauty and splendor that Agathon envisions, he wants to show Agathon through his speech that the objects of eros can only be specified by reflecting on how human nature is limited by necessity as well as how it is open to transcendence. As with Callicles, he attempts to deflate the exhilarating experience of erotic longing by forcing his listeners to clarify exactly what it is that they want and need, so that they dwell not so much on the intoxicating, unspecifiable sweep of feeling that overwhelms the expectant lover as on the correctly ordered outcome of one's relations with others.

In the *Gorgias,* we recall from chapter 1, Socrates argues as if Philosophy "herself" were the source of his attempt to persuade Callicles that he should regulate his desires according to how well they contributed to the pursuit of the good. By briefly personifying the chief object of his own eros in this way, Socrates tries to direct Callicles' longings in the same direction—a rhetorical device to which Callicles responds, as an adroit student of rhetoric, by proposing instead his own "shining" vision of the best way of life, the natural master. In the course of the *Gorgias,* as we observed, Socrates does comparatively little to fill in the middle range of civic and private friendships that might conceivably bridge the gap between Callicles' defense of indiscriminate hedonism and Socrates' rather contentless adjuration to prefer the good. In the *Symposium,* Socrates does attempt to bridge this chasm, and he again claims that his erotic insights come from beyond himself—in this instance, from a seeress who taught him all that he knows about erotic matters.

There has been much speculation about why Plato chose to depict Socrates as claiming to have learned about eros from Diotima. One reason, I think, emerges from the characteristics of the earlier speakers' understanding of eros. They saw it as an especially masculine experience, best exemplified by the kind of pederasty in which the lovers compete with each other for political influence in order to woo the younger recipients of their favors and teach them the virtues of political success. As with Callicles, this understanding of eros leads to a contest for victory in the public realm that translates into a rather one-sided expectation of gratification in the private realm. By locating the source of his own knowledge of eros beyond himself, Socrates metaphorically dampens this agonistic approach to love, placing less emphasis on his own prowess and more on his indebtedness to another. Whereas the previous speakers depicted the beloved as younger, less experienced, and generally beholden to the experience of the lover, Diotima is at once the object of Socrates' admiration and herself the authoritative figure—not in the manner of a man of affairs, but in the manner of an older woman and mother. In short, Socrates and Diotima share the roles of lover and beloved—a marked departure from

Callicles' and the other speakers' tendency to conflate victory and mastery with their personal erotic attachments. Socrates' relationship with her reflects his contention that eros properly clarified as to its objects should not lead to the one-sided gratification of passion in the lover, but the engendering of something between lover and beloved through their devotion to the common purpose of their association, the good. It is a more reciprocal relationship than the agonistic eros praised by the earlier speakers, a relationship in which nature mediates in a beneficent and orderly way between the two partners, rather than driving one of them in an urge to possess the other.[7] As Diotima expresses it, eros is "of the good," implying by this that it is not primarily concerned with the beautiful (206a). Instead, by being directed toward the good, eros "engenders" its objects "in the beautiful" and "brings [them] to birth in beauty" (206b). Beauty, then, is not so much the goal of erotic longing as it is a kind of pleasing medium through which the good is pursued and brought forth. Whereas for the previous speakers erotic longings for the beautiful drive the lover to achieve preeminence, for Diotima, eros is mediated by nature's recurrent fecundity for bringing forth the good. Socrates' professed relationship with this teacher reminds us of his characterizations of philosophizing elsewhere as a kind of midwifery (*Theaetetus* 150b–151d).

In keeping with this attempt to make eros gentler and more sober, Diotima's teaching stresses its place in the middle realm between the transcendental objects of human need and the primordial depths of ignorance and transient passion. Just as correct opinion is a middle ground between lack of understanding and prudence (phronēsis), she argues, so eros is a middle ground between the ugly and bad and the beautiful and good. Just as correct opinion is a kind of hunch about what really is that cannot as yet give a clear account (logos) of it, so does eros "hit upon what is" and point us in the right direction for further reflection (202a). In other words, our erotic needs, properly attuned to, can provide an intimation of what is closest to true being, and therefore of our transcendent satisfaction. Contrary to Agathon, however, Diotima maintains that the experience of eros is not divine in itself. Rather, eros is a "demon" between the divine and the human, an intermediary that "binds together the whole"(202e–203a). The "demonic man" is wise in his divinations in the sense that he is keen and energetic in pursuing his quarry, the beautiful and good things he lacks. He is thus not fresh and soft, as Agathon claimed, but on the contrary, an aggressive and wily old hunter: "He is far from being delicate and beautiful, as the many believe, but is tough, squalid, shoeless, and homeless . . . he is courageous, impetuous, and keen, an awesome hunter, always weaving snares, longing for prudence, and inventive, philosophizing for his entire life" (203c–d). As everyone realizes, the description suits Socrates in many ways.

We should pause for a moment to consider more closely Diotima's account of correct opinion, since it provides an interesting hermeneutical corridor to the *Republic* that will be important in our consideration of that dialogue. According to what Socrates says Diotima taught him, correct opinion occupies a middle ground that is analogous both to the place of eros in between the ugly and the bad and the beautiful and the good and to the place of the demon as the intermediary binding together the human and the divine. Diotima's parallels help us to understand how, for Plato, correct opinion—a concept more usually associated with the *Republic* (477a–480a)—is indivisible from the experience of philosophic longing, and not the rather pale reflection of true being that it is sometimes taken for. Putting her three three-sided parallels together, it seems that the demonic man is led by Eros to hit upon what is through correct opinion, which can then be further clarified according to logos. In other words, correct opinion is the erotic intuition of the "look" or form of the phenomenon, a provisional intimation of the participation of phenomena in the Ideas. Diotima's depiction of correct opinion as the first intuitive grasp of a continuous ascent to eidetic clarity guided by longing provides a ground for Socrates' lengthier and more formal presentation of correct opinion in the *Republic,* a ground that intertwines the metaphysical, epistemological, and eudaimonistic. This bridge between the *Symposium* and the *Republic* also underscores the fact that in the *Republic,* too, correct opinion is conceptually broached in the context of Socrates' first explicit discussion of eros as the chief inducement to philosophizing (474d–475b).

Socrates introduces his recollection of Diotima after a short exchange in which he tries to establish for Agathon that eros is neither beautiful nor good in itself—a conclusion to which the poet agrees in reluctant befuddlement (201b–c). Socrates' recollection of Diotima might therefore be seen as his way of presenting the same argument in a more fulsome, inspiring manner, a flow of words more congenial to the poet than Socrates' relentless parsing of terms. Like Socrates, the seeress also stresses that eros has its necessitous, compulsive dimension. But in contrast with that tough hunter, she softens this by linking erotic longing to the prospect of noble fulfilment in politics or philosophy within a harmonious cosmos bound together by the demonic power of longing.

DIOTIMAN TRANSCENDENCE AND SOCRATIC SKEPTICISM

At this juncture, I will reprise and extend my discussion of Diotima's teaching as I initially sketched it in the introduction to this book. According to Diotima's Ladder (as it has come to be known), the longing for union with the beautiful and good is directed, in ascending order, toward procreation, public life, and philosophy. Each level of union participates to an increasing degree in the good itself, which is the absolute consummation and satisfaction of all erotic longing. The good is unchanging and unaffected by becoming or decay. It is beautiful permanently and without qualification, so that whatever degree of beauty we perceive in other beings comes from their participation in the good:

> [It] is always being and neither comes into being nor passes away. . . . It is by itself and with itself, always being of a single form. . . . For this is what it is to proceed cor-

rectly in erotics, or to be led by another—beginning with the beautiful things around us, always to proceed on up for the sake of beauty itself ending at that study which is the study of nothing other than the beautiful itself. (211a–c)

Unlike Aristophanes, Diotima does not present eros as the longing for the missing half of our own bodily humanity. Rather, we long for a wholeness and unity that are ultimately the same not only for every human attraction but for everything in the cosmos. In keeping with its nature, Eros is attracted toward the good by "the beautiful" (to kalon), but in ancient Greek this also means what is noble or fine. Eros thus entails, but is not reducible to, the desire for sexual intercourse, for which there are more precise terms in ancient Greek. Diotima's use of the words "prudence" and "the beautiful and good" to describe the objects of well-directed eros and well-clarified opinion reminds us that the satisfaction of our longing is never a matter of private fulfilment alone, but is connected with the kind of sound judgment and character required by virtuous relations with one's fellow citizens.

As Diotima presents it, the longing for the noble or beautiful is simultaneously the desire to possess it for oneself and, through possessing what is most perfect and lasting, to escape the constraints of mortality in fusion with the immortal. The purpose of sexual union between men and women is procreation, because children are a literal, straightforward effort to perpetuate oneself and one's union with the beloved past a single lifespan. Political eros is more complex and admirable. As Diotima puts it, with a hint that Socrates had not examined it as closely as he should have, "if you were willing to glance at human beings' love of honor, you would be amazed at their irrationality unless you bear in mind what I have said and reflect on how uncannily they are affected by their love of renown . . . for the sake of immortal virtue and [an] illustrious reputation" (208c–d). The politically erotic, Diotima says, are those whose souls are "pregnant" with "prudence and the rest of virtue." The "greatest and noblest part of prudence" is governing cities and households so that they are moderate and just. People with this political kind of eros love others of the same kind. Out of their love for each other, they "bear" the virtues of moderation and justice with which they govern their communities and families. Here, then, the "offspring" of love is the service of the common good in cooperation with one's fellow lovers of virtue (209a, c).

In stressing that the politically erotic are attracted to each other out of love for the virtues solicited by the good government of cities and households, Diotima's Ladder addresses the concerns evinced by Callicles and Pausanias that private eros not be seen as a source of shame in comparison with the requirements of public virtue. Instead, both are to be guided by the love of the good. Just as Socrates tells Callicles that he must prove he can care for the soul of a single Athenian if he is to prove himself fit to care for Athenian affairs (*Gorgias* 515a–b), so Diotima implies that one cannot pursue either private love affairs or public fame in an honorable manner unless the erotic longing is directed toward those virtues that produce the most just and restrained character in oneself and one's fellow citizens.

One may gain immortality through the fame of this cooperative enterprise down through succeeding generations. Thus, while the previous speakers had interpreted the love of two heroes like Achilles and Patroclus as the overwhelming erotic passion of one for the other, according to Diotima's account of eros, this kind of devotion should be seen as the two friends' joint service of a standard of nobility that would perpetuate the fame of their friendship forever. As interpreted by Diotima, eros is a natural human leaning that, properly clarified and directed, provides a reasoned and psychologically persuasive substitute for the sobriety and moderation of the old traditions.

The double meaning of to kalon as noble and beautiful shows the immediate unity in Greek of the rigor and moderation of moral duty intertwined with the splendor and wholeness of a life well and graciously lived, each restraining and enlivening the other. Eros adds to this reciprocal unity of duty and satisfaction the fact that, as mortals, we cannot escape our "ownness." We long for transcendence but, like greedy lovers, we want this perfection in the mode of exclusive possession, which contradicts transcendence. As Diotima sums up this tension between mortality and eternity, "eros wants the good to be one's own forever" (206a). As we will consider presently in greater detail, according to Platonic psychology, when our absorption in the object of longing gives way to a consciousness of our failure to attain it or anxiety about keeping it for ourselves, eros shades into thumos—the seat of courage, anger, and zeal in the soul. We saw how Callicles was torn between a desire to transcend convention and a desire to enjoy the power and pleasure of conventional success. Through the presentation of his erotic longings and frustration, Plato conveys the tension built into eros between the longing to transcend the human condition and the all-too-human desire for exclusive mastery and possession. For Plato, this is the key to understanding tyrannical ambition in its pristine, spontaneous manifestations. Diotima's Ladder provides a hypothesis for how these powerful feelings might be educated toward their more considered fulfilment in private and civic friendship. It presents eros as a continuum of desires ranked according to the goodness and nobility of their objects in the world—a beauty that mediates civic virtue and public honor. If one could be educated to ascend this ladder from sexual union to the higher unions, the tyrannical desires for victory and pleasure might be assimilated and rechanneled into the honor a citizen derives from serving the common good. This understanding of political eros neither cooperates with spontaneous desire on its own level in the Hobbesian manner, nor represses desire *tout court* in the Kantian manner, but attempts to satisfy desire while elevating it. Diotima's speech thus presents in fully elaborated form what Socrates in the *Gorgias* claims to embody in his own love life but only sketches in his encounter with Callicles: a hierarchy of distinct objects of eros in which politics ("my Alcibiades") is second best to philosophy. Public life is dignified as an approximation of the consummate satisfaction of eros that philosophizing more closely approaches. Order and harmony are conjoined with noble ambition. The inchoate lusts for domination that have gripped Callicles are sublimated into noble achievements on behalf of the common good.

But *can* eros be directed and educated to "go on up" in this way? That is the question to which we must now turn, preparatory to a consideration of the *Republic*. Diotima's Ladder is certainly the most dazzling evocation of political ambition directed to the pursuit of civic virtue in classical—perhaps in all—political philosophy. At the same time, Plato does not present it as a doctrine, but as a hypothesis open to the ongoing reflection and questioning stimulated by the dialogue form. Since it seems to fit the bill for the kind of statesmanship that the *Gorgias* sketches but does not fill in, its virtual absence from the *Republic* is particularly striking. Why does this seemingly most promising therapy for directing the erotic energies of ambitious public men like Callicles toward a more moderate conception of statesmanship not have a central place in Plato's most sustained investigation of justice and the optimal ordering of the political community?

The answer, I believe, is partly provided by the arguments and action of the *Symposium* itself. Diotima's teaching is only one perspective offered by the dialogue, and is not even synonymous in every respect with what Socrates says on his own behalf about eros. As we noted, Diotima seems to have reproached Socrates for dismissing the phenomenon of political honor as irrational (208c–d). Whether or to what degree he has modified his views since then under her influence (a question I will take up in a moment), his own remarks about eros to Agathon are much less fulsome than hers. Diotima's teaching abstracts from some of the more troublesome aspects of eros to which Plato draws our attention elsewhere. The positive teaching of the Ladder does not dwell upon or elaborate the tension within the experience of eros between the longing to transcend the limitations of the human condition and the longing for mastery and possession. Diotima's majestic rhetoric directs us more toward the fulfilments that summon eros forth in its most expectant, optimistic manifestations, and only implicitly toward the anger, jealousy, and competitiveness that spring into consciousness when erotic longings are frustrated. Diotima presents eros as a steady, seamless ascent from lower to higher, from particular to more general pleasures. She does not dwell on the ways in which an erotic attachment in private love affairs or family life can distract us from public service—a problem for reconciling the good of the individual to the good of the community that is crucial in the *Republic* (e.g., 416d–417b, 420e–421c, 457d, 458d–e, 464c–d). Nor does she dwell on the ways in which even striving to serve the common good may involve as much belligerence and pain as a feeling of soaring beyond oneself toward the beautiful goal. Even granting that the desire for fame can be gratified by serving the common good rather than tyrannizing over it, what if the competition for fame in public service leads the erotic politicians to battle each other for a greater share of recognition and responsibility? Moreover, what if a statesman finds that his fellow governors or citizens are not dependably or consistently inspired by their noble longing to rise above base selfishness, but also need to be threatened with punishment or regulated with stiff laws? Although

Diotima does not stress these unedifying necessities, Socrates is well aware of them. In the *Gorgias,* he maintains that statesmen need to know not only the noble art of rhetoric, but how to be surgeons of the good, cutting vice out of the soul through legislation and castigation (*Gorgias* 480a.6–480d).

These issues of practical statecraft do not arise explicitly in the *Symposium* itself. The ground rule of the dinner party is to praise eros, which forestalls the question explored in the *Republic* of whether it has any constructive role to play in political life. But Plato does remind us even in this dialogue of Socrates' aware-ness that there is a tough side to statesmanship—the need for correction and refu-tation—and that it has a parallel in his own philosophical investigations. In con-versation, Socrates resembles Diotima's description of Eros—a tough and wily hunter of whatever good he can cull through sparking his interlocutors' self-exam-ination. Alcibiades, who did not hear Socrates' speech, says he "lies in ambush" in these discussions, unwittingly echoing Diotima's description of Eros (213c, 203d). Indeed, I think it is this toughness in refuting his interlocutors' ill-consid-ered views that helps us begin to make sense of Socrates' claim to have been the only man in Athens to "practice politics." He practiced the art of ruling by com-pelling his friends to think about the meaning of virtue before presuming to rule over others. In his attempts to move his interlocutors to reflect on their needs and improve their souls, Socrates does not trust exclusively in the beauty of the good to summon forth their best efforts voluntarily. Whereas Diotima's Ladder presents the ascent to the good as a voluntary one, Alcibiades reminds their audience what a "slave driver" and man of "force" Socrates is, terms similar to the ones Callicles uses in protesting the relentlessness of the Socratic refutation. Socrates' "philo-sophical speeches" are like the bites of a "painful viper," Alcibiades says:

> he conquers all human beings in speeches. . . . He compels me to agree that, though I
> myself am still in need of much, I neglect myself while instead I deal with the affairs
> of the Athenians. . . . I feel shame only before him. For I know within myself that I
> do not have the capacity to contradict him when he says what I must do; yet, when-
> ever I leave him, I succumb to the honor of the many. (213e, 216a–c)

Socrates presents Diotima as a goddess-like figure whose revelations over-whelm the devotee and bear him aloft. But as Alcibiades reminds us, Socrates him-self does not ordinarily use this inspirational approach. He more commonly drives and badgers his listeners in a dialectically aggressive manner. Diotima's speech flows like eros itself, but Socrates' accustomed mode is the short question and answer. As we will see in considering the *Republic,* for Socrates the civic educa-tion of the passions cannot rely on an appeal to the beauty of the good alone. Its basis must instead be a rather rigorous habituation to subordinate one's private good to the common. This civic education does not rely on properly directed eros to smooth away the belligerent, thumotic underside of the passions. Instead, it tries to convert the combative side of longing—the aggressive energies that ordinarily spring to the service of erotic passion as we seek to beat others to what we want or to defend what we have acquired—to the mastery of eros. While Diotima's Ladder implies that properly directed eros will assimilate aggressive passions to the service of the good, in the *Republic,* erotic attachments become the main obstacle to a political community's approximation of the good.

In this respect we can interpret the Image of the Cave in the *Republic* as a kind of corrective to the seamless ascent of the lover in Diotima's Ladder. Just as Diotima presents true being as the aim of all longing, so does the Image of the Cave depict the man who gets to glimpse the sun as so overwhelmed by its power and beauty that he never wants to go back down into the world of the lower desires (*Republic* 516c–d, 519d). But, whereas for Diotima the beauty of true being floods the soul and bears it aloft from lower to higher erotic attachments, the people in the Cave do not want to transcend their lower attachments. On the contrary, so attached are they to their customary loyalties and prejudices that, Socrates says, they need "someone" who will turn them forcibly around, breaking the bonds that prevent them from turning to look up at the source of light, "compelling" and "dragging" them "out into the light of the sun" by "force," even though initially the beneficiaries of this frog march to transcendence will be "distressed and annoyed at being so dragged" (*Republic* 515c–e). Only after this enforced break with one's attachments will one be in a fit condition to receive the light and progress further upward toward happiness, realizing how badly off he was before: "When he recalled his first home and the wisdom there, and his fellow prisoners at that time, wouldn't he consider himself happy for the change and pity the others?" (*Republic* 516c). Clearly Socrates fits the description of this "someone" who turns us around. His relentless skepticism about his interlocutors' and his own inadequate conceptions of the good life provides the forceful rupture, the pain of parting with our cozy convictions and lazy justifications, necessary for turning to face the light. Anyone who has had the good fortune to have a great teacher knows how exasperating their benevolence can be.

Diotima's Ladder is, of course, Socrates' own speech. He is capable of this flowing and edifying sort of rhetoric. Not only is he, to use Alcibiades' famous phrase, like the Silenus whose outer ugliness hides the beauty within (215b), but, as a wooer of Agathon, he can remedy the persuasive shortcomings of his own elenchus by garbing its hard bones in a beautiful revelation. Moreover, to consider its limitations takes nothing away from the fact that it tells us something true about the soul. Putting Diotima's Ladder and the Image of the Cave together enables us to see in a provisional way what for Plato are the two dimensions of an adequate hypothesis of civic education. There is a proper object of erotic longing—the good, whose stability and clarity order both the cosmos and human life at its most virtuous. But the soul is not automatically, spontaneously drawn toward this object. One must be brought, through vigorous dialectical investigations, to a point where one's soul is in a sufficiently healthy condition to be able to receive it and benefit from it. All in all, the education to civic virtue is a much tougher matter than Diotima's Ladder on its own would lead us to think, working with more intractable psychological characteristics.[8] As we will see in turning in chapter 4 to a consideration of the *Republic,* the subject matter of civic education comes into view in conjunction with the thematic consideration of the toughest, most belligerent part of the soul—the source of the greatest zeal for civic virtue and also one of the greatest threats to it.

ENTER ALCIBIADES: DISRUPTING THE DIOTIMAN ASCENT

In continuing our consideration of the *Symposium,* we should note that it remains an open question throughout Platonic political philosophy whether the ambition for political mastery can ever be fully reconciled to the service of the common good. According to Diotima's hierarchy of satisfactions, political eros subordinates itself to philosophy, content with a second-best approximation of the good. But in the action of the dialogue, Socrates and the beautiful, ambitious Alcibiades are competitors for the good.[9] The politician will not take a back seat, casting considerable doubt on whether or to what extent philosophy and civic virtue are intrinsically related objects of the soul's satisfaction. Socrates teases Alcibiades for using his description of Socrates as a way of winning Agathon for himself by warning the poet that Socrates always manages to "bring it about that he is the beloved rather than the lover" (222b–d). A man primarily of deeds rather than speeches, Alcibiades inserts himself on the couches between Socrates and Agathon—perhaps unwittingly at first, but deliberately in Agathon's view (213b, 222e). To Alcibiades' intense vexation, Agathon is bent on switching places to be next to Socrates, refusing to compromise by moving between Socrates and Alcibiades (222c). But no change takes place. With Socrates and Alcibiades seated on either side of Agathon, it seems as if philosophy has to compete with the beautiful for access to the good. As a lover, moreover, Alcibiades is aggressive and possessive. He wants Socrates to love only him, and he wants Agathon to be loved only by him (222d). He gibes at Socrates for trying to "conquer" everyone in speeches and monopolizing all the beauties. Hence, while Diotima's Ladder presents eros as rising from one object to another, each level superseding the last, the dialogue itself reminds us that eros can divide us in competition as much as it can unite us in admiration for the beloved. Everything that happens after Alcibiades' arrival can therefore be taken as Plato's commentary on the extent to which political honor is not governable by philosophy. As such, it already prepares us for the *Republic* and the denouement of the best regime.

Alcibiades' lengthy profession of admiration for Socrates and his awe before him are genuine enough. But he may not be quite as much in thrall to Socrates as he claims. By stressing how unworthy he is to live up to Socrates' standards of self-inquisition, he in effect gives himself an excuse for not actually reforming his life very much at all, as his drunkenly charismatic entrance into the dialogue after the orderly discussion is over would seem to attest. He claims that whenever he returns to his ambitions in politics, he knows that he has "succumbed" to the honor of the dēmos. But he does keep returning (216a). Unlike Callicles, whose shame has a lower breaking point, Alcibiades seems capable of clearly grasping what it is that Socrates objects to in his way of life, to some degree accepting it, and proceeding to pursue that way of life while maintaining his friendship with his severest critic. In some very gifted and ambitious statesmen, there is a strength to the love of honor that can sustain a large degree of clarifying reflection without withering away. Socrates may well subordinate Alcibiades to philosophy, as he says in the *Gorgias*. But it is not clear that Alcibiades ever subordinated his political ambitions to his association with Socrates. In this respect, again, we might already anticipate the downfall of the best city in Book 8 of the *Republic,* when the honor-seekers rebel against the wise. As the political leader who, according to Thucydides, was more responsible than anyone else for pushing Athenian imperialism to the height of imprudence in the disastrous Sicilian expedition, Alcibiades was the very embodiment of what Socrates calls the "feverish city" in the *Republic* (372e)—the city whose eros for wealth and pleasure makes it impossible to order the community on the initial straightforward clarity of the division of labor according to technē, occasioning a vastly more complex psychological investigation. Socrates' and Alcibiades' badinage over Agathon in the *Symposium* is playful, but it has a serious undertone. It prefigures Socrates' contention in the *Republic* that eros must be extirpated from a just constitution. For, like Alcibiades' attempt to force his way between Socrates and Agathon, eros can block the effort to order the political community on the pattern of the good.

Since Socrates is described by Alcibiades as not loving others but only being loved by them, it might seem as if Socrates himself does not begin the ascent up Diotima's Ladder (222b). [10] Moreover, as we observed, Diotima is not certain whether Socrates is willing to pay much attention to the second rung of the ascent to true being, the eros for political honor:

> If you were willing to glance at human beings' love of honor, you would be amazed at their irrationality unless you bear in mind what I have said and reflect on how uncannily they are affected by their love of renown . . . for the sake of immortal virtue and [an] illustrious reputation. (208c–d)

But I think there is a way in which we might see Socrates himself as climbing the Ladder, a way that would comport with the evidence elsewhere that he is indeed a lover and, in so doing, help us to make further sense of his strange contention to Callicles that he alone among the Athenians "practice politics."

Let us look for another moment at Diotima's remark about Socrates. Since her speech is Socrates' recollection of how she first initiated him into the mysteries of eros, the remark concerns the way he was in the past. In the meantime, he evidently must have absorbed her teachings and overcome what she predicted would be his "amazement" at the "irrationality" of political eros, since it is he who is now laying out the teaching for Agathon and the others. Because he did come to understand what she taught him about eros, Socrates is, as she promised he would be, now able to "reflect" on how eros makes the politically ambitious so "uncanny." Because she led him first to amazement at the phenomenon of eros, then guided him in reflecting on and clarifying this richest of human passions, he now has an understanding of what he once might have concluded was not even a fit subject matter for intelligent speculation.

A Socrates who might not even have glanced at political honor because of its irrationality sounds like the Socrates whom Aristophanes parodies in the *Clouds*. This Socrates pursued the study of the physical universe and did not assign the status of genuine theoretical knowledge to political and moral issues. Aristophanes' lampooning of his worship of the "convection principle" implies that, like many Sophists, Socrates conceived of the natural world in terms of a universal cosmological principle of sub-phenomenal motion. Because he believed that nature could be studied as something intelligible prior to and apart from convention, Aristophanes' Socrates concluded that politics and morality were shams, fit only to be manipulated to serve one's natural self-interest. The play uses Socrates to sum up the "sophisticated" outlook: individual profit and self-preservation are natural, and so are the most general laws of the physical universe. But the middle realm of the polis, where the lives of most people are centered on their loves, loyalties, and animosities, is dismissed as a local delusion or fraud.[11]

In the *Apology*, Socrates attempts to explain his life to the Athenian dēmos so as to counteract the impression they derived years before from distortions such as those in Aristophanes' play. He denies ever having been a teacher of deceptive rhetoric. But he does not disparage the study of the physical universe, commending it to anyone who can undertake it (19c–d). It is not that he once studied nature and now studies convention, but that, by investigating whether there might be political and moral phenomena the knowledge of which possesses the same universal validity as the phenomena of the physical universe, his approach both to phusis and nomos underwent a transformation that set him entirely apart from the other "Sophists" and cosmologists. He tells the story of the Delphic Quest so as to imply that, if he at one time did dismiss the possibility of the serious study of political and moral phenomena, he changed once "the god" sent him on his mission to test the knowledge of his fellow citizens—an activity that made him, he claims, the city's keenest guardian of virtue (*Apology* 20e–22e). In order to shed some additional light on what I have termed the erotics of statecraft, I want to suggest that Diotima's initiation of Socrates into the mysteries of eros offers us another perspective on this turn from natural philosophy to political philosophy. At the core of this turn is Socrates' experience of "amazement," to recall Diotima's characterization, at the seeming sheer irrationality and complexity of political phenomena like the eros for honor and fame. Diotima's remark can be taken as a summing up of why the "old" Socrates of natural science became the "new" Socrates whose main study is human virtue: if the study of nature cannot account for the richest and most controversial of human longings, that knowledge is defective both with respect to its methods and its objects. But whereas the *Apology* represents this dawning awareness through the mission that "the god" imposes on Socrates, the *Symposium* fills in the picture of the Socratic turn by revealing that the experience is fundamentally an erotic one.[12]

THE EROTIC CORE OF SOCRATIC SKEPTICISM

To clarify this experience, let us return to the *Symposium*. Alcibiades' description of Socrates is arguably self-serving to a degree, since it emerges in the context of a stratagem to woo Agathon away from Socrates. Since Agathon places himself in the position of the beloved *vis à vis* Socrates, he would presumably be put off by the depiction of Socrates as being incapable of loving if he came to believe it. Moreover, by recalling his famous failure to seduce Socrates, Alcibiades of course furnishes what he hopes will be decisive evidence in his attempt to persuade Agathon that Socrates is no lover. To explain what to him was obviously Socrates' dumbfounding unwillingness in this case to exchange the role of beloved for lover, Alcibiades says that Socrates, like the mythical Silenus, is ugly on the outside and surpassingly beautiful within (215b, 217a). Inasmuch as Alcibiades depicts himself as drawn to these inner beauties of soul, this remark, however genuinely laudatory in part, further justifies his claim that Socrates is a beloved rather than a lover, while Alcibiades is (at any rate in this instance) preeminently a lover.

But there is more to it than that. The strategy of seduction that Alcibiades' speech both functions as and recalls is also, in a sense, a political strategy that links the personal, private conversations about eros in the *Symposium* to the wider world of Athenian political affairs. Alcibiades' very arrival represents the intrusion of the city's popular energy and forcefulness into the private domain of the dinner conversation. Garlanded like Dionysus, his attention-grabbing entrance constitutes the demand of a man of action that these people who have been discussing the meaning of eros decide in favor of loving him. He demands that this rather cultured audience pay tribute to the wider public of Athens by paying tribute to him, their magnificent favorite. By trying to prevent Agathon from being next to Socrates alone, he tries to win the contest for Agathon through action when his words do not prove sufficient. Alcibiades' account of his attraction to Socrates, including his past failure to seduce him, is an illustration in microcosm of Socrates' political relationship with the Athenian dēmos as a whole as represented by its charismatic leader—bearing in mind, of course, Alcibiades' own ambivalence about his wooing of the people. For, like Callicles, Alcibiades is ashamed of his attraction to philosophy when he is competing for the honor of the many, and ashamed of his love of the many when he is with Socrates (217d–e).

I suggest that this ambivalence and double sense of shame help us to clarify Alcibiades' comparison of Socrates to the Silenus. In part, it is his excuse for loving someone so unprepossessing, as if he were ashamed of there being no outward beauty or evident nobility of rank and achievement to explain his recurring attraction to Socrates. The need to find such a justification was compounded by the fact that Alcibiades himself was usually the object of other people's admiration and affection. Furthermore, if Socrates is so beautiful in his inward richness of soul, this helps to explain his imperviousness to Alcibiades' own (to most people far superior) beauty, as evidenced by the famous failed seduction. And though he chooses his evidence about Socrates for self-serving reasons, Alcibiades does furnish us with a convincing insight into where these two extraordinary individuals stand with each other. Renowned for his generosity and winning ways, Alcibiades' usual experience is that people need him more than he needs them. With Socrates, not only is this relationship reversed, but, as he complains, Socrates is his major competitor for attracting the best people to himself—when Socrates is around, Alcibiades grouses, he gets hold of all the beauties for himself (223a). Odd as it may seem, the poor and powerless Socrates is Alcibiades' chief rival in Athens, a man who achieves a kind of independence that Alcibiades admires and honors in himself—but without wooing the people as he does.

Alcibiades backs and fills repeatedly between acknowledging that Socrates deserves his love and astonishment that he should be drawn toward this man, given his own popularity and success. But he will not give in. In this respect, he is a different type from Callicles. Callicles is torn between his openness to the independence vouchsafed by philosophy and a prospective natural master of politics whose advent he can only hope for from afar. Alcibiades, however, sees his own life as embodying all that is most admirable about political excellence on the contemporary scene. Thus, although he is in some measure torn between political mastery and philosophy, he is also more resolute than Callicles about maintaining his own way of life. He has seen the future, and it is him. This makes him more magnificent and less prickly and vulnerable than Callicles. While Socrates is able to deflate Callicles' boasted lack of shame with his barb about the catamite, Alcibiades displays his extraordinary self-confidence by freely recalling his own attempt to play the catamite to Socrates and how he was rebuffed (219b–e). Such reserves of self-esteem and resourcefulness does he possess that he is willing to use an episode that most people would conceal as a secret source of shame for the sake of a larger strategy for defeating his rival—an eristic display that gives us some insight into his ability to dominate the political scene. His speech is an elaborate rhetorical effect designed to give Socrates his due while pursuing the honor of the dēmos anyway. And, of course, he aims tacitly to have the final victory over this man before whom he professes to abase himself by frustrating Socrates' wooing of Agathon. Drunk or not, he remains a politician.

By trying to seduce Socrates, Alcibiades was attempting to practice his well-known generosity as an aristocratic and political patron. In this unique instance, he literally presented himself as the gift, reserving what he took to be the supreme favor he could bestow so as to convert Socrates into one of his clients. (As he arrogantly announced upon offering himself, "In my opinion, you have proved to be the only lover worthy of me" [218c]. Because it was a last-ditch effort to convert Socrates into one of his admirers in the dēmos, Alcibiades was willing to exchange his usual role of beloved for that of lover, in the sense of seducing Socrates into seducing him (217c). Given his failure to add Socrates to his client group, Alcibiades must afterward depict his continuing love for Socrates as an extraordinary exception that proves the rule of people ordinarily loving him, by lending Socrates a kind of superhuman status and strangeness as a love object. When Socrates ironically replies to Alcibiades' recollection that he may be "nothing" (129a) rather than beautiful within, he in effect is telling Alcibiades: The inner richness you attribute to me is a reflection of your longing for the fullest, choicest beauty, the *summum bonum*. But while you sense that this object is beauty of soul, you are ashamed of appearing to be ashamed before the dēmos of your more conventional longings for pleasure because of your devotion to me, and ashamed that you cannot conquer me by means of the beauty and power that ordinarily make you the center of people's desires. So you make me beautiful "within" to excuse your attraction to an ugly old man who will not reciprocate your advances.

We might say that this is the one contest on his rise to power that Alcibiades did not win, and it perhaps explains the sense one has of him in his later years as a wounded sort of personality. It is interesting to speculate whether his failure to woo the one man in Athens who most manifestly stood apart from the dēmos helped fuel his ambitions to move beyond the confines of Athens through the expedition to conquer Sicily and later, his ability to treat with various foreign powers as if he were himself a country. Did he try to compensate for his inability to embrace fully the universality of thought to which he was unquestionably attracted with an ambition for universal horizons of political fame?

Of course, Alcibiades as we encounter him in the *Symposium* and in his historical career has to some extent been shaped by Socrates from his late teens. Hence, the question arises: To what extent was Socrates himself responsible for how he turned out? As we observed in the last chapter, in the *Alcibiades* I, Socrates inflames the young Alcibiades' eros with a vision of world-scale ambition and monarchy. Socrates' original approach to Alcibiades may therefore provide us with an illustration of how Socrates set about to explore Diotima's teaching that eros properly guided can be the source of civic virtue, prudence, and the subordination of statesmanship to wisdom. Since the dialogue took place fairly early in Socrates' life as narrated by Plato, Socrates' direct appeal to Alcibiades' eros for fame arguably demonstrates the psychological insight into love and honor that Socrates in the later conversation of the *Symposium* depicts retrospectively as his "initiation" into the rites of eros by Diotima, symbolizing his "turn" from natural science to political philosophy.

Socrates' unfolding relationship with Alcibiades sheds some further light on our leitmotif for the Platonic understanding of tyranny, the problem of Callicles. In comparison with his original approach to Alcibiades, with Callicles Socrates takes a more sober approach, doubtless because Callicles has a different sort of eros but perhaps also as a consequence of how Alcibiades' life has unfolded since Socrates first approached him. Rather than stimulate an eros for honor as a continuous ascent to virtue, Socrates stresses from the outset its fecklessness and instability—how eros has made Callicles "double," internally divided and love's slave. Moreover, while Alcibiades' eros is powerfully focused on his own prospective mastery of politics and undistracted by shame, Callicles is, despite his professions of shamelessness, vulnerable to shame over his passions and divided between a longing to be the master himself and a longing to revere and serve a higher authority. Unlike Alcibiades, his eros is from the outset less focused, more riven with doubt, and accordingly offers little prospect of the innate capacity for an ascent to wisdom through politikē that evidently sustained Socrates' longing for Alcibiades. The therapy that Socrates explores for Callicles' eros is accordingly more repressive and ascetic: eros is tamed and chastened, not by its own immanent higher potential, but by its enemy, moderation, grounded in the soul's intimation of the mathematical harmony of the cosmos.

In the *Republic,* as we will see at length in chapter 4, eros is even more thoroughly discouraged, rejected in favor of thumos as the basis for civic virtue and paideia. When reintroduced in Book 5, eros does make possible the ascent from civic virtue to philosophy, and from the third level of mathematical reasoning to the forms. But, rather than being, as in Diotima's speech, a continuous ascent from political virtue to philosophy, philosophic eros in the *Republic* performs a kind of end run around civic virtue rooted in thumos. Within the internal Socratic biography of the Platonic dialogues, the *Republic,* I would argue, reflects Socrates' considered assessment of eros in contrast to what he presents as his original initiation into Diotima's teaching. Accordingly, the results of Socrates' encounters with Callicles and Alcibiades are very different. Alcibiades' eros having been inflamed, he tries to conquer the world, inflaming Athenian imperialism and ultimately leaping beyond the city to become, as Thucydides says, like a city all on his own, treating with other countries as if he were their equal. By contrast, Callicles vanishes. There is no record of his having made the mark in politics he so clearly intends when we first meet him in the *Gorgias.* His silence at the end of the dialogue could be the silence of refusal, but it could also be the silence of an inner gestation as he ponders what he has heard. Without being convinced by Socrates about the best way to live, he may have absorbed enough doubts about the life of mastery to spoil him for political greatness.

Alcibiades and Callicles both stop listening to Socrates at a certain point. Alcibiades affects to lament his periodic returns to the dēmos, and he may feel genuine remorse, but he does it just the same. The reasons for Socrates' limited success in persuading Callicles and Alcibiades are not the same in each case. Callicles is more prone to shame than Alcibiades. Whereas Alcibiades is ready to recount how he tried to play the catamite if seducing Socrates was all he could do to convert the other into one of his lovers, Callicles is shamed by Socrates' mere imputation in speech that either he or his beloved is too wanton. Alcibiades' shameless attempt to turn Socrates from beloved into lover can be taken as emblematic in his private life of how he conducts his relations with the Athenian dēmos in his public life. He inflames their longing for him, as it were, by the tantalizing prospect of the conquest of Sicily.[13]

By contrast, Callicles' shame over the imputation of wantonness in his private love life reveals—in contradiction to the argument he maintains so as to prevent himself from contradicting himself—that he might place certain limits on his love affair with the Athenian dēmos, limits on how much pleasure and honor he would promise them and how much he would demand in the way of gratification for himself. This unspoken and unadmitted moderation is in keeping with Callicles' spoken admission that he himself is not likely to prove to be the natural master: he reveres something or someone higher than himself. His nobility of character is revealed by his selfless longing for a superior ruler, although the "doubleness" of soul Socrates diagnoses in him stems from the fact that, in keeping with his exposure to the Sophists, he interprets perfection in statesmanship as the perfection of selfishness—that is to say, tyranny. Alcibiades, by contrast, believes himself to be this naturally superior ruler, and while aware that Socrates is his superior in other respects, cannot help but regard him as a rival for "all the beauties" and would like to settle their rivalry by establishing that Socrates is also his lover, even chief among his lovers—that is to say, a particularly esteemed client.

Now that we have considered Socrates' relationship to Athenian politics from Alcibiades' perspective on their erotic relationship, let us turn the account around and trace it from the Socratic side. Self-serving as Alcibiades' descriptions of Socrates may be, they do contribute to the truth about Socrates when taken in the total context of the dialogue. They give us a sense of how Socrates can claim to "rule" and "practice politics," at least within the small circle of his conversational partners. Since Socrates on more than one occasion depicts himself as skilled in erotics, we are warranted in assuming that we can learn something about him from how others react to and depict him in these friendly contests for influence and affection—especially when we put these accounts together with what Socrates says about himself.[14] For Socrates implicitly offers us another account of himself in the *Symposium* that reverses Alcibiades' comparison of him to the Silenus— one in which he is, as it were, beautiful on the "outside" rather than the inside. He is able to garb himself in an outward discursive beauty by his rhetorician's ability to fabricate Diotima's revelations about eros.

This rhetorical skill, I now want to suggest, is as much an illustration of Socratic "political science" as it is a strategy of seduction, since Socrates woos his friends in order to benefit their souls. Diotima's speech about what is truly beautiful and good is itself a noble depiction of the world. It answers Agathon's wish for a new kind of poetry to replace the old poetry of necessity with a praise of eros as the god of the modern age. But it does so in a sober manner, subordinating love to the good, so that the proper understanding of eros can serve as a guide for the true art of rhetoric. The speech of Diotima, then, can be taken as a paragon of that "noble art" of rhetoric whose prospect Socrates sketched for Callicles, but that could not be elaborated in the absence of a full account of eros. Socrates employs it to provide some content and structure for Agathon's intimation of the need for a new poetic morality to replace the departed standards of the past. The speech therefore illustrates rather well what Socrates means by his claim to undertake the proper art of statesmanship. Since Socrates must make his friendship appealing to Agathon before he can practice this beneficial art upon him, the speech sheathes the analytical and refutational side of Socratic philosophizing in a beautiful medium that is more palatable to a gracious poet like Agathon. In this respect, Socrates' strategy for wooing Agathon illustrates what Diotima herself says about eros in the speech: eros properly understood is not primarily drawn to the beautiful, but rather is drawn to the good (*to agathon*) through the medium of the beautiful, engendering something beautiful "in" this medium (*Symposium* 206a–b). The speech depicts the beautiful as Agathon needs to find it so that Socrates' dialectical advances will be pleasing, leading to a fruitful friendship between them. Eros (the wily hunter Socrates) pursues the good through the medium of the beautiful (Diotima's teaching)—*if* the beautiful Alcibiades' love of victory will sit still for the philosopher's triumph in their contest to possess the good.

But what, then, is Socrates truly like "within," since both Alcibiades' account of him and his account of himself are elaborated in the context of strategies of seduction? "Perhaps," he says to Alcibiades, "I am nothing" (219a). As Al Farabi remarks, Socrates is so ironic that, on occasion, he can state the truth simply and baldly because it will go unnoticed compared to the dense ambivalence that surrounds it.[15] I think this may be one of those moments. As I interpret it, however, this nothingness is more a source of hope than despair. Socrates' suggestion that he might be "nothing" is a further reason for thinking that Diotima's description of eros as needy and impoverished applies especially well to him. And here is where I think we can put together Socrates' self-absorption as a needy lover with the beneficence of his claim to practice the art of ruling. Socrates' description of himself as "nothing" is the description of his need, his lack. It comports with his description of himself in other texts as, on the one hand, knowing that he knows nothing (*Apology* 21d) and, on the other hand, of being a skilled knower of erotics (*Symposium* 177e, *Theages* 128b–c, *Theaetetus* 150b–151d). For the full pursuit of erotic satisfaction is, as Diotima describes it, a kind of technē of nothingness or lack. And this is how Socrates can be both skilled in erotics and inwardly empty. Knowing that you know nothing is to know the limits of your knowledge in every area, which is to know that you are fundamentally needy—the core of Diotima's description of eros.

We can flesh out this supposition with some pertinent passages from other dialogues. What Socrates says to Theaetetus about the connection between dialectic and eros may be another example of the truth stated playfully and simply amidst graver half-truths about nature and being: Socrates would like to be able to ask questions forever of this young soul that flows like oil (*Theaetetus* 144b, 146a).

With Theaetetus, Glaucon, and others, Socrates acts as a midwife who helps bear the child of discourse with which the young men are made pregnant through his questions (*Republic* 506e–507a). As he tells Theaetetus, he cooperates with "the god" to do this, while the "demon" (Diotima, we recall, characterizes eros as a "great demon" who binds gods and men together) guides him away from souls incapable of this kind of gestation (*Theaetetus* 151a). Through his questioning, he engenders in eligible souls a long labor pang of self-doubt and self-examination. Socrates himself remains "barren" at the end of this gestation—the positive outcome is their own clarification of how to live. Through dialectic, then, Socrates traces and tests the limits of his own knowledge—his emptiness and lack—through others, whom he "slave drives" (as Callicles and Alcibiades complain) to self-reflection.

SOCRATES' PHILANTHROPIC AGGRESSIVENESS

The Socratic elenchus is aggressive and wily on behalf of eros. It is therefore philanthropic, because it results in greater self-knowledge for his partners.[16] Socrates' philosophical erotics shed some light on Nietzsche's claim that Socrates offered a kind of replacement for the old Homeric and tragic morality.[17] As traditional standards collapse, Socrates' certainty that he lacks certain knowledge itself becomes a powerful standard of intellectual sobriety, steadfastness, and rigor, a wall to cling to in the storm (*Republic* 496d). His seemingly disinterested pursuit of the truth is the outward consequence of his single-minded pursuit of the pleasure of bringing the souls of others to term. Thus, Socrates is "amazed" that Theages would turn to him, of all people, as a guide for kalo kagathia: the "beautiful and good" standards traditionally said to guide the conduct of a gentleman of birth and means in the polis (*Theages* 127a–d). This short dialogue illustrates particularly well Nietzsche's claim that Socrates replaced the moral authorities that had customarily guided the gentleman. It depicts an old-fashioned father from the countryside bringing his son to town to learn virtue from Socrates. But Socrates finds that the young man himself wants to be a tyrant, since that is what all the other smart young men in town believe to be the best and most natural way of life (*Theages* 124e–125a, 126a). In this simple drama, we encounter the conflict between the old and new moralities—between the two strata in Athens represented by the Just and Unjust Arguments in Aristophanes' *Clouds,* or by the Athenians in Thucydides who viewed the plague as a punishment for impiety as opposed to the cool amorality of the generals on Melos. Moreover, the dialogue apes the plot of the *Clouds*—where another father originally from the country brings his citified son to study with Socrates—in order to reverse its meaning: far from corrupting the youth, Socrates tries to mitigate the corrupting influence on them of the city itself, "the great Sophist," as Socrates calls it in the *Republic* (*Theages* 121c–122b).

Socrates is sober and, as he says to Callicles, always says the same things when those around him are constantly changing their minds (*Gorgias* 482a–b). But because eros guides his life, Socrates is also playful. He can be surprised by the passions he stimulates. He does not "already know all the answers" to the questions he launches, as first-time readers often feel. For example, he might have divined Callicles' character in its basic outlines from having previously overheard Callicles talking with his friends about how much philosophy is too much (487c–d), enabling Socrates to begin their encounter with his psychoanalysis of the "doubleness" produced in Callicles' soul by his dual attraction to philosophy and political mastery. But Socrates could not have predicted the energy and complexity of Callicles' great speech extolling injustice in response, stimulated by Callicles' desire to convert Socrates to his own view, and so outshine Socrates before their audience of connoisseurs of oratory, including the renowned Gorgias. Often one has the impression that Socrates has come prepared to a discussion with a few ready-made themes in mind—the craft analogy being perhaps his single most preferred gambit for opening the conversation. But this observation is in no way incompatible with Socrates' frequent expressions of amusement and surprise at his interlocutors' responses, and the ways in which those responses compel him to change his tack.

Once a logos is launched—such as the formal comparison of a virtue to an art— it bobs along on currents of feeling in those to whom it is directed, whose precise variety and intensity cannot be predicted. "Following the logos" is therefore not simply a matter of deductive necessity, with personal reactions thrown in as a sort of second-order dramatic device to make the foregone conclusions more easily communicable. Nor, of course, is following the logos a matter of whim, intuition, or authentic mood. Socrates makes it abundantly clear that a formal argument like the craft analogy must proceed deductively toward a certain kind of conclusion once it is launched in a certain direction—applied to a specific phenomenon or action. (For example, insofar as justice is analogous to an art, it cannot do harm to anyone, even to an enemy [*Republic* 335d–e].) But there is no way of telling ahead of time, or with certainty throughout a dialogue, in which direction Socrates' psychological interaction with his interlocutors will launch such an argument, or how the eruption of different feelings or the entrance of new characters might change its course from one direction to another. Different sorts of *logoi* suit different sorts of souls, and the truth of the encounter resides precisely in tracing the varieties of these couplings. Nothing else can properly explain the fact, apparent even to a casual reader, that Socrates presents formal arguments whose premises and conclusions flatly contradict each other from one dialogue to another, or even within the same dialogue. The mathematician Theaetetus needs a logos that stresses the unity of the soul's parts, while the erotic and ambitious Glaucon, for reasons we will examine in the next chapter, needs one that stresses its differentiation.

One could adduce many similar examples. The point they convey can be summed up as follows: Socrates not only refutes and criticizes—he dances. There is room in his life for erotic spontaneity, flow, chance, and play. Tuchē is released within the "concept nets" (to use Nietzsche's phrase) of the elenchus as the consummation of Socratic probing. If this gestation leaves Socrates barren, he has the pleasure of the procreation itself. Time and again we see Socrates marveling at the twists and turns his investigations take, his attraction to certain types of encounters from the outset, and how encounters that he did not initiate surprise him and capture his interest in a way he did not anticipate. This "amazement" at the complexity of the human soul, I surmise, made Socrates' experience of his need to clarify his ignorance through testing the ignorance of others so rich. For him, as perhaps for no other philosopher, thinking and conversing were indivisible. The fact that Socrates wrote nothing himself can be explained in part by his belief that the outcome of his conversations as "barren" apart from the beneficial self-reflection he sparked in others. But it must also derive, in my view, from the fact that he found these daily encounters so consumingly interesting that he was unwilling to detract from his immediate pleasure at philosophizing by taking the time to write.

By helping the young to see how their need for knowledge emerges from their need to understand their own desires and ambitions, Socrates fulfills the role of demonic eros in Diotima's Ladder, linking man with the gods. Our growing awareness of how much we lack a connection with true being vouchsafes us a glimpse of true being at the top of the ladder, "always being, neither coming into being nor passing away, always being of a single form" (211a–c). Socrates' knowledge of limits is a knowledge of the extent to which each phenomenon fails to be a consistent and noncontradictory eidos. It enables him to do his friends the benefit of testing their unconscious ignorance against his own conscious ignorance. He takes advantage of them in order to gratify his eros for their need of his clear and certain ignorance. In this sense, Socrates' erotic career constitutes a kind of pleonexia and immoderation that indivisibly entail friendship and justice. In contrast with Richard Rorty's entirely plausible suggestion about Heidegger, Socrates is not an SOB. But he is not exactly nice either. He is mild, but not sweet: not sarcastic, but ironic.

In my view, this philanthropic aggressiveness is the core of Socrates' personal claim not merely to speculate on, but actually to undertake, the art of ruling and to practice politics. Since he does not in fact rule or have any major political responsibilities, the best sense we can make of this seemingly absurd contention is that, in devoting himself to the pursuit of pleasure through the impregnation of others with a dawning awareness of what they would truly need to know in order to be good citizens, rulers, and family members, Socrates more than anyone else in Athens is devoted to the necessary propaedeutic to any elaboration of a truly good and just political community, as opposed to (as he puts it to Callicles) politics "as they are now practiced—acting like a 'real man'" (*Gorgias* 500c). The true art of politics begins with the real human beings around you, regardless of how the larger political order is currently constituted. For as Socrates tells Callicles, if you cannot point to a single friend who has ever been improved by intercourse with you, you can hardly hope to be considered fit to lead an entire people. If we are capable of caring for our friends, to that extent we might hope for further improvements in the direction of a city constituted in such a way that its citizens are friends. As I will argue in connection with the *Republic,* understanding the soul begins by considering it "writ large" in its involvements with others through the pursuit of justice. But once the soul's nature is clarified by seeing its relation to an optimal politeia, the chief practical outcome is that one can found this constitution in oneself while living in a defective regime. Thus, even if there is little prospect of major political reform, one can begin to live as if one were a citizen of the best constitution by practicing its virtues among one's friends and, where possible and prudent, gradually bringing their influence to bear on wider political affairs.

In sum, philosophical erotics are at the heart of Socratic political science. If, as Leo Strauss has written in connection with Hobbes, modern scientific optimism about understanding and reconstructing the cosmos is based on an ultimate skepticism that anything exists that could be known independently of the categories of anthropocentric instrumental reasoning itself, Socratic skepticism about the adequacy of our beliefs is based on an ultimate optimism that there is a good that we can and must seek in order to fill our emptiness.[18] "The god" sets the aim and the boundary: knowledge of the whole in union with the beautiful and good. In the *Apology,* "the god" bears down on Socrates with a mission to expose the limitations of people's knowledge. As Strauss suggests, in that work of Plato's, the skeptical side of Socratic philosophizing is housed within an overarching wonder at the mystery of the whole and of service to the Oracle.[19] Because he serves the god, he must be the gadfly. The Delphic Quest and the Gadfly are the two poles of Socrates' public self-vindication: the one submissive to the dawning wonder of the complexity of political and moral affairs, the other aggressive in the hunt for clarification of this wonder. As I will suggest at greater length in my consideration of the *Republic,* Socratic philosophizing is made up of both dimensions, the holistic (represented in the *Apology* by the Delphic Quest) and the analytical (represented by the Gadfly). But their full characteristics cannot be grasped from the *Apology* itself, because, of the two dimensions, the holistic one is the primary and unifying dimension, and it can be grasped only in erotic terms.

As Socrates' one truly public speech to the dēmos, the *Apology* abstracts from the erotic continuum linking skepticism with wonder because it is more "politic" to represent philosophy as a selfless dedication to the study of virtue than as a devotion to pleasure, even the pleasure of self-perfection (*Apology* 31b–c). And this is why the *Apology* is a kind of gateway to the Platonic world, outlining problems that the dialogues themselves more adequately explore. The "politic" defense makes sense in the dire situation of Socrates' trial, especially given the imperviousness of Meletus to reflection and debate. But upon consideration, it is, I believe, inadequate to explain and justify the mission of service that Socrates claims to perform for the city by discussing virtue. For if a devotion to the political community's virtue contradicts the pursuit of self-perfection, then civic virtue can be based only on venal self-interest, compulsion, or unreflecting conformity. The dialogues themselves fill in the missing core of the *Apology* by showing us a Socrates who has the leisure to explore how pleasure and duty properly clarified might have a common aim. Among these more discriminating audiences, Socrates' apparent selflessness in urging people to think more carefully about virtue proves to be a consequence of his own pursuit of satisfaction. The god sets the boundaries for this mission in Diotima's Ladder just as in the *Apology*. But in the *Symposium*, Socrates is a gadfly because he is a lover who needs the need of his interlocutors for knowledge. To the extent that philosophical erotics can help others clarify the meaning of the soul's natural excellence, virtue need not be seen as unnatural (painful, foolish, or compelled). And to this extent also, Socratic political science will be political philosophy. That is to say, it will not be only a Stoic carapace or "politic" exoteric defense of philosophy (although it will include this), but the intrinsically philosophical study of the naturally best constitution for the soul and the city.

But if I am justified in arguing that civic virtue is the central subject matter of Socrates' philosophical erotics, and that Socratic philosophy is therefore indivisibly political philosophy, does it necessarily follow from this that Socratic political philosophy serves rather than undermines the civic association as it is understood and experienced by most citizens? Even after the "turn," the Platonic Socrates is still a strange being, even inhuman in some ways, like Aristophanes' Socrates in a basket. He is not an ascetic in the sense of being oblivious to human pain (flea bites) or eros (proffered buttocks), as he and his pale students are lampooned in the *Clouds* (190–198, 630–635). But he does possess an almost inhuman moderation in withstanding the tug of bodily pleasure. This is revealed by his ability to outlast everyone else at the *Symposium* (223c–d), and by his comparative self-control at the sight of the beautiful Charmides (while everyone else present sees no one but Charmides, Socrates is both smitten by Charmides and has the presence of mind to observe everybody else's rapture as well [*Charmides* 154b–c]).

Moreover, Socrates does not join his fellow Athenians in everyday politics, does not lead or advise, is not a partisan of any faction or regime. Hence in the *Apology*, while drawing the audience's attention to his friendship with Chairephon, a partisan of the democracy, and by so doing distancing himself from his aristocratic friends such as Critias, Socrates carefully refers to Chairephon before the dēmos as "your" Chairephon (21a). He knows he cannot go so far as to claim that he is "their" Socrates. The most he can plausibly maintain in his one speech to the dēmos is that his ceaseless pursuit of an understanding of virtue makes him unable to devote himself to any one government or party, that he might better serve them all through improving public discourse.

Very much unlike the Aristophanean Socrates, Socrates in the *Apology* does try to make himself intelligible to the dēmos and to justify himself according to the city's religious and moral beliefs, that is, as the servant of the Oracle.[20] For in ordinary politics, the heat of factional strife and controversy traces back to a belief in what the gods want, and indignation that one's opponents cannot or will not recognize it. Neither a political partisan nor (as in the *Clouds*) a scientist detached from the moral and religious controversies that often give rise to political partisanship, the Platonic Socrates is justified before the city as embodying the standards of knowledge for assessing such disagreements over the meaning of virtue, justice, and nobility, thereby serving Apollo. The dialogues provide an enduring image of that life, "a Socrates become beautiful and new," as Plato puts it in the *Seventh Letter* (314c).

However, while Socrates presents himself in the *Apology*, before his largest and least discriminating audience, as the selfless umpire and guardian of virtue, it transpires in the *Symposium* and other dialogues that the source of Socrates' interest in virtue is his eros for wisdom, mediated by his attraction to souls whom his demonic sign approves for conversation. In this sense, for Socratic philosophizing, the civic virtues cannot stand on their own, cannot justify themselves in their own terms. They are grounded in the best case as no more than adumbrations of philosophy, a propaedeutic for a good higher than themselves. Hence, if we probe behind the Stoic carapace of selfless umpirage in the *Apology*, we find that, although Socrates is indeed every bit as much of a nonpartisan as he presents himself at his trial, his detachment from political faction does not stem simply or primarily from a concern for the good of the whole city, but because he is absorbed in conversations that keep him from demonstrating many of the citizen's ordinary attachments or commitments.

What Socrates and his friends share in common is a discussion of whether there is a "common"—of whether virtue exists by nature and what it truly is. For this reason, there does seem to be a common good among the philosophic, based on their shared speculations. From observation, one can also say there is a common good of which citizens are capable, most often expressed as a party or regime that asserts its view of justice at the expense of other views. The question undertaken by the *Republic* is whether there can be a regime, a political common good, that embodies the philosophic common good of logos—if not in the literal sense that all citizens might philosophize, then in the proximal sense that a reformed paideia or art of rhetoric might link the polis with the cosmopolis without dissolving the civic-spirited bonds peculiar to the being of the former. In short, to anticipate Socrates' peculiar proposition in Book 2 of the *Republic*, can thumos "see"?

NOTES

1. Translations of the *Symposium* are my own. I have also consulted with profit the translation by Alexander Nehamas and Paul Woodruff.

2. See the discussion in David Sachs, "A Fallacy in Plato's *Republic*," in *Plato II*, ed. G. Vlastos (Indiana: University of Notre Dame Press, 1978).

3. Consider Zeiger, "Plato's *Gorgias*."

4. Cf. Hesiod *Theogony* 116, 117, 120.

5. As Athenian power rose and fell between the final defeat of the Persians and Athens' defeat in the Peloponnesian War, there was a widespread perception that the old moral and

religious authorities were melting away, leaving a vacuum. See Dodds, *Gorgias,* 291–292 and Guthrie, *The Sophists,* 106–107. In Thucydides' memorable presentation, the destabilizing effects on the Greek polis of the geopolitical struggle between Athens and Sparta revealed an underlying moral rot: "Thus every form of iniquity took root in the Hellenic countries by reason of the troubles. The ancient simplicity into which honor so largely entered was laughed down and disappeared; and society became divided into camps in which no man trusted his fellow. . . . In the confusion into which life was now thrown in the cities, human nature, always rebelling against the law and now its master, gladly showed itself ungoverned in passion."(Thucydides *The Peloponnesian War* 3.83–84). In the *Republic,* Glaucon claims (albeit somewhat self-servingly) that contempt for justice and the belief that selfishness is the natural life are views he has heard from "thousands of people" (*Republic* 358c).

   6. Consider Stanley Rosen, *Plato's "Symposium"* (New Haven: Yale University Press, 1968), 44: "In terms of Phaedrus' speech, the cosmic Eros of preSocratic physics is difficult if not impossible to reconcile with the human Eros ostensibly being praised. This is the theoretical background against which Phaedrus' speech must be studied."

   7. As Nussbaum notes: "A central feature of the ascent is that the lover escapes, gradually, from his bondage to luck. . . . [The philosopher's] contemplative love for all beauty carries no risk of loss, rejection, even frustration" (Nussbaum, *The Fragility of Goodness,* 181).

   8. Nussbaum comments on the two paths in this way: "We see two kinds of value, two kinds of knowledge; and we see that we must choose. One sort of understanding blocks out the other. The pure light of the eternal form eclipses, or is eclipsed by, the flickering lightning of the opened and unstably moving body. You think, says Plato, that you can have this love and goodness too, this knowledge of and by flesh and good-knowledge too. Well, says Plato, you can't. . . . The *Symposium* now seems to us a harsh and alarming book. Its relation to the *Republic* . . . is more ambiguous than we originally thought. . . . It starkly confronts us with a choice and at the same time makes us see so clearly that we cannot choose anything." (Nussbaum, *The Fragility of Goodness,* 199). Nussbaum's essay on the *Symposium* is powerfully argued. As I argue in the next chapters, however, there remains the prospect in Plato that a properly elaborated civic *paideia* might ameliorate the tension in the human soul between passion and the good. On this prospect, consider Gadamer, *Dialogue and Dialectic,* 54–59.

   9. See Lowry Nelson, Jr., "Alcibiades' Intrusion in Plato's *Symposium*," *Sewanee Review* 94 (1986): 203–204.

   10. The observation is Rosen's (*Hermeneutics as Politics,* 160).

   11. See Nicholls, *Socrates,* 26.

   12. Diotima's implicit criticism of Socrates for having originally dismissed political psychology as an irrational subject is usefully compared with the *Statesman.* There, the Eleatic Stranger defines statesmanship as the art of herding featherless bipeds. "Young Socrates," a mathematician, accepts this reductionist definition of *politikē* without objection. See the illuminating essay by Charles Griswold, "*Politikē Epistēmē* in Plato's *Statesman,*" in *Essays in Ancient Greek Philosophy,* vol. 3, ed. John Anton and Anthony Preuss (Albany: State University of New York Press, 1989), 141–167.

   13. Thucydides *The Peloponnesian War* 6.16–24.

   14. See Leo Strauss, "Plato's *Apology of Socrates* and *Crito,*" in *Studies in Platonic Political Philosophy,* ed. Thomas Pangle (Chicago: University of Chicago Press, 1983), 46–47.

15. Al Farabi, "Plato's *Laws*," in *Medieval Political Philosophy,* ed. Ralph Lerner and Muhsin Mahdi (Ithaca: Cornell University Press, 1972), 84–85.

16. Here and in the following pages, then, I am arguing that there is at bottom no conflict between Socrates' self-perfection as a lover and his care of the beloved for the beloved's own sake. On this supposed dilemma, see the influential essay by G. Vlastos, "The Individual as Object of Love in Plato," in *Platonic Studies* (Princeton: Princeton University Press, 1981) and the response by A. Kosman, "Platonic Love," in *Phronesis,* supp. vol. 2, ed. W. H. Werkmeister (1976).

17. Friedrich Nietzsche, *The Twilight of the Idols,* in *The Portable Nietzsche,* ed. and trans. Walter Kaufmann (New York: Viking Press, 1974), 473–479.

18. Leo Strauss, *What Is Political Philosophy?* (Westport, Conn.: Greenwood Press, 1973), 196.

19. Strauss, "Plato's *Apology of Socrates* and *Crito,*" 41, 46–50.

20. Consider Thomas Pangle's introductory essay to *Studies in Platonic Political Philosophy,* by Leo Strauss (Chicago: University of Chicago Press, 1983), 14 ff.

Chapter Four

The Education of the Civic-Spirited

In the last chapter, we considered the erotic ascent to transcendence as illustrated by the *Symposium*, especially the speech of Diotima. We turn now to the *Republic* in order to consider the other route sketched at the end of chapter 2—the steep and rocky ascent, to use the language of the Image of the Cave, whose primary basis in the soul is spirit. Within political psychology, the *Republic* implies, the eidetic clarification and ordering of the soul's actions, especially the desires, requires a critical rigor more characteristic of Socratic refutation than Diotiman rhetoric—always bearing in mind, of course, that both must be integrated if we are to arrive at the fullest consideration of the soul's potentialities, political or otherwise.

In the following chapter, I will trace some of the main features of Socrates' arresting proposal that thumos can be educated to be both civic-spirited and, in a manner, philosophical. By making thumos rather than eros the source of civic virtue in the *Republic,* Socrates extends the critique of Diotima's teaching that is already implicit in the *Symposium* to the thematic consideration of the best constitution. Having explored the prospect that eros might provide a "demonic" basis for civic and philosophical friendship that would mirror the holistic unity of the cosmos, Plato now asks us to consider whether the refutational side of philosophizing—reflective of the clear and distinct "forms" in which the whole is articulated—might aid in educating citizens to a more aggressive and self-regulating kind of service to the common good.

The prominence of the spirited part of the soul is established very early in the *Republic*. The word for spirit (thumos) is related to the word for desire (epithumia), a connection that Socrates plays upon to depict spirit as a sort of engine of the desires in general.[1] Spiritedness may thus be considered, along with eros, as one of the primordial passions of the soul, the winged horses whose energies can plunge the charioteer of mind into the abyss if he does not direct them toward their proper ends. Each passion has a comprehensive scope, but a markedly different content. When we are overcome with eros, it tends to make us forget ourselves. We are carried away with longing or admiration for the beloved. Eros enlists all our energies, including the aggressive energies of thumos, in the pursuit of the object of longing (*Republic* 572e–573e). But when our way to the object of longing is blocked, the spell of eros is broken, and thumos comes to the fore. Instead of losing ourselves in the beloved, we become self-conscious. We become painfully aware of our selfhood and its limitations—we feel anxious, weak, and isolated, or jealous and angry that we cannot get what we desire.[2] These moods can combine in an outburst of daring rage.

Before examining the role that Socrates assigns to thumos in the optimal community elaborated in the *Republic,* it will be useful to get a sense of its traits from other sources. For it is an unusual, complex, and in some ways disturbing dimension of political psychology. According to the *Laws,* in its pristine condition prior to a proper education, thumos is more of a defect of the soul than an advantage. Along with "fear, pleasure, pain, envy" and other desires, as the Athenian Stranger puts it, thumos can tyrannize over the soul and make us behave unjustly toward others (*Laws* 863e). Thumos is closely connected with fear and pain—in the words of the Athenian, pain is a "form of fault" in the soul that we name "thumos" and "fear" (864b). In its pristine emergence, ungoverned by virtue, thumos is like the desperation of a cornered animal, lashing out at whoever or whatever might pose a threat. Longings for pleasure undermine courage and "turn thumos to wax" (633d). But as a passion, thumos is distinct from the experience of pleasure because it is quarrelsome and pugnacious, whereas pleasure gratified is an experience of ease and contentment (863b). Prior to education and redirection, spiritedness can erupt in impulsive killing or premeditated murder arising from a perceived slight to one's honor. In the latter case, we might say that it makes use of a certain cold-blooded rationality in plotting its revenge that places reason at the service of an irrational concern with one's honor. In Platonic political psychology, thumos is altogether the most ambiguous source of moral agency, strung between the purely involuntary—when passion overwhelms us—and the purely voluntary, when the tug of the passions is subordinated to prudent counsel (866d–867b). In order that its fears and longings be combated, thumos must be governed by the virtue of courage, which is instilled by an education in correct opinion. But—this is equally important—the belligerent side of thumos must not entirely disappear under the virtue's restraint. For, according to Plato, every citizen of a well-governed community must be both spirited and gentle. The man of "perfect virtue" in the city is the spirited citizen who reports injustices and inflicts punishments. Such a citizen must be gentle toward those whose infractions are not deliberate or who can be cured by persuasion, while "letting anger have free rein" against the incorrigible (730b, 731b–d).

As this preliminary consideration of its traits reveals, spiritedness is a troublesome steed to hitch to the chariot of political justice. If thumos has been properly educated, it can be a source in the soul for the energy of moral conviction and righteous zeal in the service of civic virtue. But the capacity of spiritedness for punitive and indignant excesses must be guarded against, lest such excesses become a source of danger to the stability and moderation of the political order. Put bluntly but not misleadingly, the pedagogical aim of Platonic political psychology is to shape a civic character somewhere between the extremes of Stanley Baldwin and Torquemada, and somewhat closer to the former than the latter. As we will see, everything hinges on the possibility and extent of this relative proximity of belligerence to reason in the good organization of the soul and the city.

THE PRIMORDIAL EXPERIENCE OF THUMOS

Before turning to the discussion of thumos in the *Republic,* we should also be aware of its wider, pre-philosophic context, since this will give us a better sense of what Plato views as the good and bad potentialities of this aspect of human experience. In the earliest poetic sources, thumos is the source of some of the strongest emotions like anger, revenge, grief, victory, hope, and fear. Sometimes it is used to describe thought, but the sort of bold practical judgment that a ruler must exercise in a crisis rather than contemplative reflection. Hence, Odysseus "spoke to his proud thumos" when considering his options on the battlefield.[3] We often get the impression from these sources that thumos is not so much a feeling that an individual may be said to possess as a kind of force that possesses the individual, sweeping him into a daring action. Thus, Achilles' "brave thumos roused him" to find Aeneas and fight him to the death in order to avenge his beloved Patroclus. After Patroclus was killed, the Trojans' "thumos strongly hoped to pull away Patroclus' body from under Ajax." When Hector challenges the Greeks, Menelaos "complained loudly in his thumos."[4]

Thumos is variously described in terms of a swoon, breath, or as a life force that is "blown forth" from the body. In certain contexts, it seems to be coextensive with life, heart, and soul—that is, with the primary forces of human existence altogether. We might connect this with the etymology that links thumos with the verb *thuein,* meaning to rush on like the wind, the sea, or a swollen river, or to storm and rage both in the meteorological and anthropological senses, or for the earth to "seethe with blood." In other words, we might see thumos as the welling up and eruption in human existence of a more primordial force of motion, turmoil, and disruption in the world at large. Such speculation is borne out by the fact that, in its earliest usages, thumos seems to be especially connected with the bodily, mortal, most vulnerable dimensions of human experience. It is especially manifest at moments of death, particularly when someone is killed or wishes to kill another. It is at the moment of death that thumos is often spoken of as being "blown forth" or otherwise departing from the body.[5] And yet, while the "soul," strictly speaking—the *psuchē* or source of life—continues after death and represents the individual in the afterlife, thumos is less often mentioned as departing to the afterlife (although it is sometimes found intact among the shades of Hades, as when, for instance, the shade of Ajax is said to feel unbending anger for Odysseus [*Odyssey*

11]). It seems to be a force particularly connected with, dependent on, and expressive of the most finite, time-bound, perishable dimensions of our existence. Similarly, while mind (nous) and soul are virtually never attributed to animals in these poetic sources, many animals (oxen, swine, horses, wolves, and lambs, among others) are said to possess thumos, again most often at the moment of dying. Once more, it would seem as if thumos was particularly characteristic of the perishable aspect of existence that we share with other organisms rather than what might be thought of as the soul's capacity for transcending such mortal limitations.

These various manifestations of thumos—anger, hope, fear, and the experience of death—thus give rise to a sort of ontological reflection. Thumos seems to be that passion through which existence brings us face to face most jarringly with our finitude and perishability. It causes the soul, in its anxiety, to wonder about the character of the world and the place of human beings in it. Are there gods, or is existence nothing but hostile happenstance? If there are gods, do they care about human beings? Do they defend justice and decency as these are understood by humans, or are they indifferent, or hostile, or able to be swayed by sacrifice and homage from the unscrupulous? As we will see, a part of the Platonic therapy for thumos is to isolate it from the fullest range of these anxious and gloomy ruminations, treating it as a more strictly delineable psychological property confined to the familiar issues of everyday politics and statesmanship.[6] But Plato is aware that the straightforward manifestations of thumos in anger, envy, or indignation through the competition for goods, status, or honor in everyday political life are underlain by a more profound and general anxiety about the seeming vulnerability of human existence in a mysterious if not downright hostile cosmos. One of the main grounds on which Socrates takes the poets to task and proposes the censorship and even expulsion of their works from a well-ordered politeia is that they inflame this gloomy sensibility by depicting it so vividly as to make whining and complaining seem like a profound and soulful stance toward the world. Socrates uses the Homeric Achilles as an exemplar of thumos in its pristine, uneducated manifestations, before its energies have been converted to a constructive zeal for civic virtue, and in his portrayal, Achilles veers between extremes of unseemly cowardice and mad daring (*Republic* 386a–391a). These extremes issue, in Plato's understanding, from the same root cause—the tendency of the man overwhelmed by thumos to feel as if he is in a pitched battle with all the forces of a hostile world, sometimes shaking his fists madly at the gods or doing battle with rivers, at other times paralyzed by sorrow or fear. In this connection, we should note other etymologies connecting thumos with smoke and the vapor arising from warm blood. Taken together with its other associations (such as the earth seething with blood), it might seem as if the pre-philosophic meaning of thumos carried a profound, very ancient intimation of the ontological riddle of tragedy: the mystery as to whether human existence with its varied woes might be a sort of sacrifice, a sort of Dionysian dismemberment, through which the gods or some unfathomable necessity recurrently shatter human hopes.[7]

In Book 10 of the *Laws,* Plato writes sympathetically of how thoughtful young men are often led by their pride to rather gloomy reflections on the meaning of life. Their awareness of how often injustice goes unpunished, of how certain people succeed in enjoying huge degrees of pleasure and glory at the expense of others and die peacefully of old age, makes them wonder whether any rational and beneficent order governs the world (*Laws* 899e–900a). There is, in sum, a close connection between the primordial meaning of thumos and the tragic sense of life. Even when poets and tragedians urged just and moderate conduct, they did so in a way that might be thought to undermine their own advice. As Adeimantus complains in the *Republic,* he and his friends have been brought up according to such poetic authorities as Hesiod, Homer, and Simonides to believe that justice and moderation are preferable to vice, but that, while vice is easy and pleasant, virtue is harsh and difficult—which leads one to wonder how virtue could ever be considered preferable (*Republic* 363a–364e). One of the poetic answers was that Necessity recurrently purges the passions of their hubristic sweep, reestablishing the proper relation between a chastened city or human being and the gods.[8] The downfall of Oedipus from a *turannos* renowned for his skilled daring to a blind exile leaves him a man of deepened awareness, while his former subjects gaze in awe and dread at the fate of a man whose ambitions and eros carried him above the station proper to mere mortals. But in the Platonic critique of this tragic account of morality, these cycles of human daring and divine punishment lead less to a chastened reconciliation to divine Necessity than to an Achillean sense of cosmic victimization—as if the rule of justice and moderation can only be reestablished at the expense of human nature and happiness. As Socrates replies to Adeimantus's complaint, this is precisely the danger of exposing the young—especially the spirited class of the city—to the traditional depictions of Achilles and other heroes:

> For my dear Adeimantus, if our young should seriously hear such things and not laugh scornfully at them as unworthy speeches, it's not very likely that any one of them would believe these things to be unworthy of himself, and would reproach himself if it should enter into his head to say or do any such thing. Rather, with neither shame nor endurance, he would chant many dirges and laments at the slightest sufferings. . . . We'll beg Homer and the other poets not to be harsh if we strike out these and all similar things. It's not that they are not poetic and sweet for the many to hear, but the more poetic they are, the less should they be heard by boys and men who must be free and accustomed to fearing slavery more than death. (*Republic* 388d, 387b)

Thus, while Plato wishes to show that the energies of thumos might be converted to the service of a well-ordered community, he is emphatic that this can only be done by purging it of the gloomier existential undertow so vividly evoked—hence exacerbated—by the poets. The image of the chariot of the soul from the *Phaedrus* with which this book began offers a sharp corrective to the primordialist experience of thumos. It implies that thumos, like eros, is a passion that opens up the question of the prospects for transcending the limitations of human existence. But it also implies that thumos will best realize this longing for transcendence, not by descending deeper into the primordial depths of chance and disorder that ground the disorderliness of the passions and the consequent despair of finding a home in the world, but instead by being directed toward the stable order of the cosmos and participating in it through a virtuous ordering of the soul.

As we will see in greater detail in the following discussion, the Platonic critique of tragic poetry is thus a facet of the larger enterprise that we saw emerging through our earlier consideration of the Socratic response to Sophistry and the ontology of primordialism. This enterprise is nothing less than the possibility of "political science"—a clear and rigorous knowledge of statesmanship that does not separate political convention *tout court* from nature, thereby rendering it a mere artifice useful for camouflaging one's natural intentions but not worthy of studying for its intrinsic contribution to natural human satisfaction. For both the Sophists and the poets, in the Platonic presentation, human nature is at odds with political convention. For the poets, this is a tragic conflict; for the Sophists, a recipe for individual liberation. For the poets, the tension can only be resolved during periodic, transient cycles through the recurrent destruction of human longings and ambitions. The proud and clever ruler Oedipus goes down to his doom as Dionysus, betrayed—as he complains—by Apollo, the very god of art, form, and intelligent achievement whom he might have thought to be his friend. Justice can only reemerge at the expense of mortal hubris, which must be ground down by Necessity so that Apollonian stability can be reborn out of Dionysian motion. For the Sophists, on the other hand, the disjunction between human nature and convention means that all laws and civic moralities adjuring us to prefer the common good to our own are nonbinding, except insofar as one needs to appear to honor them so as to pursue pleonexia with maximum safety and efficiency. In contrast with both the tragic and Sophistical responses to the tension between the individual and the city, Platonic political science argues that human nature need not be seen as collapsing into the pre-political origins of chance and necessity. The art of ruling, then, as Socrates claims to undertake it in the *Gorgias,* stems neither from the tragic insight that natural satisfaction and conventional justice are existentially incompatible, nor from the Sophistical teaching that natural selfishness is both unavoidable and (because natural) just in contrast with the artificiality of convention. While both tragedy and Sophistry transcend convention by a descent into the invisible origins of phusis as polemos, Platonic political science investigates the possibility of a natural knowledge *about* convention—about whether a certain set of conventions might be naturally satisfying and just in contrast with other defective sets.

CAN THUMOS "SEE"? THE NATURE OF CIVIC-SPIRITEDNESS
IN THE SOUL AND THE CITY

Let us begin our consideration of thumos in the *Republic* by recalling some of the main issues in that dialogue. The goal of the discussion is to explore the question of why or whether we should practice justice for its own sake as opposed to its consequences according to law and convention. Glaucon poses this challenge by presenting the view of the Sophists, according to which justice is good only by convention, and not at all by nature: "For I desire to hear what each is [justice and injustice] and what power it has all alone by itself when it is in the soul—dismissing its wages and its consequences"(358b). Adeimantus supplements the question by adding some troubled observations about the ambiguity of traditional moral authorities like Homer and Hesiod. While adjuring us to justice and moderation, he complains, they depict the gods as indifferent to these virtues or capable of being swayed by the sacrifices of the wicked. Socrates' way of taking up the question is to propose the construction "in speech" of a city where they can watch justice come into being. Having seen it "writ large" as a virtue of the whole community, he avers, it will be easier to trace what it is in the individual soul and why it is good.

The Nature and Origin of the City

It should be noted that, by examining the question of justice in this way, Socrates rejects at the very outset the grounds on which the Sophists distinguished between nature and convention. By making the city the pattern for the individual soul, Socrates implicitly repudiates Glaucon's contention that the nature of justice can only be delineated when "its wages and consequences" are dismissed. The point is not to find natural justice by abstracting it from conventional duties and rewards, but to elaborate the specific set of conventional duties and rewards that permits the individual to pursue justice in a natural—rational, fulfilling, and noncoerced— way. For the Sophists, human nature is spontaneously motivated by self-interest and desire. It is not shaped by political society or convention, and obeys conventional authorities only from fear of punishment or because the law has an instrumental value in protecting each individual from harm by others. But Socrates will not concede that the proper way of investigating the status of justice is to ask how it affects this allegedly natural individual, an approach that would guarantee ahead of time that justice could never be viewed as directly satisfying our natural needs. Instead, he implies that justice cannot even be delineated as a phenomenon for observation unless it is seen from the outset in its public as well as its individual dimensions. Justice is a pattern. By setting up the parallel between the just soul and the just city, Socrates implies that the nature of the individual cannot be fully understood except as it is manifested in his or her relations with others in the civic association.[9]

Echoing the Sophists, Glaucon was inclined to search for the "nature" of justice as being coeval with its "origin" and "becoming" (358e)—to view the nature of politics as residing in its pre-political substratum of self-preservation, struggle, and fear, regarding convention and law as artificial constructions. Justice, he suggests, is a compact originally made among naturally selfish individuals to limit the more drastic consequences of their competition with each other. Socrates, however, argues that the satisfaction of our needs even on the simplest level of bodily self-preservation already entails the practice of the arts and, therefore, a community organized according to the division of labor: "On this basis each thing becomes more plentiful, nobler and easier, when one man . . . does one thing according to nature." 370c). In other words, even granting that human nature is primarily concerned with self-preservation, we cannot survive apart from some sort of ordered association, so that, while there are certainly individuals, "individualism" is not a natural given. Thus, whereas the Sophists distinguished nature on the one hand from art and convention on the other, as Socrates sketches the first primitive association, the "city of sows," phusis and technē come into being together. Whereas Glaucon, echoing the Sophists, had proposed looking for the nature and origin of justice together (358e), in Socrates' discussion of how the city originates, phusis does not emerge with the original becoming, but is coeval with the specificity of the tasks for which different types of human natures are fitted (369b, 370a). Here, then, as in the *Gorgias,* the Socratic paradigm of art is used as an exploratory analogy for virtues like justice. In contrast with the Sophists' understanding of art as a creative matrix, for Socrates art points toward the ends—the finished products—for which we employ the arts. The distinctness of the arts and the clarity and stability of their objects intimate the character of the cosmos and the soul as a noetically structured whole.

The city of sows and its division of labor among the banausic arts corresponds to the level of pedestrian desire (epithumia) in the individual soul—our simplest material needs for survival. In this way, much as he does with Callicles in the *Gorgias,* Socrates attempts to unpack Glaucon's indiscriminately jumbled desires for sex, food, and other lusts from his desire for honor, and to show him that his basic bodily needs can be easily satisfied within an austere, temperate type of political community, without any need to aim for tyranny. Much like Callicles, however, Glaucon is put off by the low and boring quality of the desires served by the banausic arts. However, just as with Callicles, it is precisely Glaucon's impatience with the reduction of natural satisfaction to these pedestrian material needs that proves Socrates' larger point—that it is not possible to articulate the full range of the soul's longings on the basis of the sophists' sub-political account of human nature. By remarking that he wants to see added to their hypothetical city whatever luxuries and refinements of pleasure are conventionally and customarily accepted (*nomizetai,* 372d–373a) in a rich and sophisticated city like Athens, Glaucon implicitly identifies through a natural conversational response to the Socratic craft analogy one of the germs of Platonic political science: the hypothesis that the fullest human satisfaction can only come to sight by way of convention, not prior to and apart from it. As Socrates puts it in reply, it is only now when they are introducing these conventionally sought-after pleasures that they will really be able to see how justice and injustice "naturally grow" (372e), since only now will the full range of vices be present with which to contrast the life of justice. The city of sows is left behind in the discussion because eros longs for more than the pedestrian sorts of satisfaction serviced by the banausic arts. It craves luxuries, and in order to acquire them, the city must go to war. Eros as a quality of the public soul leads to imperialism, and is perhaps itself satisfied in part by the scope and grandeur of imperial politics, as Alcibiades intoxicated the Athenians with the splendor of their own military forces and the prospective conquest of Sicily.[10]

The Separation of Civic-Spiritedness and Eros

At this point, Socrates persuades his listeners to agree to a crucial psychological premise that shapes much of what follows: the distinction between pedestrian desire (for which he reserves the word epithumia) and spiritedness.[11] As I have already mentioned, epithumia and thumos are etymologically related. For reasons I will presently discuss, they can also be related as a matter of experience and observation. By insisting that the distinction between desire and spiritedness is as clear as the distinctions among the various arts that they agreed would provide the analogy for their discussion of justice in the soul and the city, Socrates rigorously separates the part of the soul that *strives* for the grand objects of eros from the *enjoyment* of those pleasures. He does this by asking Glaucon whether a class of warriors will be needed to conquer what the city requires for its "feverish" new pleasures, now that the austere city has been superseded. Glaucon agrees only too eagerly, both because it was he who instigated the transition from simple to feverish pleasures and because he admires martial prowess. Socrates often remarks upon Glaucon's manly courage (*andreia*), which seems to make him a suitable interlocutor for some of the more radical transitions in their conversation (357a). Later, Socrates places him in the male role for their joint bearing through dialectic of a "child of the good," the Images of Philosophy in Books 6 and 7 (506d–507a).

However, when Socrates asks him if desire and spiritedness are two parts of the city or the same part, Glaucon is initially inclined to view them as the same (374a–e). Within the little history of the hypothetical city's emergence, it could obviously be the case that the artisans, their desires newly inflamed, took up arms and made their own conquests. They would be both desiring and spirited. But Socrates reminds Glaucon of their earlier agreement to search for the meaning of justice on the analogy of technē with its division of labor. Because of this principle of "one man, one job," now explicitly extended from the parts of the city to the parts of the soul, they must see the warlike part of the soul and the city as distinct from the desiring part. In this way, Socrates drains eros from desire, or, more precisely, from the combativeness of desire—a seemingly small step in the argument, but one that has a profound effect on the dialogue's positive prescriptions for education and statecraft. By making the belligerence needed to acquire the objects of erotic longing a separate, distinct psychology from the hedonistic life itself, Socrates chops up the erotic continuum that, according to Diotima, links even pedestrian bodily pleasures with the noblest activities of public life as ascending levels of satisfaction. Although Glaucon wished to see the bodily needs expanded to a more fully erotic scope, the city now unfolds in such a way that the rigor and discipline that were meant to procure these refined and expanded pleasures are robbed of any connection with hedonism itself. The combative part, thus eviscerated, has the drive eros needs to achieve its pleasures (the Auxiliaries will fight and conquer on behalf of the now-lustful Artisans), but has been drained of the longings for the substantive satisfactions themselves. It is a little as if Robespierre were sent to rule over Las Vegas.

Glaucon agrees, not merely because of their earlier agreement on the principle of "one man, one job," but because—as with Callicles—a part of him is indeed attracted to a courageous self-overcoming that disdains the soft life of luxury now shifted to the Artisans. Whereas in his speech Glaucon had revealed his attraction to the Sophists' claim that they could teach an art of rhetoric for disguising one's acts of injustice against one's fellow citizens, he is now starting to become attracted to an art of soldierly perseverance on behalf of both the common good and a steady character. The comparison of the soul's virtue to the paradigm of technē, with its clarification of distinct means toward distinct ends, helps Socrates to distinguish and clarify the parts of an ambitious young personality.

The Double Nature of Thumos and the Need for Philosophy and Education

Thumos comes to the fore now as the chief characteristic of the warlike part of the city and the soul. Socrates uses the word or its cognates no fewer than five times in the first passage introducing it (375a–d). His way of using it is also noteworthy. In discussing the qualities of a brave soldier or army, Socrates' interlocutors would probably have proceeded directly to a discussion of courage, a word that in Greek is not only specifically human, but specifically masculine, literally a synonym for manliness . Socrates instead rather emphatically makes spiritedness the basis of courage, not only in people but in "any animal"—"Then will a horse or dog, or any other animal whatsoever, be willing to be courageous if it's not spirited? Haven't you noticed how irresistible and unbeatable spirit is, so that its presence makes every soul fearless and invincible in the face of everything?" (375b). In other words, instead of making the usual identification of courage with manliness, Socrates reduces the specifically masculine quality of andreia to a mere *instance* of spiritedness—a quality that, as he depicts it, is universal in scope, cutting across distinctions of gender and species. In this elevation of the more universal natural trait of spiritedness as the source of what the ancient Greeks usually considered to be a gender-specific virtue, we can already anticipate Socrates' arguments later in the *Republic* that men and women should be educated to the same civic responsibilities, inasmuch as merit is a quality of "every soul" rather than of body, hence universal rather than restricted to one sex.

According to Socrates, spirited animals—he uses dogs as an example—have "sharp senses, speed to catch what they perceive," are swift and strong and "ready to fight it out with their catch" (375a). We might be reminded here of Diotima's description of Eros as a wily, combative hunter, characteristics attributed by Alcibiades to Socrates himself. Here, unlike the *Symposium,* the combative, hungry part of the soul is being explored in abstraction from any specific object of erotic longing. As I will argue presently, however, there are reasons for thinking that the reformed psychology of thumos that Socrates elaborates in the *Republic* as the basis for the civic training of the Auxiliaries represents the importation of certain Socratic traits into the education of a citizen body. But at this early stage a problem arises, one so critical that Socrates is almost prompted to give up their whole search for justice in the soul and the city. Like a watch dog, he observes, spiritedness is capable both of gentleness and savageness. But this means that the nature of thumos is "double"—whereas, Socrates reminds Glaucon, they had agreed that every nature is single, since, on the analogy of virtue to technē, each is defined by one specialized activity alone. If any nature is conceded to "possess opposites," Socrates says, they will have "abandoned the image we proposed" (that is, the craft analogy) for tracing the emergence of justice (375d). We should note that, in objecting to characterizing the nature of a thing as "possessing opposites," Socrates is objecting to a typical Heracleitean formulation about phusis. Broached here, this critique is more comprehensively stated in the context of the fully elaborated division of labor within the soul in Book 4 (436b.12).[12]

But then Socrates qualifies his description of spiritedness. Dogs can be trained to be gentle with those they know and savage toward those they do not know. Although their primary nature is savageness, gentleness is an "ethos" instilled by training. This ethos is also "by nature," a kind of second nature cultivated through the right breeding (375e). Spiritedness therefore need not be seen as double in the drastic Heracleitean sense of "possessing opposites"—a phenomenon whose transient presence is established by the temporary concatenation of contradictory forces.

It is equally true, however, that spiritedness is not quite single in the simple, straightforward sense that the parts and functions of human nature were single when they first came to sight in the primitive city of sows. As its nature begins to emerge in the more complex civic association solicited by the inflamed longings of eros for satisfactions beyond the necessities of survival, it transpires that thumos is neither a simple unity, nor a simple opposition, but a compound "nature" of two traits harmonized by education. The coeval emergence of phusis and technē still holds: Socrates does not abandon the "image" of one man, one job. But eros has introduced the prospect of a choice among pleasures beyond the level of survival, hence the possibility of unjust as well as just behavior toward one's fellow citizens and other cities. The possibility of injustice disrupts the direct parallelism between technē and the soul. The possibility of this parallel—put another way, the possibility that politics and the soul can be governed according to "political science"—can only be saved by the mediating relationship provided by education.

KING ALFRED'S COLLEGE
LIBRARY

Socrates therefore concludes, in a rather tentative and qualified way, that they can proceed after all with the investigation, since the education of spiritedness to be both gentle and savage toward the appropriate objects is at least not "against nature" and "is possible" (375e).

Given the equivocal sense in which the unity of thumos has been rescued, it is rather breathtaking when Socrates next proceeds to link the doubleness of spiritedness directly with philosophy, arguing as if the guard dog's or loyal citizen's distinction between friends and enemies parallels the distinction philosophy makes between what is known and ignorance. As he asks Glaucon to agree:

> does the man who will be a fit guardian need, in addition to spiritedness, also to be a philosopher in his nature? . . . since [this soul] defines what's its own and what's alien by knowledge and ignorance. . . . So shall we be bold and assert that . . . the man who's going to be a fine and good guardian of the city will in his nature be philosophic, spirited, swift and strong?(375d–376c).

Why does Socrates ask the courageous Glaucon to make this bold leap—the identification of the loyal citizen's distinction between "friendly and hostile looks" with philosophizing—at this early juncture? I make the following suggestion. If the ambiguous double-nature of spiritedness is not to blow the city apart with the tension between its loyalty to its friends and its savagery toward its enemies, then the distinction citizens make between their fellow citizens and the enemies of their community must possess the same certainty and objectivity as the distinction philosophy seeks between being and nonbeing. The order and stability of the polis must be grounded in the order and stability of the cosmos. If spiritedness "sees" in this way, Socrates says (using one of his prime metaphors for intellection), then it will be "orderly" (kosmion)—the word he uses in the *Gorgias* to connect a well-ordered soul with the orderliness of the world (376a). Because of the problematic nature of spiritedness, then, the *Republic* ceases at this point to be merely a discussion of the meaning of justice. In the course of searching for an account of justice that would possess the clarity of technē, it launches the hypothesis that a particular ordering of the political community could in some manner reflect the universal good of the cosmos. We have to wonder: What particular set of political conventions, however well-considered, could possibly be at the same time universal in character and validity? How can one be loyal to a particular, exclusive association and simultaneously transcend such local attachments through the universality of knowledge? How can one be a partisan of the nonpartisan?

Socrates' terminology reflects the paradoxicality of this strange proposition: The well-bred guardian's attachment to "one's own" will be synonymous with "learning" (376a–b). Yet the very word for "one's own"(*oikeon*) directly evokes the household (*oikos*), family, and private property—the ties and commitments that, as the Image of the Cave later sums it up, ordinarily make it extremely difficult if not impossible for citizens of a particular community to look beyond their own local conventions and prejudices. The proposition that "one's own" could, in this optimally ordered city, have as its particular local content the transcendental good already implies the destruction of the conventional oikos, including the abolition of property and the family. Equally strange is Socrates' contention that a love of learning can be bred "in the soul" of precisely that type of psychology ordinarily most fiercely attached to its own honor and possessions.

Glaucon is nothing if not spirited, according to Socrates, and Socrates needs the young man's spiritedness to energize their conversational leap from spiritedness to philosophy. Socrates' need to appeal to Glaucon's boldness in making the leap from thumos to philosophy as the ground for the civic ethos that blends savagery and gentleness illustrates the dilemma underlying the leap. It recapitulates the dilemma Socrates faces with Callicles: he has to appeal to Callicles' pride in order to try to establish the government of reason over passion, but Callicles' pride limits his openness to reasonable persuasion to this position. As he does with Callicles, here, too, Socrates contends that the gentleness that philosophizing can breed in a savage nature will make that man gracious and refined (376a, cf. 505b). But his prospects for success are at least more promising with Glaucon. Glaucon is younger, so the love of the dēmos may not have taken root in his soul as Socrates concludes it has done with Callicles. All in all, however, the equation of well-bred thumos with philosophizing remains a breathtaking leap.[13] It is a particularly apt example of what Aristotle means when he criticizes the divine madness of Platonism. For Aristotle, the subject matters of politikē—statesmanship, ethics, and civic education—cannot emerge in their own right until philosophy's concern with first principles recedes. For Plato, as soon as the need for ethics and education emerges, we must go straight to philosophy.[14]

Let us recall the main point: they can continue with the discussion because the doubleness of thumos is mitigated by its receptivity to an "ethos" that knows how to distinguish friendly from hostile looks. It is not an accident that education now becomes the guiding theme of the rest of the *Republic* (376c–d). Paideia is the fragile link between the partisan commitment of a citizen to the community and an openness to the universal truth that transcends partisanship. The possibility of a political community whose particular conventions have the status of natural principles will stand or fall by the possibility that there is a certain way of educating the human character to participate in the order of the whole. The tenuousness of this proposition is underscored by the tenuousness of thumos itself as a bond within the civic association. Can people whose souls are predominantly characterized by combative zeal be given an authoritative training that enables them to transcend all zealotry and "see" the universal? Can warlike ambition become the ally of reason? It is little wonder that Socrates warns his listeners that their discussion must now take a very long time and verge on the "mythological."

As we have seen, for the Sophists and pre-Socratics, nature is generally to be understood in terms of accident, change, and contrariety. The strife at the roots of

the world in turn encourages us to see human nature as predominantly characterized by disorderly passions and impulse. Socrates alludes to the primordialist
ontology when he reminds Glaucon of their agreement, stemming from the craft
analogy, that no nature should be said to possess opposites. By arguing instead that
phusis and technē emerge coevally within human associations, Socrates tries to
break down the dichotomy erected by the Sophists between nature and convention, bringing nature into the political community through the clarification of the
virtues on the analogy of the arts. In the Socratic approach, nature does not point
toward the primordial substratum of an artificial political convention, but rather
toward the articulation of the different faculties and talents displayed by citizens
and statesmen. Thus, while Socrates is aware that human nature often manifests
markedly contrary, contradictory, aggressive behavior, he does not agree with the
Sophists that we need conclude from this that the human capacity for virtuous
associations is a superficial camouflage for the more natural disorderliness
papered over by convention. Indeed, by squarely facing the difficulty of reconciling the most belligerent, ambitious, and troublemaking part of the soul to any sort
of moderate civic pattern, Socrates wishes to demonstrate that the contraries and
contradictions of the soul do not undercut the very possibility of an ordering of the
community that might satisfy human nature. Instead, these contraries in human
nature are transposed to the realm of civic education itself. They no longer place
human nature across a divide from the political association in a stance of Herculean predation or tragic despair. Rather, these contraries are investigated, clarified, tamed, and domesticated, becoming the subject matter for the attempt to fashion laws and conventions in such a way as to solicit and satisfy natural human
energies in the service of the common good. The nature of man emerges through
the correct conventions by way of education. Socrates makes the education of
thumos a kind of test case for this enterprise.

As a consequence of Socrates' separation of thumos from desire, the thumotic
capacity for discipline and self-control is drained of eros's attachment to specific
substantive objects. In other words, thumos is drained of the longing to possess the
beloved that stretches along the erotic continuum in Diotima's Ladder from bodily desire to the boldest ambition for civic fame. The warlike Auxiliaries of Socrates' hypothetical city will protect and oversee its productive capacities. But they
will not possess and consume its products. As we saw in chapter 1, Socrates tries
to convince Callicles that this conception of governing must follow from the identification of the art of ruling with prudence, and of prudence, in turn, with technē.
Just as artisans such as cobblers have authority over shoemaking by virtue of their
superior knowledge, but do not for that reason get to own the greatest number of
shoes, so rulers, to the extent that they are practitioners of the art of ruling and
nothing else, only manage the city's goods and do not consume them. The Auxiliary class of the optimal city in the *Republic* represents the fully elaborated outcome of this comparison of ruling to technē. Thumos trained according to certain
conventions is the psychological basis for the art of governing. Because it is

abstracted from eros, its ability to "see" clearly what is and what is not is thereby unclouded by passionate longing.

In this sense, the *Republic* is—at least hypothetically—the answer to what Socrates tries to achieve with Callicles but cannot, because from an early age Callicles' spiritedness has been too deeply entangled with his eros for geometrical proportionality to take root in his character. In the *Gorgias,* as a result of Callicles' stubbornness in arguing for the purblind version of hedonism according to which every bodily desire is good, Socrates arrives at an equally extreme formulation, according to which the desires are entirely reducible to the bodily, while order resides entirely in the soul. This bifurcation of order and pleasure makes it difficult for Socrates to impart much content to his advice that Callicles should prefer friendship within a moderate city to the extremes of eros. In the *Symposium,* by contrast, eros is shown to be a route to the good, including civic friendship, thus mitigating the bifurcation of order and pleasure. But the holistic solution limned by Diotima's Ladder is proffered at the expense of the analytical, refutational side of Socratic philosophizing. In the *Republic,* an attempt is made through civic education to find a place in the political community for the more aggressive dimension of the Socratic pursuit of knowledge. Thumos is the candidate for this psychological experiment. In contrast with the other two dialogues, where passion is either banished from civic virtue (the *Gorgias*) or treated as its main motive (the *Symposium*), in the *Republic* passion is first de-eroticized and then made the basis of good citizenship. Although ordinarily experienced as a passion, thumos is explicitly treated as a part of the soul. Although it is bodily, Socrates tries to detach it from bodily gratification.

An Education in Cosmic Beauty and Steadfastness

We should note, however, that although Socrates excludes eros from the investigation of the thumotic soul and governing class, he does not altogether attempt to deny the Auxiliaries an indirect kind of erotic satisfaction. Although denied the direct pleasure of possessing and consuming the objects of the "feverish" passions now banished to the lower class of banausic artisans, the Auxiliaries are offered through their education a kind of indirect aesthetic replacement that will also consolidate the proper training of their savage and gentle potentialities. The educational reforms that Socrates sketches in Books 2 and 3 are meant to reinterpret the world for the Auxiliaries in order to make it beautiful in the sense of being harmonious and orderly, so as to instill in their characters the same soberly gracious traits. The poets are taken to task for depicting the gods and life as a whole as random, unpredictable, often hostile forces. Instead, Socrates proposes a clear and consistent theology. The gods, he says, are the source only of good things, never bad. They do not change shape miraculously or assume false appearances "like wizards," but retain at all times a stable "look" or "form" (eidos, 380d). Moreover, they do not lie, although rulers may sometimes have to. In the primordialist ontology, as in the

poetic genealogies, good and bad fortune spring indiscriminately from the origi-
nating motions of necessity and chance. For Socrates, however, the good is the stable perfection at which things aim to the extent that they participate in being—not
the generational origins of stable and unstable appearances alike. Both morally and
metaphysically, being is not the same as existence. What is true does not cause
everything, only what is good. We must not believe that Zeus capriciously doles
out good and wretched fates (379b–380c). Nor should we believe that the gods are
overwhelmed by their own chance passions and whims, boozing, raping, and
choosing favorites on impulse. The gods of eidos are not a generational necessity
out of which all things unfathomably emerge, but a transcendental necessity that
solicits beings toward their various distinct fruitions (380d–381e, 390b–e, 391c–e).
     A decent person, Socrates argues, must be educated to believe that virtue is
grounded in a world where permanence, harmony, and intelligence prevail over
chance, strife, and disorder. Virtue is the approximation of this cosmic stability in
one's own character through the restraint of selfish passions, just as wanton passion is the human equivalent of decay and chaos in the world. In this way, Socrates seeks to reassure young men like Adeimantus and the unnamed young men
described in Book 10 of the *Laws* that they need not despair about their place in the
ultimate scheme of things. He wants to disabuse thumos of its tendency to dwell
gloomily on its root anxieties and fears, projecting them onto the world at large.
Of course, Socrates implies, unmerited reverses and setbacks occur in life. Sometimes good people do suffer unjustly while the wicked prosper. But these misfor-
tunes should be seen as accidental exceptions to the stability that is more prevalent within and typical of the cosmos, not elevated—as the pre-Socratics, poets,
and Sophists tended to do—into a cosmic principle putting chance and disorder at
the very heart of existence. The reform of "music" (tragic and lyric verse) to reflect
the stately repose of the highest beings will further inculcate in the Auxiliaries the
virtuous restraint of passion. "We would use a more austere and less pleasing poet
. . . one who would imitate the style of the decent man (398)," Socrates tells Glaucon and Adeimantus in describing the reform of poetry in the optimal city. "Good
speech, good harmony, good grace and good rhythm accompany good disposition"(399d). "We'll never be musical . . . before we recognize the forms of moderation, courage, liberality, magnificence and all their kin" (402c).
     The example of Achilles, Socrates points out, shows what can happen when a
spirited young man does not receive a proper education but instead believes in the
primordialist ontology. If life is at bottom a flux, disorderly passions are profoundly natural. Bravery in the service of the passions is a kind of heroic madness
into which the thumotic man whips himself, goaded by competitors or fear. Cowardice is actually the more sensible response to a world of unremittingly hostile
fortune—which is why, Socrates says, Homer attributes to Achilles the disgraceful belief that life is preferable to death at any cost, including dishonor and insubordination (*Republic* 386b–388b). We feel life to be tragic because it fuels our passions and then dashes them. Nature's awesome, frighteningly random accidents

and reverses goad us to fight back in furious self-assertion, as when Achilles does battle with the river, alternating with despair of achieving anything. By purging "music" of this irrational Dionysian undertow, the wordless moodiness that senses the flux and indeterminacy behind the stable appearances, Socrates tries to insulate the thumotic soul from these tragic extremes of fury and hopelessness. The stately calm and lucidity of poetry and prose as Socrates reforms them are meant to give the soul an anchor. The Achillean type of person, educated in this way, will avoid sinking into the primordialist undertow to become a sort of existential revolutionary, and will become instead the paragon of dignified and gracious self-control.

The reform of Achilles' type of spiritedness into the steady, sober courage of the Auxiliaries is a good illustration of the hypothesis that the spirited citizen of a well-ordered city might in some manner philosophize, his aggressiveness controlled by a knowledge of friendly and hostile "looks." In contrast with the manly daring traditionally associated with Achilles, the virtue of courage recommended by the *Republic* bears a much closer resemblance to the "steadfastness" (*karteria*) that, according to the *Symposium,* Alcibiades admired in Socrates' behavior on the battlefield (and in his bed [*Symposium* 219d–221c]). Socrates was neither cowardly nor rash, but vigilant, steady, and self-controlled. Socrates' "eyes [darted] this way and that," according to Alcibiades, just as "sharp senses" are said to characterize thumos in the *Republic* (*Symposium* 221b, *Republic* 375a). One of the aims of the new poetry outlined in Books 2 and 3 of the *Republic* is, I would suggest, to impart to the more widespread and representative "manliness" (andreia) of the Auxiliary class a habituation to this Socratic quality of patient endurance. As Socrates puts it, the task of civic poetry is not to imitate the furies and laments of the Homeric hero, but instead to "imitate the sounds and accents of a man who is courageous in warlike deeds and every violent work, and who in failure or when going to face wounds or death . . . in the face of all these things stands up firmly and patiently against chance" (399a). As characterized in the *Republic,* courage, although it does not flinch from combat, does not actively seek out war and struggle so much as it behaves in a steadfast and disciplined manner when such dangers strike the community.

Socrates' proposals for educating the Auxiliaries in how to believe in the gods necessarily reminds us of his own eventual conviction for impiety. Inasmuch as the education of the Auxiliaries imparts certain Socratic traits to the civic-spirited, the *Republic* can be said to make Socrates into a kind of exemplar of good citizenship (including pious citizenship), thus anticipating (within the dramatic chronology of the dialogues) and refuting for posterity the indictment brought against him in Athens. In concluding our provisional overview of the civic education set forth in the *Republic,* let us consider for a moment what light it sheds on the troubling question, raised recurrently by Plato in the dialogues we are considering, of Socrates' own fitness as a citizen.

Socrates' theology in the *Republic* is, like the civic education of which it is a component, supposed to narrow the gap between civic virtue and philosophy. But upon consideration it creates at least as many problems in this regard as it solves. Since the gods do not change or assume different shapes, they do not intervene in human affairs or appear among humans, as do the Homeric gods. Although this may banish caprice from their behavior, we also have to wonder how they can be "friends" of the city, as Socrates maintains. Given that the prime task of the Auxiliaries is to distinguish between friends of the city and outsiders—a "philosophic" distinction, as we have been told, because it corresponds to the distinction between what is and what is not—we have to wonder whether the Auxiliaries would not regard these distant, changeless, noninterventionary beings as outsiders to the city. Purging the gods of their capacity to intervene unpredictably in human affairs is necessary, in Socrates' view, in order to purge thumos of its ordinary tendency to extremes of punitive zeal and righteous wrath by depriving the zealous of a divine ally. The problem is that it is hard to see how gods so thoroughly purged of any interventionary capacity in human affairs retain any connection with civic virtue at all, whether for good or ill.

As Benardete observes, Socrates "desanctifies the city in the name of the sanctity of the gods."[15] We might alter this formulation slightly to say that Socrates desanctifies the gods in the name of the sanctity of the gods. He banishes their inconsistencies so that they might provide stable, steadily impersonal standards of justice. He thereby also robs them, however, of their awe-inspiring capacity for miraculous intervention in human affairs in order to make them nonpartisan and noncapricious. Such gods would presumably never support one army's slaughter of another, or command a man to make his son into a human sacrifice. Nor, it is important to note, could such gods as these be invoked by a Meletus to prosecute a Socrates. They do not lend themselves to human indignation, even over a charge of impiety, and altogether make rather pallid figures for which to die, fight, or punish others.

The *Republic* is an elaboration of Socrates' basic contention at his trial that his kind of philosophizing, far from corrupting the city, is the true guardian of its virtue. The optimal political community is one in which men like Socrates, true rather than sham philosophers, might rule (495b–e), an issue I will examine at length in chapter 5. While the Auxiliaries need a theological basis for their education in cosmic harmony and orderliness, it cannot be a theology that would lead to a philosopher (perhaps one of their own rulers) being charged with impiety. If the Auxiliaries believe in wrathful gods, their righteous zeal on behalf of the city's ways could boil over into an intolerance of their own philosophic Guardians. On the other hand, if the gods of the citizenry are too tepid, too detached, too unconcerned with fighting on behalf of the just, will there not be a weakening of the zeal necessary for the Auxiliaries to act as good guard dogs, repelling foreign aggression and policing internal lapses from virtue?

The theology of the *Republic* definitely tilts in the nonwrathful direction as opposed to the wrathful one, more (to return to my earlier comparison) toward

Baldwin than Torquemada. And in this way it points to one of the most difficult obstacles to the projected reconciliation of philosophy and civic virtue that forms the cornerstone of the whole civic education. The gods of the kallipolis cannot easily be invoked as the partisans of Achillean anger and indignation. From among the gods of the conventional Greek pantheon, only the Apollo of Delphi makes it into the public religious rites of the best regime (427b–c), and what is noteworthy about Apollo among the other Olympian deities is his relatively cosmopolitan character. Apollo was one of the least polis-bound of the gods; his chief oracle at Delphi was respected by all the cities, and internationally maintained by them even during periods of conflict. Not coincidentally, he is also the god with whom Socrates links his fortunes in the *Apology* through the story of the Delphic Quest. Half in the polis but half out of it, Apollo is the appropriate conventional religious capstone for the blend of civic commitment and openness to universality summed up in the proposition that thumos can "see."

But even the Apollo of ancient Greek religion was capable of capricious, lethal incursions into human affairs, praised by the beneficiaries as just and lamented by the victims as unfathomable betrayals. In the *Republic,* he is no more than a figurehead for the public rituals of the kallipolis, not a living presence of dreadful beauty, the "far darter" invoked by Oedipus. The theology of the best regime leads us to wonder whether the Platonic Socrates was ever able to reconcile the conflicting requirements of civic gods and philosophic gods, emblematic of the conflicting requirements between civic zeal and philosophy. Indeed, in the *Euthyphro,* after he has already been indicted, we find Socrates conducting a dialogue to search for a way of relating himself to the piety of his fellow Athenians—a dialogue in which, just as in the *Republic,* Socrates begins exploring the true meaning of piety on the analogy of a stable, unchanging eidos. The *Euthyphro* illustrates the fundamental tension between the kind of piety that supports the city and the kind of piety that philosophers can plausibly claim to exercise, and forces us to wonder whether thumos can "see"—whether, that is, philosophy and civic virtue are intrinsically related objects of the soul's satisfaction, or mutually exclusive paths.

Euthyphro goes too far in imitating what he understands to be the gods' standard of justice, so pious that he commits the impiety of prosecuting his own father, just as Zeus punished his father Chronos (*Euthyphro* 4c–e, 5e–6a). But Euthyphro's impious zeal is closer to the pious zeal of Socrates' accusers (although a relatively unconventional version of it) than is Socrates' lack of zeal. Indeed, there is a family resemblance between the zeal of Euthyphro and Meletus, since both are prosecuting elderly men. Euthyphro's zeal, although an eccentric variation, is closer to the nexus of family, law, and retribution that the city's gods support, whereas Socrates' gods are never angry. While Euthyphro invites ridicule because he has chosen the wrong object for his zeal in prosecuting his own father, the Socratic gods do not support prosecuting a father because they lack zeal for any prosecution. As Socrates argues to Polemarchus in the *Republic,* justice may well require us never to do harm to anyone (335d), and as he argues to Meletus in the *Apology,* if people do wrong, the best response is to rehabilitate them by teaching them to see their own ignorance (26a). Education is always to be preferred to punishment, although sometimes punishment is unavoidable.

All in all, the stable, remote, and impersonal gods of the *Republic* encourage us to be gentle. Natural human spirit is assumed to possess more than enough aggressiveness on its own to energize the virtue of the Auxiliaries. The Athenian dēmos is capable of gentleness and compassion, but it is also capable of spasms of wrath against someone perceived as insufficiently loyal to the city's ways. Hence, the dēmos merely laughs at Euthyphro when he speaks of his divine wisdom in the Assembly—they regard him as "touched" (*Euthyphro* 3c). They are indulgent toward him because, while a son should not prosecute a father, it is unquestionably right to prosecute wrongdoers. But their feeling for Socrates is angry thumos, not indulgence (3d). They suspect that he does not care enough about matters like murder or treason to want to punish those who commit such acts. Even in the *Republic,* as we will consider in chapter 5, Socrates recognizes that the thumotic citizens, educated to forestall such spasms of moralistic rage, may at length feel anger for the philosophic rulers if they catch onto the fact that the rulers regard their own citizens' moral education as mere opinion rather than the truth. Even after passing through the elaborate pedagogy of the best regime, thumos remains combustible, ready to explode in Achillean indignation, invoking righteous gods to punish the wicked. Just as Strepsiades ultimately burns down the think tank in the *Clouds,* so too in the *Republic* the men of civic zeal ultimately overthrow the philosopher-kings.

The education in civic virtue sketched in Books 2 and 3 is a less heady prospect than Diotima's Ladder, which entertained the possibility that a life of noble public service could be directly possessed and enjoyed like a loved one, creating "offspring" in the form of friendship and fame. But if the outcome of this education is less exhilarating, it does not pay the price of abstracting eros from the less tractable, more aggressive sides of human nature, as does Diotima's account. In the *Republic,* Socrates attempts to achieve a more detailed and realistic synthesis of the belligerent, self-conscious passions with a selfless absorption in the beautiful—albeit an indirect absorption through the cultivation of gracious, balanced tastes and sentiments rather than through the direct consummation of erotic longing. Whereas Diotima overlooked the combative dimension of longing, Socrates lays emphasis on it when proposing his own way of moderating passion. He attempts to sublimate the aggressiveness of thumos by reforming its view of the world, while eschewing the optimism of Diotima's Ladder that the satisfaction of civic virtue could be as palpable as the satisfaction of a private erotic attachment. As we will see, only when Socrates departs from the subject of civic virtue strictly speaking and considers the philosophic life does he reintroduce the prospect of direct erotic satisfaction that he has expelled from the optimal city.

Thus, while Diotima's Ladder expresses the idea that there is a continuous ascent from private eros to civic virtue and philosophy, Socrates' fully considered view seems to be that the respective satisfactions of civic virtue and philosophy are, while not altogether discontinuous, considerably more discrete and compartmentalized than Diotima presents them—corresponding, moreover, to the predominantly thumotic and erotic dimensions of the soul respectively. At the same time, of course, while politics and philosophy may be relatively discrete activities, they cannot be absolutely dichotomous, because if that were so, it would make no sense for Socrates even to explore the hypothesis of a civic paideia that in some measure reflects the knowledge of being and nonbeing sought by philosophy. The view of the world sketched in Books 2 and 3 as being characterized more by the visible stability of eidos than by the invisible motions of tuchē is meant to be a precondition for, and transition to, the education in philosophy that is set forth in Books 6 and 7. There is a progression from the friendly and hostile "looks" or "forms" that are "seen" by the Auxiliaries (376b) to the stable "looks" or "forms" that characterize the gods (380d) to the "looks" or "forms" glimpsed by philosophy as the stable ground of phenomena (475b, 479a). But, as we have already had occasion to consider, the transition is not a smooth or unproblematic one. For the question still looms: Can the spirited part of the soul really "see?" In order to explore this question further, we must consider Socrates' completion of his argument about the tripartite soul in Book 4.

THE DOCTRINE OF THE SOUL IN BOOK 4

In Book 4 of the *Republic,* Socrates formally completes the comparison of the soul "writ large" as the city with the soul of the individual, having previously separated out from the original Auxiliaries a third class of Guardians, whose task is the wise guidance of the whole (412b–414b). He then proceeds to search for justice among four cardinal virtues that, in addition to wisdom, include courage, wisdom and moderation. Most pertinently for our theme, Socrates further clarifies the precise nature of thumos as it emerges in comparison with the faculties of desire and knowledge in the city and the individual citizen.

We recall that in the *Gorgias,* Socrates appeals to his and Callicles' "common feelings" as lovers in order to clarify the goals of erotic longing. Here, by contrast, Socrates emphasizes the "opposite actions and passions" that characterize the soul (437a–b). He excludes from the outset the possibility that the desires of the soul could be unified by an eros for the beautiful and good. The principle of "one man, one job" derived from the division of labor inherent in the analogy of virtue to technē, and the further compartmentalization of the soul's capacities through the suppression of bodily pleasures by thumos, leads to a strikingly analytical kind of political psychology in comparison with the holistic approach that emerges from an emphasis on the erotic dimensions of political ambition.

One other point will help to put what follows into sharper focus. The formal doctrine of the tripartite soul set forth in Book 4 does not stand on its own as a separate theme from the civic education of the Auxiliaries that has just preceded it in Books 2 and 3. On the contrary, for reasons I will discuss below, it is the summing up of what was implied about the soul of a citizen educated in such a manner. Not only does it sum up the civic education, but the doctrine of the soul in Book 4 is itself a part of this civic education, meant to be absorbed by citizens and legislators. It is a political psychology in the sense that this is how citizens and legislators should study the soul if the political community is to be educated in the manner established by Socrates' proposals for educational reform in Books 2 and 3.

Desire, Calculation, and Spirit

Socrates begins by maintaining that the parts of the soul do not form a whole, and that the entire soul is never manifested through an action of any one of its different parts. In establishing this premise, Socrates gets Glaucon's agreement to a series of propositions about the soul that sum up the elevation of the clarity and stability of eidos over the chance becomings of the primordialist ontology—a clarity and stability that first emerged from the initial search for justice on the analogy of an art, and at length became the cornerstone of the education of the Auxiliaries to see the cosmos in a way different from the accounts of the poets. They must "necessarily" agree, Socrates now tells Glaucon, "that the very same forms and dispositions as are in the city are in each of us" (435c).

Moreover, each of these parts acts in one way only. This is backed up by the rather dubious comparison of the tripartite soul to a man who stands still while moving his arms and head. Rather than describe this man as standing still and moving "at the same time," Socrates claims, it would be better to say that one part of him stands still and another moves. The point of the comparison is to criticize once again the Heracleitean contention that "something that is the same, at the same time, with respect to the same part and in relation to the same thing, could ever suffer, be, or do opposites" (436c–437a). And yet, the comparison itself reminds us of how one-sided this approach to the soul is, abstracting from the prospect of the soul's unity that other dialogues—and other parts of the *Republic*—explore at length. For it is in a sense absurd to argue that a single body that moves one of its parts is more like two different parts than a composite unity capable of different actions. After all, it is the body as a whole that stands still while it moves its arms and head. The limbs are not floating autonomously on their own. Socrates so lightly suppresses the implicit unity of the body in this example that his very choice of this example reminds us that there are ways of understanding bodies and other beings as combining unity and difference without thereby granting the Heracleitean understanding of nature according to which "nothing is." To say nothing of other dialogues like the *Symposium* or the *Theaetetus* (where, in contrast with the argument here, Socrates convinces Theaetetus to consider the soul in terms of an oil-like flowing unity rather than in terms of mathematical distinctness [144b,

146c–147c, 148d–149a]), even in the *Republic* Socrates concedes, as we have observed, that thumos is not an absolutely self-identical nature, but a nature with two conflicting potentialities whose unified ethical development is guided by education.

Socrates is pretty explicit here that their premise is more ad hoc than rigorously demonstrated: "So we won't be compelled to go through all such objections and spend a long time assuring ourselves they're not true, let's assume that this is so and go ahead, agreeing that if it should ever appear otherwise, all our conclusions based on it will be undone" (437a). They must soldier on with the "image" (the division of labor) that enabled them to launch the city in speech early in Book 2, or everything will fall to pieces. Socrates will have missed the festival of the goddess for nothing, and might even miss the torch race on horseback! Socrates' ironic plaintiveness in asking his young interlocutor that they not examine the premise *too* rigorously reminds us that the analytical account of the soul is only one kind of logos—valid to a point, but not necessarily or always supervening over other kinds of demonstrations and observations. Socrates' purpose here is heuristic, not to say playful. He means to push the eidetic division of labor in the soul and the city as far as it will go. This is one of the ways in which the Gadfly tests the Oracle. Only if the holistic unity claimed by the common good of the city can be shown to be able to embrace and withstand the analytical clarity that the Socratic elenchus brings to the examination of such claims about the meaning of virtue and the good life will it be possible to argue that a certain set of conventional political arrangements is "according to nature." In order to test the possibility of thinking unity and difference together, one must push difference to its extreme.

The division of labor among functions of the soul is underscored by Socrates' denial that desire as such is concerned with what is good. Our desire is for drink, Socrates claims, not for cold or delicious drink (437d–438a). Much as in the *Gorgias,* Socrates derives clear knowledge about the desires and their objects from the analogy to art (for example, the art of house-building [438c-d]). And the problems with this analogy are much the same as in the *Gorgias.* As before, Socrates uses as examples the kind of pedestrian desires served by the banausic arts (hunger for food and thirst for drink). But even these simple needs are arguably inseparable from an experience of *good* food and drink, although it is at least more plausible to divorce them from some larger sense of satisfaction than would be the case with more complex desires (honor, for example, or, of course, love). Moreover, while it is clear that house-building produces an object, one must wonder in what sense the desire of hunger, to use one of Socrates' examples, produces anything. Is pleasure the object or the product of an art? Or might pleasure not more plausibly be considered as a scale of intensities of feeling? If this is so, then the craft analogy is a shaky one for clarifying the nature of the desires, pointing to the need for a complementary holistic approach. As depicted here, however, the soul is not directly motivated by substantive pleasures, but by the "opposite actions and passions" of willing and not-willing such pleasures. The concrete aims of the desires themselves are reduced to a sub-set of these more general levers of volition. Socrates also insists that the soul behaves according to the principles of identity and contradiction. In characterizing the levers of volition as opposite actions and passions, he holds firm to the proposition that these levers perform one kind of operation at one time and another kind at another time. They are not "opposite" in the Heracleitean sense of a concatenation of contradictory motions "at the same time," but in the eidetic sense of a series of self-identical operations performed at successive stages over time.

We recall that Callicles was reluctant to restrain the desires even to the extent of qualifying them as aiming for some good. At this juncture, Socrates makes an equally extreme type of argument for the opposite reason. He is so bent on excluding hedonism from the meaning of the soul's excellence that he will not qualify his critique of the desires by allowing that some of them at least to some degree aim for the good. Whereas, with Callicles, he argues for the regulation of desires by the good, here he treats the desires as inherently so recalcitrant that they must be excluded from any connection with the good so as to preserve it from their taint. Thus, he goes on, when we refrain from or act upon a desire, this does not proceed from the comparative intensity of the desires themselves or from the comparative goodness of their objects, but from "calculation" (*logismos,* 439d). Calculation is a faculty that reckons the sense of an action from outside the context of the desires themselves and where they beckon. It is perhaps because it directs the desires by standing apart from them that Socrates uses a term ordinarily associated with mathematical deduction to describe it. (These passages as a whole are filled with mathematical terms and comparisons, as if to drive home the idea that contradiction should be understood in terms analogous to number rather than in terms of the primordialist ontology.) Because calculation directs the willing of desire, it is the seat of volition in the soul in the political psychology of the *Republic*. The moral bearing of this volitional arithmetic is clear when Socrates says that it "leads thirst like a beast to drink," a metaphor that further denigrates the independent capacity of the desires themselves to aim at some good (439b). In the opposite case, he goes on, calculation "masters" desire so as to achieve our abstention from it. Socrates' choice of words again stresses that desire can only be governed in the manner of a beast or servant, and cannot be relied on to aim voluntarily for a sensible goal.

The elevation of calculation over the desires as the seat of volition has the effect of lowering the status of the desires to mere random impulses, alike in their senselessness and with no natural intrinsic potential for aiding the soul's transcendence of its basest, most primordial compulsions. The desires are, as Socrates puts it in a phrase that became a favorite of the Stoics, "affections and diseases" requiring harsh medicine. [16] In first introducing the civic psychology of the Auxiliary class in Book 2, Socrates drained eros from thumotic combativeness so as to sever the erotic satisfactions of the "feverish" part of the soul and city from the vigor of the Auxiliaries' public-spiritedness. In Book 4, he draws out a further implication of that initial distinction between epithumia and thumos: not only is civic virtue not to be seen as pleasant, but pleasure is not to be regarded as civically virtuous.

By "pleasure" I mean here, specifically, the "feverish" pleasures of spontaneous eros—the longing for all varieties of luxury and refinement—that Glaucon introduced in Book 2 when he rebelled against the sobriety of the City of Sows. By agreeing to banish these unreformed pleasures and longings from the class of Auxiliaries, Socrates and Glaucon excluded from the outset the possibility that eros could be rehabilitated by the kind of educational and eudaimonistic ascent to virtue that Diotima thought inherent in the nature of eros itself. At the same time, however, they have educated the Auxiliaries in such a way as to make them friendly—a friendship mediated by the harmoniousness of the cosmos instilled in their characters through their poetic and gymnastic training. In other words, unlike Diotima, Socrates in the *Republic* explores, through the elaboration of a civic education, the prospect that citizens can be friends without being lovers of the beautiful and good. The dialogue is in this respect a compromise between the assimilation of civic philia to well-educated eros propounded by Diotima, and the sketch of civic philia bereft of passionate content offered by Socrates in the *Gorgias*. The beautiful and harmonious tastes inculcated in the Auxiliaries by their education are meant to balance these extremes of longing and self-control.

As Socrates sums it up, there are two "forms" in the soul. The term he introduced in the theology of Book 2 to stress that true being is absolutely stable and self-identical, always distinct from other beings, and never mixed with them in Heracleitean becoming, now characterizes the inward structure of the soul as well as the gods and the world around us. The higher "form" of the soul reckons according to the calculative faculty (*to logistikon*). The lower of the two forms is erotic. As Socrates puts it, this part "loves" in accordance with the irrational, the appetitive underside of the soul of which, Socrates here implies, one cannot even give an intelligible account (it is *alogiston,* the part without logos). From its majestic power in Diotima's speech as the unifier of the noblest human aspirations, guiding the desires toward the beautiful and good so as to unite pleasure with duty, eros is reduced to the tawdry role of being a mere engine of the most senseless appetites in the lower "form" of the soul. As the single, diminished reference here to erotic longing reveals (439d), eros all but vanishes in the political psychology of the *Republic,* which brings pedestrian appetite and moral zeal into the foreground as the most pressing alternatives.

At this juncture, we should bear in mind that Socrates' ability throughout this argument to diminish so markedly the role of eros in the soul goes together with the fact that he has as yet given no clear account of wisdom (*sophia*) in the *Republic.* Only by means of this omission can Socrates argue as if it were possible to give a definitive account of political psychology before the nature of knowledge as a whole has even been provisionally clarified. When turning to the role of wisdom in the soul and the city later in Book 4, he merely asserts the synonymity of wisdom with the calculative faculty (441e). But he makes no attempt to elaborate the distinct qualities of sophia until late in Book 5—when, not accidentally, eros makes a startling comeback in the exploration of the soul's natural satisfaction (474c–475b). In sum, Socrates introduces "calculation" as a place-holder for something he cannot as yet properly discuss—or, more precisely, return to discussing. For as Adam notes, at this point in Book 4 we can only infer that the calculative faculty said to govern the soul will eventually be equated with the full-blown philosophical capacity that Socrates had daringly ventured in Book 2 would enable the soul of the citizen to distinguish between what is and what is not. In presenting the formal completion of the *Republic's* political psychology in Book 4, Socrates does not yet claim the status of philosophizing for the faculty that directs desire and spiritedness. Indeed, as we will see in the next chapter, there are serious difficulties with making this equation. The psychology of Book 4 emphasizes instead the education of the spirited, honor-seeking type of human being, and not primarily the philosophically inclined. Nevertheless, in order to hold to the grounds laid out in Book 2 for tracing the nature of the soul as it is writ large in the nature of the city, Socrates cannot sunder civic virtue from philosophy. The precise nature of the connection, however, is left in abeyance. For now, the place eventually to be held by wisdom in the governance of the soul is held by a sketchy concept of the minimal orderliness needed for keeping the desires at bay.[17]

The Root of Civic-Spiritedness

Having thus distinguished desire from calculation, Socrates' next step is to ask Glaucon if spirit is a third part of the soul or of "like nature" with the other two. Glaucon's initial, unprompted response is Plato's way of reminding us that there are alternative ways of envisioning the soul to the analytical one Socrates offers here—ways articulated in the *Symposium* and later in the *Republic* itself when the theme changes from the satisfactions of civic virtue strictly speaking to the satisfactions of philosophy. We remember that in Book 2, Glaucon was inclined to think that the people in their imaginary city whose desires had been inflamed beyond the basic necessities would themselves do the fighting to expand their city's possessions. So now, in a continuation of that tendency to assimilate courage to the pursuit of the pleasures for which it fights, Glaucon's first inclination is to think that spiritedness might be the same as desire (439e). As we saw in considering the erotic psychology of Callicles, and indeed as much ordinary experience appears to confirm, it is at least plausible to argue that erotic longing itself entails spiritedness; that, rather than oppose eros as Socrates is adamant in maintaining here, spiritedness serves it. Having been overwhelmed with the desire to possess someone or something, our longing for this good can summon from us the energy and daring to fight for it, motivating us to derive our self-esteem from possessing it and to grow indignant at the threat of someone taking it from us. In other words, eros itself might arguably fill the role Socrates assigns here to calculation, leading and organizing the desires, bidding and forbidding them in accordance with the best route to the goal of the greatest satisfaction. This is the role eros plays in Diotima's Ladder and, when it comes to the philosophic life as opposed to the political, the *Republic* eventually argues for its plausibility as well. Even if we did not go the full length of conceding the argument made by Diotima for the unifying role of eros and the existence of a consummate pleasure that could organize the other desires in its pursuit, it is still arguable that, among a plurality of diverse desires of differing intensities, one desire could at least for a time gain the upper hand, uniting other desires or shunting aside those that interfered with this particular pleasure.

However, just as Diotima's Ladder presented the pure paradigm of eros by abstracting from the more aggressive dimensions of civic and philosophic education, Socrates here presents the pure paradigm of civic-spiritedness by abstracting from the discrete, substantive satisfactions of the desires and the possibility that happiness could be achieved by a certain economy—a certain ordering and harmony—of the pleasures themselves. His purpose here is to explore the extent to which spirit could act as the auxiliary, the police arm, of calculation in ruling the desires like a "master." He must therefore push Glaucon away from his inclination to consider thumos itself as a desire. Just as he did in Book 2 when Glaucon was inclined to merge the two "opposite actions" of desire and spirit, here too Socrates obtains agreement by reminding Glaucon of their basic premise that the soul has three distinct parts according to the principle of "one man, one job" (439e–441a). We are reminded again that, to the extent that eros subsides as a principle for the unity of the soul, the analytical account of the soul comes to the fore. As the tripartite division of the soul replaces the erotic continuum of Diotima's Ladder, there is a corresponding emphasis on the need to repress one's aberrant passions and those of one's fellow citizens rather than relying on their voluntary longing for transcendence. This shift in emphasis is similar to the one that Aristotle describes as the transition from the "ethical" part of "political science" to its strictly "political" dimension. The art of ruling, viewed from this perspective, has more to do with punishment and castigation than with a noble rhetoric of persuasion.

A Troublesome Steed: The Story of Leontius

Socrates backs up the role of thumos as the enforcer of reason's rule over the passions with a story that he says he "trusts" (439e). The very peculiar story of Leontius is, we should note, the only concrete illustration offered of this crucial stage in the moral psychology of the *Republic*. Leontius wants to look at the corpses in the executioner's pit beyond the walls of Athens. He is disgusted with himself for this desire. His spirit reviles his desire for being able thus to "master" him—a disgraceful reversal of the coercive authority that Socrates has just maintained calculation should exercise over desire. From Leontius's self-disgust Socrates draws the conclusion that spirit "sometimes . . . makes war on" desire as if it were something alien to itself (440a).

When Socrates introduced thumos in Book 2, he likened it to a well-bred dog whose spirit was supposed to work hand in hand with philosophy, identifying its "enemy" with ignorance and repelling it through knowledge. At least in a formal sense, spirit in the Leontius story fulfills the role sketched for it in that initial discussion. Here, the battle against ignorance is internalized and the enemy identified with the irrational "diseases" of the lowest, least rational "form" of the soul. This internalized battle is a consequence of the education Socrates outlined in Books 2 and 3, whose results are summarized in the schematic presentation of the soul in Book 4. The citizen will be able to combat aberrant desires (equated with ignorance) in other citizens not because of mere external habituation or propaganda, but because, owing to the characterological transformation effected by the civic education, he first combats them in himself. Socrates stresses how "nobly bred" the spirited citizen is when he castigates himself or accepts his punishment from the civic authorities. Well-educated thumos is the bond that links the parts of the soul in such a way as to breed the correct ethos of savagery toward enemies and gentleness toward friends. As Socrates contended in Book 2, only such an ethos can save the passion of thumos from undoing the whole argument for the optimal politeia with its doubleness and contrariety. Once again, we are reminded that, in contrast to the smooth ascent from pleasure to civic virtue presented in Diotima's Ladder, Socrates' road to political justice is a rougher one. There is a place for anger in the optimal community. Ordinarily anger serves the love of one's own. The striking hypothesis of the *Republic* is that the ill effects of anger on justice, moderation, and political stability can be remedied, not so much by repressing or extirpating the sources of anger from the human character, as by educating a citizen to regard "his own" as synonymous with the impartiality of reason. He will be wrathful on behalf of what transcends wrath. He will bear arms to defend the rule of a man who, if Socrates' discussion with Polemarchus in Book 1 is anything to go by, doubts whether justice considered on the analogy of a curative art would ever do harm to anyone.

Behind Socrates' proposals for reforming rhetoric and education looms the larger question of whether and to what degree philosophy can vindicate itself before the larger political community, a prospect called radically into question by Socrates' eventual prosecution and trial. In considering Socrates' proposed reform of rhetoric in the *Gorgias,* I earlier raised the question of who exactly this new kind of orator might be—the philosopher himself, or a statesman strictly speaking who relied on the philosopher's guidance for practicing the art of rule? That question will re-emerge fully in our consideration of the philosopher-king in chapter 5. At this point in our consideration of the *Republic,* the Guardians have not yet fully emerged from the Auxiliaries as these optimal governors. Although the Guardians are introduced at the end of Book 3, they are at this point still more of an upper tier of the Auxiliary class than a separate class with their own education and psychology. In Book 4, the rule of wisdom—sketchily evoked by the faculty of "calculation"—is still being effected mainly by means of the education and psychology of the thumotic Auxiliaries. So I want to pause for a moment to consider whether the civic paideia of the *Republic,* considered more or less in its own right before it is overshadowed by the proper emergence of the philosopher in Book 5, might provide the kind of mediation between philosophic self-awareness and political ambition that Socrates' proposals for reforming rhetoric aim at providing for Callicles.

There is a difference between dialectical conversation such as Socrates undertakes with Callicles and Glaucon and his one attempt at a conversation with the dēmos in the *Apology.* As we have seen at different junctures in this study, Socrates may convince someone dialectically while failing to convince them in their inner feelings. In his encounter with Callicles, Socrates appears to test his effectiveness as a rhetorician by searching for a mixture of demotic and dialectical speech. In this instance, he appeals not only to the standard of noncontradictory logos but to the "common feelings" shared by lovers. Callicles himself is a blend of the demotic and the philosophic. He is a Meletus who is willing to converse for considerably longer before refusing to allow himself to be put in a position to contradict himself. In this sense, the question posed by the *Gorgias* and expanded upon by the *Republic* is: How powerful an authority can logos be in politics? How wide and compelling a consensus among citizens can be forged through the standard of noncontradictory speech? In short, can reason rule? Even if reason can rule, it may require a demotic intermediary—a Callicles—to reach the citizenry. But will these intermediaries consent to second place under the authority of reason?

As Socrates says in the *Gorgias* (503a), there *can* be a kind of rhetoric that is a real art and makes human beings better. Here, he relaxes somewhat his earlier dichotomy between the sham art of rhetoric and the true art of statesmanship. This opens the way for the demotic intermediary, the rhetorician-statesman who serves the authority of reason. Who, then, is the person best suited to practice the noble art of rhetoric? Could it be Callicles? If so, he would have to become a "cosmologist" of proportionality in order to rule, or at least absorb such a teaching. Could it be Socrates? But Socrates would rather question than rule. If the unexamined life is not worth living (*Apology* 38a), then even ruling one's fellow citizens justly and benevolently would be a distraction from the only activity that truly makes life bearable. Moreover, if Socrates knows that he knows nothing (except, perhaps, erotics), how would he have the certainty necessary for governing decisively? As we will consider at length in chapter 5, this turns out to be one of the most serious flaws in the logic of the best regime, given the crucial premise that philosophy and the art of ruling are deemed to be one "job."

Another intriguing possibility is Gorgias himself. His interest has clearly been aroused. Although Socrates' success with Callicles is limited, Gorgias himself may be the ultimate addressee. By reaching him through his admirer, Callicles, Socrates is able to spare the eminent Sophist a direct refutation while telegraphing a potent challenge: Here is what you, Gorgias, should be doing. The Sophist need not, as does Socrates in the *Clouds,* make a division between the irrational conventionality of politics and the study of nature according to the canons of epistēmē. He need not be vulnerable—as Gorgias is vulnerable in his dialogue with Socrates—to having his view exposed that justice is only in the realm of seeming.

When Callicles threatens to storm out of the argument, Gorgias instructs him to continue to its conclusion, and to submit to as much refutation as Socrates pleases (497b). Callicles obeys Gorgias in a way that he never obeys Socrates, whom he treats first with good-natured condescension and later with truculence. Indeed, Callicles obeys Gorgias in the prompt way that he might obey the natural master he extols in his speech, submitting himself to the pain of Socrates' refutation in order to gratify another man whom he honors, behavior that contradicts his professed creed of maximum pleasure for oneself. The famous and politically experienced Gorgias is arguably far more of a personal authority for the ambitious Callicles than Socrates could ever be, the seeming exemplar of someone who has moved beyond the childishness of mere philosophical disputation to a manly role as a political actor. One of Socrates' purposes, therefore, may be to reach the rhetorician through Callicles. By arguing with the younger man, he spares Gorgias's feelings while using Callicles as a stalking horse for a sketch of how rhetoric must be reformed so as to allow the wise to rule and to protect them from the fickle backlashes of the dēmos.

Nothing in the sequel, however, in the Platonic dialogues or from other sources, suggests that Gorgias took up this enterprise. Socrates' evident failure to persuade the gifted Sophist throws into clear relief the starker alternatives that we begin to see emerging in the *Republic*. There is no demotic intermediary between philosophy and demotic virtue, no rhetorician-statesman. Philosophers (in the Socratic sense) must themselves rule, or the men of action will take over. Although Socrates claims in the *Gorgias* to "practice politics" in Athens because he searches for a rigorous epistemic basis for statesmanship, only the Sophist and rhetorician Gorgias actually comes close to performing a ruling action in the dialogue itself (just as in real life, he advised rulers and headed delegations, rather than merely talking about virtue as did Socrates). For it is only Gorgias' intervention that keeps the dialogue with Callicles going. The only way that Socrates can rule Callicles—that is, get him to submit to the elenchus—is through interesting Gorgias sufficiently to get him to make Callicles obey. Nothing could illustrate more simply and straightforwardly that philosophy can exercise political authority only intermediately through rhetoric.

In this specific instance, the citizen-philosopher Socrates, who never left Athens, can only rule his fellow citizen Callicles because Callicles has been attracted to the concept of nature through the influence on him of an itinerant Sophist from another country. It is Callicles' confidence that he understands the difference between nature and convention that prompts him to set Socrates straight by means of his opening speech, introducing for the first time in the dialogue an explicitly philosophical criterion for the assessment of happiness, virtue, and politics. In this way, too, then, the *Gorgias* is a kind of rehearsal for the complexities of the *Republic* we are unraveling here. It is not just a matter of philosophy needing rhetoric so as to reach the citizens in a way that is compatible with their closed horizon of beliefs and customs, but rather of finding a rhetoric through which the proper Socratic understanding of phusis can appeal to sophisticated citizens like Callicles who have already had their closed horizon opened up by theoretical speculations. The more sophisticated kind of citizen (a Glaucon, Callicles, or an Alcibiades) will obey the kallipolis only through the cosmopolis. As Socrates puts it in launching the theme of paideia in the *Republic,* the thumos of a citizen must "see" the difference between being and non-being, befriending only what is and husbanding it within the polis. The citizens of the feverish city, whose longings need restraining through justice and education, have already been exposed to philosophy along with other erotic superfluities. The aim of the civic paideia set forth in the *Republic* is not simply to make such people behave themselves, but to show how the cardinal virtues are derived from and confirm the understanding of the cosmos as being primarily characterized by eidetic stability rather than Heracleitean flux. Paideia must provide a window on the world, a combination of the universality of reason with the particularity of the political community. In light of Socrates' apparent failure to persuade either Callicles or Gorgias to re-examine his view of statesmanship, the *Republic* leaves for posterity the suggestion that paideia might embody the rule of philosophy over the civic-spirited.

We recall from chapter 1 that Socrates hoped to divert Callicles' aggressive qualities from the service of his erotic longings and enlist them in achieving a moderate ordering of the desires. He hoped, in other words, to enlist Callicles' own pride at his capacity for self-discipline to achieve the transition in Callicles' soul from a passion for ruling others to self-rule, and thence to a new conception of friendship and statesmanship subordinating pleasure to the good. In his dogged challenges to Callicles' understanding of his own prospects for happiness, and through the spirited badinage and gibes they exchanged, Socrates in effect made war on Callicles in the hope that, by thus goading Callicles to make war on him in return, out of their dialectical contest would emerge the opportunity to clarify and redirect his needs and ambitions. In the end, Socrates had to concede that the love of the dēmos was too deeply rooted in Callicles' character, and that he should have been inculcated with a taste for "geometrical proportionality" earlier in life. In the story of Leontius we might say, then, that Socrates holds out the possibility that if someone like Callicles were to undergo the elaborate civic pedagogy from earliest youth to adulthood set forth in Books 2 and 3 of the *Republic,* the aggressive criticism of indiscriminate hedonism that Callicles suffers at Socrates' hands might be approximated and internalized through careful habituation to a code of moral and cosmological stability. Whereas Callicles and Alcibiades bewail the "slavedriving" force of Socrates' critiques of their lives, a well-educated civic guardian might exercise this "mastery" of himself guided by an understanding of the cosmos in which the rational stability of eidos supervenes over the disarray of chance and motion. The civic education of the spirited might provide them, in short, with a kind of philosophic temperament by remote control.

This is the larger moral-pedagogical purpose behind Socrates' doctrinal equation of volition with calculation. As I suggested in the last chapter with reference to the Image of the Cave, if a soul cannot provide direction for itself, it will need "someone" who is willing to do us the rough benefit of turning us around. In the *Republic,* Socrates is examining the hypothesis that every citizen of a well-ordered politeia could, through education, provide this guidance for himself or herself, at least to some degree. By arguing that calculation is to be seen as the seat of volition, Socrates is propounding a doctrine of the soul that it will be necessary for citizens to believe if they are to internalize a degree of mathematical clarity about the passions—the moral geometry of whose worth he failed to convince Callicles. Earlier, we saw how the Auxiliaries might internalize a degree of the sober steadfast Socratic kind of courage to insulate them from the madness and despair that naturally seize the thumotic Homeric warrior. The education of the Auxiliaries, including the correct way of understanding the soul that Socrates propounds in Book 4, are facets of Socrates' speculative enterprise of seeing whether thumos might philosophize—whether citizens might be inculcated with a degree of Socrates' own moderation and tough-mindedness through civic education.

Of course, as we noted earlier, it is far from clear that a habituation to repress one's passions in accordance with the received authority of a civic education, however thoughtful an education it may be, is the same thing as a reasoned demonstration through an ongoing, unconstrained dialogue that this is the best way to live. This is where the thinness of Socrates' discussion of wisdom in connection with the political psychology of Book 4, and the mere assertion of its identity with calculation as the ruling element in the citizen's soul, become especially telling. The Auxiliaries' lives as described in Books 2 and 3 will possess a stately calm and certainty. But Socrates was the gadfly of Athens, the relentless questioner who could not imagine living without daily skepticism. This is why the Leontius story only formally satisfies the requirement Socrates set for himself in Book 2 that thumos be shown capable of "seeing" philosophically. The sketchiness with which, as we noted above, "reason" has so far been elaborated in the parallel between the tripartite soul and city proves to be more pronounced than ever as we think through the argument.

As if to remind us of the provisional and hypothetical character of the whole investigation, therefore, Socrates is careful not to claim more for this illustration than it really furnishes. The story of Leontius shows it is *possible* that the aggressive side of the soul might turn against the desires *if* we can be educated to believe that these desires are low and disgusting. In this sense, the kind of desire with which Leontius must wrestle is especially suitable for making Socrates' point. Leontius's desire to look at corpses is obscure and can be interpreted in a number of ways. But it is disgusting on the face of it. It suggests, among other possibilities, an unwholesome dwelling on the agony and disgrace of others, or perhaps an unhealthy attraction to the role of executioner, or a sado-masochistic identification with the role of victim, or an obsession with criminality. It also leads to dwelling overmuch on the nasty and oppressive side of all political orders, the side where persuasion and deterrence shade away into the inspiration of fear; on the fact that even a relatively just and well-governed society has to punish and coerce, and that even when the rule of law prevails, the innocent may be punished wrongfully and the government may confuse dissidents and nonconformists with those who actually threaten the civil peace.

A good citizen who dwells on this underside of authority is likely to be driven by such gloomy reflections to become subversive, disillusioned, and incapable of wholehearted belief in the decency and justice that all political orders claim to stand for. There is a hint of this alienation in the setting of the story, which has Leontius walking outside of the city along its north wall (439e). The city tries to keep the violent underpinnings of its established authority out of the sight of decent citizens in the center of town. A government that claims to be based on the virtue of citizens able to participate in the direction of their community's affairs under the rule of law cannot flaunt its power of life and death without creating the offensive impression of being tyrannical. Within the citizen body, no one is supposed to be punished in a humiliatingly public or degrading manner, even though guilty. Leontius's attraction to the obscene spectacle on the outskirts of everyday civic life has quite literally alienated him, drawing him away from the center of citizen affairs.

Looking ahead to the Image of the Cave, where people are bound to their places beneath a wall (514a–b), the setting of the Leontius story along the north wall may suggest that Leontius's taste for violence roots him to the deepest recesses of the Cave, the primordial passions of fear and mastery that lurk in the gloomiest recesses of thumos. If this seems farfetched, or to do violence to the order of the argument, let us bear in mind that there are other anticipatory references in Book 4 to the Cave image. When Socrates initiates the search for the virtue of justice in the completed tripartite hierarchy of the soul and the city, he calls for Glaucon to follow him along a rugged and shadowy track where they find justice "rolling around" at their feet (432c–d). The language anticipates the description in Book 7 of the philosopher's descent from the sunlight back into the Cave, while the description of justice as "rolling around" specifically anticipates Socrates' characterization of opinion in Book 5 (including the "correct opinion" of which the civic virtue of the kallipolis is an instance) as "rolling around somewhere between not-being and being purely and simply" (479d). Finally, at the end of Book 4, Socrates remarks that, having delineated justice and the other virtues, they have reached a "lookout" from which "we are able to see most clearly that these things are so" (445b–c). As we will consider in the next chapter, the Leontius story is arguably one of Socrates' most tangible illustrations of how civic morality altogether might look from the standpoint of the philosopher, for whom the stability and coherence of the city are rendered evanescent, mere opinions rolling around in the gloom.

But, for now, let us resolve to remain firmly within the element of civic morality as it presents itself in its own right, for in Book 4 of the *Republic,* as we have
already observed, the philosophic life has not yet emerged as a distinct alternative
to political life. Altogether, then, because Leontius's desire is of this rather morbidly pathological kind, we have little difficulty sharing his disgust with himself
for wallowing in it. But what if Leontius had been tempted instead by some
innocuous private pleasure, some unconventional but harmless sexual enjoyment
that conventional morality might also deem indecent and unhealthy? Or, what if
Leontius had been motivated by a desire for knowledge (for example, medical
knowledge) that would require the same sort of dwelling on corpses?[18] Because
he has a morbid longing to look at corpses for no constructive reason, Leontius's
disgust with himself seems much more deserved than if he had lusted after, say,
someone's beloved, or after fame or martial honor, because the motives for such
desires, while they often lead to morally dubious or compromising situations, are
not so self-evidently revolting as dwelling on violent death. As is clear from the
Symposium, following the desires does not always lead to the primordial underpinnings of the political order in violence, fear, and power, or to an obsession with
mastering others and fighting to avoid being mastered. Desire can arguably lead
us toward the transcendence of such fears and aggressions by way of the political
community at its best and noblest. If this is so, then the desires should not always
or simply be mastered. Socrates makes this very argument later in the *Republic,*
but only on the level of philosophy, not—as Diotima argues—on the level of civic
virtue in its own right.

Another noteworthy feature of the story is that Leontius's spirit does, in fact,
fail as the ally of reason. He *is* "conquered" by the desire to look at the corpses
(440a). If, as Socrates earlier suggested, the analogy for the properly clarified relationship of the soul to its parts is a man who stands still while moving his arms and
head, Leontius fails the test. He tried to stand stock still, but ended up running
wild-eyed and shouting toward the pit. On the face of it, then, even Socrates'
choice of a successful example of the alliance between spirit and reason against
desire confirms to some degree Glaucon's inclination to see spirit as being of the
"same nature" as desire. Of course, Leontius could not have received the elaborate habituation of thumos set forth in Books 2 and 3, since he is a figure from real
Athenian life. So Socrates can make the minimal claim that the story illustrates a
capacity on the part of spirit to battle desire that, if properly educated and reinforced, can become the chief characteristic of thumos, assimilating its more dangerous extremes of despair and insubordination to a constructive zeal on behalf of
public morality. The near-absurdity of Leontius's struggle, however, points to how
delicate a matter this civic psychology is. Leontius's actual behavior is almost
comically inconsistent. He does not run away from the pit as he would if his spirit
were completely victorious. Instead, he stands there with his cloak over his eyes
to hide the corpses from his vision, then runs *toward* the pit shouting at his eyes
for being such swine (439e–440a). He knows he is in the wrong to be running in

the direction of the corpses, and, while he cannot overcome his desire, he converts some of its energy, in the very act of giving into it, to despising himself, singling out the particular criminal sense organ deserving retribution. Even his self-reproach, however, could be interpreted as an unconscious sophistry, inasmuch as it acts as a moral camouflage for the fact that he is running toward the bodies all the while that he is reproaching himself. The thumotic power that is fueling his self-reproach is also making him run so that he can get to the corpses before the well-behaved dimension of his spiritedness has time to stop him. (And swiftness, we recall from Book 2, is a trait of every spirited organism [376c].) There can be no better illustration of the way in which a passion can rule us—can take us over and impel us toward its object—while giving us the sensation of releasing our own energies and giving free rein to our own wishes. Nevertheless, according to Socrates, it is possible in principle to achieve a more balanced approach aided by the right kind of education. Recognizing that the horses are pulling us, we can guide those horses as best we can and so tap their power—tap the passion that bids to overwhelm us—into our own virtuous behavior.

The Leontius story confirms some further implications of Socrates' argument for the tripartite division of the soul and the city. Socrates does not appear to believe that the willing and unwilling actions that he introduced as the levers of volition before discussing the role of spirit are themselves sufficient for restraining aberrant desires. The vigor of spirit is needed as well to win the inner battle for self-mastery. But at the same time it is clear that, for Socrates, spirit is not the faculty of willing as such. The volitional capacity to bid or forbid the desires clearly has its seat in the calculative faculty. Instead, spirit seems to function as a kind of moral depth charge in the soul. The desires themselves as presented here are capable only of random, paltry lusts. The logistikon is poised to move the levers of volition into place so as to restrain these witless "diseases" of impulse. But a kind of explosion of moral energy is needed (such as Leontius's anger at his weakness of character) to set the levers in motion.[19] Thus, while Socrates erects the levers of volition over the various bodily desires so as to deny that the latter contain any independent capacity for transcendence, he then (as it were) reintroduces passion through the back door into the economy of the soul by arguing that volition requires a kind of forceful push from thumos. This passion, as we observed in Book 2, is made into a fit ally of reason by being drained of the substantive content of bodily hedonism, and is thus converted into a kind of general ferocity. Thus, although in a loose way the *Republic* seems to make a Kantian argument for the repression of natural inclinations by reason in contrast with the *Symposium's* unabashed eulogy to eros, the political psychology of the *Republic* in fact amounts to the regulation of the natural passions by a natural passion. It stresses the thumotic dimension of an overall ensemble of the passions that is the same for both dialogues. Eros and thumos each have their virtues and liabilities within the sound housekeeping of the soul.

Thus, while Socrates is careful to distinguish spirit from desire so as to prevent eros from assimilating civic ambition, he is equally careful to distinguish spirit from calculation. One reason for this is to prevent anger from gaining too much authority in the soul and the city, usurping the control of reason in the name of a more savage and relentless defense of the decencies. I will explore this danger at greater length in chapter 5. But another reason is to prevent reason itself from usurping the moral vigor of the spirited part of the soul and city. This may sound like an exaggeration, given that the famous climax of the parallel between the soul and the city is Socrates' contention that only when philosophers rule will the "ills of the city" be cured (473d). But let us remember that, although Socrates maintains that the moral energy of the Auxiliaries must take a backseat to the authority of the philosopher-king in the optimal politeia, he never argues that the tasks of statesmanship and government could dispense with the energetic traits of character that, in the *Republic's* tripartite division of labor, are located in the thumotic part of the soul. Each part of the soul and city has a distinct job that best fulfills its nature, according to the "image" with which Socrates and his companions launched the city in speech. Socrates, in other words, denies the possibility that reason can assimilate the unruly passions directly and immediately to its own agenda. This is brought out by a line Socrates quotes (approvingly) from Homer as he completes the discussion of spirit's role: "He smote his breast and reproached his heart with word" (441b–c). The main point of the quote is to assert reason's sovereignty over anger. But the illustration is nuanced, suggesting a *spirited* castigation by reason of irrational spiritedness. Lest "calculation" emerge as too wan a commander, Socrates allows the distinction between the two faculties to blur a little into an irrational thumos and a rather thumotic reason. The example might seem small in itself, except that it points to a serious logical difficulty with the soul-city parallel that I will explore in greater detail in chapter 5. My point for the time being is this: By insisting as much on the incapacity of reason to assimilate thumos as on the incapacity of desire to do so, Plato has Socrates concede the full weight of Callicles' emendation of Socrates' definition of true rule on the analogy of technically skilled production to include courage and an experience of the rough and tumble of political action. Reason cannot rule, either in the soul or in the city, without the alliance of the civic-spirited.

To sum up: thumos remains a troublesome steed to hitch to the chariot of justice. The analytical account of the soul and of the role of thumos in Book 4 conjoins technē and combativeness—conjoins epistemic rigor and moral rigor. It enhances the epistemic rigor of statecraft and the moral rigor of a civic education by minimizing the erotic continuum between the primordial and the transcendental. But the middle term is this still-volatile passion of spiritedness, strung between the compelled and the voluntary. In describing spirit's capacity to castigate desire and accept punishment on behalf of reason, Socrates moves back and forth between "him" and "it" (440b). The alternating personal and impersonal pronouns remind us of the ambiguities of thumos in its pristine manifestations. Does the man employ the passion, or does the passion employ the man so as to manifest itself through his actions? At bottom, thumos remains mysterious.

CONCLUSION

I began my discussion of the *Republic* by observing that the pre-philosophic experience of thumos tends to shatter the restraints of law and governance, flooding the soul with daring or despair. Plato does not attempt simply to repress or reason away the power of this passion. Instead, he seeks to enlist its energy in the service of moderate statesmanship while educating it in such a way as to insulate it from its primordialist undertow, so clearly revealed by the defects of the Homeric hero Achilles. In the political psychology of the *Republic,* the spirited part of the soul is hemmed in between, on the one hand, a de-eroticized controlling reason and, on the other hand, desire drained of the erotic scope that would summon forth thumotic aggressiveness in its service. This is accomplished in two main ways. First, the theology of Books 2 and 3 that grounds the education of the Auxiliaries provides a horizon of transcendental orderliness that directs them toward the eidetic stability of true being and insulates them from the mad daring or tragic ruminations to which spiritedness is spontaneously prone. Second, the anger and belligerence of thumos, having been safely limited in this way, is released in a selective manner as a moral depth charge of energy for the enforcement of reason's commands over desire. By exploring the prospects for this civic paideia in which anger may licitly serve reason in the enforcement of the optimal city's conformity to the good, Socrates tries to find a constructive moral purpose for this troublesome aspect of human nature.

In discussing the *Republic,* I have laid emphasis on the way in which Socrates transforms the role of spiritedness so as to enlist it in the service of the common good. By maintaining at the outset that thumos must be clearly distinguished from epithumia, Socrates resists the tendency in much of ordinary experience—a tendency confirmed by Glaucon's initial responses to his arguments—to view anger and belligerence as being among a jumble of desires for pleasure, power, and prestige. By calling this assumption into question, Socrates analytically isolates certain pristine traits of the spirited part of the soul from the wider continuum of the passions: its severity, austerity, and capacity for moral indignation. By abstracting these traits from the erotic and ambitious passions with which they often cooperate, Socrates lends them a greatly heightened clarity and independence—a stringent vigor that can, with the proper habituation, be turned against the other more naturally hedonistic, sensuous passions as a watchdog. In this way might a Callicles, properly reared from an early age, find his pride in ruling himself rather than mastering others. Socrates and Callicles have met too late: an eros for the dēmos has taken over Callicles' soul, and since he did not study mathematics early on, there is nothing in his character to fortify him against the onslaught of the passions.

In elaborating his proposals for the education of the Auxiliaries, Socrates is in effect telling us how he believes men like Callicles should be brought up.

But for all that Socrates abstracts thumos from the other passions and purifies its capacity for self-command and righteous wrath, we should note that Socrates never suggests that spiritedness can be considered as anything other than a passion. This is a crucial matter for distinguishing Platonic political morality from moral idealism of the Kantian sort. Socrates argues in the *Republic* that thumos is not epithumia—not a leaning toward bodily gratification. But it is a passion nonetheless, an emotional experience that the soul undergoes. Thus, we should beware of misidentifying the carefully channeled role of thumos in the political psychology of the *Republic* with the modern Kantian conception according to which the will considered as an agency outside the determinations of nature acts to repress the natural inclinations, and whose success in achieving moral freedom is measured by the degree to which it is undetermined by any substantive content of the natural passions.

The chief guarantor of virtue and human dignity for Plato is not autonomy, but education. As we have seen, Socrates explicitly distinguishes thumos from volition or willing. Moreover, the terms Socrates uses to describe volition itself—the soul's movements toward, or aversion from, certain actions—do not possess the monistic specificity that the word "will" does when it is used in its philosophical or theological meanings to describe the capacity of God or of human freedom to oppose itself to nature. Words like *boulē* have a variety of meanings such as will, wish, plan, and counsel. Unlike the Christian and post-Christian conception of the will, which begins with the radical abstraction of effectuating agency from the context of given experience, these Greek terms are colloquially intertwined with the experiences of everyday life. Socrates, then, does not identify spiritedness with the will, but on the contrary with a burst of passionate natural energy that fuels volition. Thumos does not repress the natural passions, but is itself an emotion whose particular characteristics of severity, masterfulness, and wrath can be educated in such a way as to achieve an overall economy of the inclinations and feelings—the correct harmonizing of the affects so as to inculcate in the soul the geometric proportionality that orders the cosmos. This is an instance of the "pathological" approach to virtue as a matter of "inner perfection" that Kant found objectionable about ancient moral philosophy as a whole. The concept of a will that opposes itself to nature and human nature is a specifically modern, post-Christian criterion for moral and civic virtue, an ontological shift that places the meaning of rule and statesmanship on a new basis.

NOTES

1. Quotations from the *Republic* are from the Bloom translation, occasionally amended.

2. See Pangle, "Political Psychology" and Ricoeur, *Fallible Man*, 161–163, 184–185.

3. Homer *Iliad* 11.403, 407. See especially Bremmer, *Early Greek Soul*, 54–56, 74–75, 126–127.

4. Homer *Iliad* 17.234, 7.95, 20.174.

5. Homer *Iliad* 22.475, 5.697, 4.524, 16.468.

6. On the continuity between poetic and Platonic thumos, consider Tait, "Spirit, Gentleness and the Philosophic Nature," 209–211.

7. Bremmer, *Early Greek Soul,* 56. Heidegger approvingly contrasts the Homeric understanding of being with the Platonic: "*ta eonta,* so-called beings, does not [in Homer] mean exclusively the things of nature. The poet applies eonta to the Achaeans' encampment before Troy, the god's wrath, the plague's fury, funeral pyres, the perplexity of the leaders, and so on. In Homer's language ta eonta is not a conceptual philosophical term but a . . . thoughtfully uttered word. It does not specify natural things, nor does it at all indicate objects which stand over against human representation. Man too belongs to ta eonta." Tragic poetry, in other words, is linked to the ontology of primordialism, the issuance and passing away of beings out of necessity. Platonic ontology, by contrast, privileges the moment of permanence, with the "danger that lingering will petrify into mere persistence." Heidegger, *Early Greek Thinking,* 37–38.

8. On this theme, see Mircea Eliade, *A History of Religious Ideas,* vol. 1 (Chicago: University of Chicago Press, 1978), 259–264 and Dodds, *The Greeks,* 29–50.

9. This is surely the basis for the alleged fallacy in the argument of the *Republic.* See Sachs, "A Fallacy in Plato's *Republic,*" 141–158.

10. Thucydides *The Peloponnesian War* 6.15–23.

11. James Adam, ed. *The Republic of Plato* (Cambridge: Cambridge University Press, 1920), 1: 99–100.

12. See the discussion in Adam, *The Republic,* 1:246–247.

13. Consider Seth Benardete, *Socrates' Second Sailing* (Chicago: University of Chicago Press, 1984), 56–57.

14. Aristotle *Nicomachean Ethics* 1.6–7.

15. Benardete, *Second Sailing,* 25.

16. For a useful discussion of the different accounts of the unity of the soul given in the *Republic, Laws,* and *Phaedrus,* see Robert Hall, "Psyche as Differentiated Unity in the Philosophy of Plato," *Phronesis* 8 (1963): 63–82.

17. Adam, *The Republic,* 1:259. See the discussion in R. C. Cross and A. D. Woozley, *Plato's Republic: A Philosophical Commentary* (New York: St. Martin's Press, 1966), 115.

18. See the discussion in Bloom, *The Republic,* 375–377.

19. As Zeigler observes, the seat of volition in the Platonic account of the soul is *boulēsis.* This does not mean "will." It is more akin to a rational wish. It entails a particular end or counsel advantageous for the situation. ("Plato's *Gorgias,*" 126–127). So Platonic volition cannot be equated with the modern Kantian concept of "autonomy," the striving to exert a pure will unmediated by empirical correlates. Consider also Drew Hyland, *The Virtue of Philosophy* (Athens: Ohio University Press, 1981), 7–9.

Chapter Five

Virtue, Eros, and Transcendence

Before turning to the problem of the disjunction between reason and civic morality in the *Republic*, let us review some of the main issues that have emerged from considering the complex place of thumos in the optimal politeia. Socrates' proposals for the education of the Auxiliaries are a way of redirecting the primordial energies of thumos to the service of the common good while shaping the character of the citizen in such a way that his now licit anger does not draw him downward into the spiral of the pre-philosophic experience of thumos—the morass of mad daring, self-pity, and despair irresponsibly praised and embellished by the poets. And yet, clearly this is a kind of playing with fire. For the very energies that Socrates argues might be educated to support the common good are, in their original and spontaneous manifestations, among the passions likeliest to challenge civic authority. Thumos is a horse that might at any time plunge out of control. The energy that Socrates summons to the service of the community issues from the individual's experience of being driven back upon his naked selfhood, his sense that he is threatened and powerless and must look out for himself or be crushed by his foes.

As we have noted, in the Platonic account of the soul, eros lifts us out of ourselves toward transcendence, while thumos makes us self-conscious. If we cut away the objects of erotic longing, as Socrates does in the tripartite political psychology of the *Republic*, we are left with the engine of longing itself, the warrior who wants victory. When Achilles battles the river, he personifies the world, endowing it with a will so as to prove that his failures are not simply his own fault, but result from the active opposition of hostile gods and forces. This is the lamenting and whining view of life as tragic that Socrates criticizes the poets for making seem attractively profound. This consciousness of an enemy also lends one's struggles the dignity of a battle to overcome a foe and prove one's manly worth, so that one's struggles are more than a mere succession of whims and impulses. It is this energy, this consciousness of dignity through struggle, that Socrates suggests might be tamed on behalf of a morality grounded in a cosmology of eidetic stability and rational purpose. The individual educated in this way will gain his sense of self-respect by punishing the enemy of aberrant desire within himself. Furthermore, bearing in mind the parallel between the soul and the city, the spirited class of citizens will make war on aberrant desires within the community. The guide for their struggle for transcendence, the orderly cosmos sketched in Books 2 and 3, mirrors back to them the orderliness of soul that will bring them repose by elevating them above the hedonistic temptation to possess and consume the community's goods.

The whole analytical account of the soul—the division of labor that narrows and specifies the role of thumos—provides the reins of the chariot for the direction of this powerful steed. The energy flow of thumos in its pre-philosophic experience, its unpredictable spasms of daring, rage, despair, and revenge, are sluiced off into the complex series of locks and breakers with which Socrates delineates the soul in Book 4. But while the hedonism thus dampened can plainly be a threat to the common good, so can the zeal thus liberated. Although in a sense Socrates tames thumos by severing it from the erotic pleasures for which it ordinarily fights, in another sense he renders it stronger and more dangerous by purifying its belligerence and stubbornness precisely by removing the distraction of occasional erotic satisfactions. Here is one of the roots of the difficulty that Hobbes believed central to classical political philosophy as a whole: that it encouraged "vainglorious" young men mad about war and honor to usurp conventional authority by flattering them that their ambitions were in the service of a higher natural standard of justice.[1] Socrates himself incorporates this kind of objection in the course of following the logos from its basic premise in Book 2 that thumos might, properly educated, in some manner philosophize—although not on the same grounds or with the same consequences as Hobbes. The rebellion of the Auxiliaries against the ruling order of Guardians in Book 8 is, indeed, the very reason for the downfall of the kallipolis in the history of its hypothetical unfolding.[2] The danger, in other words, is not only that thumos may not be persuaded to commit its energies to the defense of the community, but that it may make this commitment with altogether too much ferocity and zeal, so that it eventually comes to regard the rulers themselves as fainthearted or tenuous in their devotion to the morality that provides the warriors with their sense of honor and self-esteem. In making the rebellion of the Auxiliaries against the Guardians the denouement of the optimal community, Plato reminds us of the tenuous and exploratory character of the whole exercise of questioning whether and to what degree a vigorous civic-spiritedness might be compatible with the clarity of unprejudiced philosophical reflection.[3]

PHILOSOPHY AND CIVIC MORALITY

The Leontius story is a kind of intersection for several ways of looking at civic morality and its relationship to philosophy in the *Republic*. As I have observed, the location of the episode below the "north wall" makes us think ahead to the famous Image of the Cave in Book 7, where the poets and other fashioners of opinion are said to walk along a wall. When one rereads the *Republic* in light of the image of the Cave, it provides a sort of retrospective illumination of the entire dialogue. Socrates' descent to the Piraeus at the beginning of the dialogue may be compared to the philosopher's descent back down into the Cave from the transcendental illumination glimpsed through philosophizing. For the first time, he sees the polis in its entirety from above and outside. He returns and sees the shadows at the base of the cave as shadows, not as the realities they are mistaken for by most. From this perspective, the city does not possess the impressive unity and stability that the shadow-watchers in their bonds take for granted. Instead, as its nature comes into clear view for the first time as the philosopher returns back down, the city dissolves into its constituent elements—the household (oikos) represented by Cephalus and his sons, and the various activities of commerce and war. As the apparent unity of the city dissolves in these distinctions, philosophy begins the discursive search for its true unity according to logos, the "city in speech."[4]

Justice is apparently the binding element, but its meaning is elusive. Seen from the viewpoint of transcendental illumination, the nature of the city is closer to "the Piraeus"—closer to water and the busy harbor, to the hazy play of light and shapes in water. These fuzzy impressions are said to characterize both the depths of the Cave (516a) and the first level of the Divided Line (509e–510a). The Divided Line is the image Socrates uses to give a brief sketch of the progress of a philosophic (as opposed to a merely civic) education. It is an epistemological schema that abstracts from the passions found in political life. But when we integrate this schema with the Image of the Cave, it suggests ways in which the passions ordinarily encountered in political practice can be clarified in light of the requirements of knowledge. The interplay of light and shadows at the bottom of the Line and the Cave corresponds to the level of unclarified phenomena. It is dialectic, the sifting of the various contradictory opinions about (in the case of this particular dialogue) justice through the search for its non-contradictory eidos, that helps more solid shapes emerge from these fuzzy impressions, shapes that one can "trust."

Trust (*pistis*) is the faculty corresponding to the second level of the Divided Line (511e). Trust is not yet rigorous knowledge, but it is an intimation of such, whereby one is able to distinguish real beings from mere shadows cast by their manipulation or distortion. As Klein suggests,[5] to distinguish clearly among different objects and their properties, to begin sorting out what is the same and what is not the same in an object with respect to other objects and with respect to itself at different times, is already a kind of "counting," a comparison of identity and non-identity, such that the relative solidity of the objects whose existence we trust has already been lit up in some measure by the higher levels of intellection proper: mathematical knowledge and, implicitly, knowledge of the forms that ground both the self-subsistence and heterogeneity of all beings. Thus, the "calculation" (as we recall, originally a mathematical term) that Socrates suggested might be bred in the soul of the citizen is a necessary if not sufficient beginning for thinking through the prospect that thumos might philosophize; that political authority and civic commitment might have their bases in reason rather than coercion or blind obedience.

Socrates says that the Leontius story is one that he heard and trusts (439e). In light of the preceding remarks, I make the following suggestion about the status of the knowledge that Socrates assigns to this kind of moral illustration. The content of the story corresponds to the second level of the Divided Line, whose faculty is trust. The Leontius story thus appears to exemplify the type of preliminary knowledge one gains when one first sees the objects that cause the shadows on the wall of the Cave—the authoritative opinions and convictions that most people believe are true. It is an account of the basic elements of moral conviction from a perspective that has begun to transcend the prejudiced attachment that characterizes those who possess moral conviction. It must be emphasized that this latter category includes the Auxiliaries. For the Image of the Cave limns the nature of the polis itself. There are better and worse caves, but even the optimal city is a cave. And this is the root of the problem that eventually brings down the kallipolis. For it is precisely in distinguishing between clear knowledge and mere opinion—including the correct opinion that characterizes the knowledge that the Auxiliaries possess through their education—that Socrates warns Glaucon they must beware of making "these men" angry.

> What if the man of whom we say that he opines but doesn't know, gets harsh with us and disputes the truth of what we say? Will we have some way to soothe and gently persuade him, while hiding from him that he's not healthy? (476d–e). . . . So, will we strike a false note in calling them lovers of opinion rather than lovers of wisdom? And will they be very angry with us if we speak this way? (480a)

"These men" include the noble protectors of public morality that they have been educating ever since Book 2. They must beware of making the Auxiliaries angry by revealing to them that their most cherished convictions are, if not groundless, not sufficiently grounded to warrant the loyalty to them that is the heart of their honor as citizens.

One need not open up any Nietzschean abyss in order to claim that the political morality of the *Republic* is insufficiently grounded from the perspective of philosophy. For our purposes, it is sufficient to distinguish between an analogy and a proof. In the Image of the Ship of State, for example, an analogy is posited between the pilot who studies the heavens and the philosophic ruler who knows statecraft (488a–489a). But the sober beauty of the image obscures the fact that, while we can demonstrate our knowledge of the heavens through observation and measurement, it is an open question whether knowledge of this kind can be derived from politics and morality. Conversely, while politics requires a more or less settled epistēmē of rule that will help the community achieve stability and order, the philosophic quest for knowledge about nature is open-ended and impossible to complete. All of Socrates' arguments are heuristic. The beauty of these images softens the edges of the analytic incommensurables they purport to join together. Each one of them engages our reflection on how it is that man needs both wholeness and clarity, eros and analysis, and in this sense they are the jewels of Socratic dialectic, showing how we must alternate between disjointed particularism and empty unity guided by the archetypal particularity of the forms. That is why Plato wrote dialogues rather than treatises. Every positive assertion of Socrates is undercut by the ironies of his own rhetorical appeals to different types of interlocutors and by his own relentless skepticism about any settled answer to the question of how to be a kalos kagathos. And it does not need to be more than an open question in order to threaten the edifice of the kallipolis, since the best city is premised on the hypothesis that thumos *can* philosophize—that a citizen's attachment to a particular, settled ordering of the political community can possess the status of the kind of knowledge philosophy seeks. As the nature of wisdom finally begins to emerge in the *Republic,* filling the earlier aporia signified by the place-holding role of calculation, a gap opens up between those who are educated in a way that may be a precondition for philosophizing but who cannot grasp the grounds of the limited truth of their beliefs and those who can progress in such studies.

The entire kallipolis is based on the hypothetical comparison of virtue to technē and technē to epistēmē. It is a kind of reasoning that, as Socrates intimated earlier, is valid to a point, but cannot on its own power progress further than the mathematical, which forsakes the specificity of the phenomena it tries to illuminate. The further leap to the forms is necessary so that the heterogeneity of the world from which mathematical knowledge is abstracted can be restored to it, making the archetypes of natural beings both universal and particular. Socrates intimates the difficulty in Book 4 when, in discussing how we might gain knowledge of the nature of desire, he implies that he is not sure what the object of knowledge *itself* is ("learning [*mathēmatos*] itself, or whatever it is to which knowledge [epistēmē] should be related") as opposed to the objects of distinct *kinds* of knowing like the different crafts (438c). When he tries to compare the object of knowledge itself to the specificity of crafts like medicine, he must resort to circumlocution ("knowledge . . . of that alone to which knowledge is related"[438e]). Technē has clear aims and objects. But although knowledge—and therefore the knowledge of desire—can initially be clarified by the craft analogy, it is ultimately less clear in the case of knowledge than in the case of techne what its objects are or should be. Mathematics is not the object of knowledge in the same way that a house is the object of house-building. The forms as propounded in Book 7 rescue the heterogeneity of the cosmos from the overly formalistic universality of mathematical knowledge. In this sense, the forms also rescue and elevate to a cosmological principle the diversity manifested by the banausic arts themselves with their various actions and objects. But this ascent is, as Socrates makes abundantly clear by the end of Book 5, an erotic one. The craft analogy is not enough. On the level of philosophizing, the heuristic value of its clear distinctions must be reintegrated with the hierarchical continuum linking high to low that only eros divines.

If philosophizing were *only* a technē, we might be forced to agree with Heidegger's contention that Platonic reasoning is already incipiently the global domination of technology. But, as we observed in chapter 3, the only knowledge that Socrates unambiguously claims for himself is a skill in erotics, which amounts to saying he is so rigorously attuned to his lack and uncertainty that, although reason may enable him to trace and "bear" the varieties of human ignorance through conversational "intercourse" with less self-consciously ignorant interlocutors, he will never possess the kind of certainty necessary to launch a project for the assimilation of Being to technē imputed to Platonism by Heidegger.

Or, to take the argument of the Heideggerian Marxist Kojève as to why Platonic political rationalism differs from the modern kind, it is not simply that the rational political order of the *Republic* does not "have time" to be implemented in Plato's era but must await the whole outcome of history with its cumulative struggles to impose human mastery over nature.[6] Rather, Socrates' exploration of the meaning of a rational political order is at bottom for the sake of something else that he has all the time in the world to enjoy, and which evidently so absorbed him that he did not even take time out from it to write. This is the entirely now-oriented activity of philosophical erotics — the hunt for a young interlocutor like Theaetetus whose soul is so smooth and flowing that, as Socrates playfully implies, his prize in their conversational ball game will be to ask whatever questions he wants of the young man without limit (*Theaetetus* 146a).

The chief flaw in the Heideggerian interpretation of Plato is that it derives the "metaphysics of presence" from the reification of the projects of historical striving to which time and care compel us. In other words, to use the terms of this interpretation, it depicts Plato as if he regarded thumos to be the only meaningful experience, both practically and philosophically, such that the quest for stable "forms" can be understood as the (perhaps unself-conscious) projection of human mastery upon Being. Heidegger overlooks eros. For Plato, eros, not thumotic mastery, is the primary locus for our openness to "presence," to the stable perfection that we intuit as the proper goal of our own longings, and that leads us to contemplate the whole. Analysis and the "masterful" elements of reason are for the sake of this self-forgetting rapture.[7]

The pursuit of the Ideas is grounded in eros — in the soul's neediness. Philosophy is a directed longing. The Ideas point the way to a reasoned articulation of the cosmos. But philosophy is a longing without completion, a cycle of recurrent need and partial clarification. Because of his absorption in this cycle, Socrates has no political project, no ideological agenda. The phenomena of political life — including the question of who or what the gods might be — provide the richest possible subject matter for clarifying the soul's neediness. The education of the Auxiliaries is not primarily intended to provide a recipe for training model citizens here and now — although, as transmitted through the philosophical schools of classical antiquity, it had something like this effect. Its primary purpose is to provide a kind of curriculum to help Glaucon and Adeimantus — and young people like them who might hear or read the *Republic* in later generations—to reflect on what it *would* mean to be properly educated, which is to say, educated to consider one's political commitments in light of the whole.

Socratic and Tragic Wisdom

Before exploring the political dimension of the disjunction between reason and morality in the *Republic* more directly, let me bring out some of its features by returning to the Socratic critique of poetry that the education and psychology of Books 2, 3, and 4 are meant to embody. Earlier, I suggested that Socrates' proposals for educating the spirited part of the soul and class of citizens were intended to provide a corrective to the tragic embellishment of spirit's spontaneous excesses. In keeping with this, I suggest that the rather comical story of Leontius is meant to provoke a comparison with the tragedy of Oedipus.[8] By covering his eyes to avoid seeing the corpses, Leontius tries to protect a kind of prejudice in the Burkean sense—a kind of moral certainty about how to live. The greatest example from Greek poetry of blindness as a kind of moral wisdom is the tragedy of Oedipus. The outcome of Oedipus's unbridled passion is that he blinds himself, as Leontius tries figuratively to do by covering his eyes. Just as Leontius vents his moralistic wrath by personifying his eyes and castigating them ("wretches, take your fill!" [*Republic* 440a]), so does Oedipus curse his eyes as he dashes them out after gazing on the broken naked corpse of his mother and wife:

> He tore the brooches—the gold chased brooches fastening her robe—away from her and lifting them up high dashed them on his own eyeballs, shrieking out such things as: they will never see the crime I have committed or had done upon me! Dark eyes, now in the days to come look on forbidden faces, do not recognize those whom you long for. With such imprecations he struck his eyes again and yet again. (1266–1275)

Oedipus thus learns horribly the wisdom of the blind Teresias that it is better to be blind about the deepest, most primordial truths of life. It is better not to think that our reasoning powers can gain complete insight into, and control over, forces and destinies beyond our control—including, at bottom, our own passions. By contrast, Socrates' illustration of the salutary effects of blindness is much closer to comedy than tragedy. Indeed, it is possible that Leontius was a character in a play by Theopompus, who specialized in comedies of manners and burlesques of the grand mythologies treated seriously by the tragedians. While Leontius tries to preserve his moral bearings by covering his eyes, for Socrates, unconstrained seeing is the chief metaphor for intellection and the soul's grasp of the order of the whole. The word for "form" (eidos), a cognate of the verb "to see" that literally means the "look" of a thing, suggests that the stable aspect of visible phenomena is the manifest sign of the degree to which they participate in true being. We recall that when Socrates tried to save the analogy of virtue to an art from the doubleness of thumos by broaching the subject of an education that might mitigate its contradictions, he leapt rather breathtakingly from the mere prospect of educating thumos like a well-behaved hound to the identification of civic-spiritedness with the philosophical capacity to "see" what is and is not. Leontius's need to hide his eyes from certain phenomena that would corrode his virtuous moderation is an apt measure of how tenuous this hypothesis has proven to be. Unlike Teresias, Socrates would never maintain that a deliberate blindness toward the possible illumination of human ignorance could ever be regarded as wisdom.

I do not mean to suggest that Socrates might not conceal his thoughts, or remain silent, if he thought it would be better for the other person. But even Socrates' evasions are chatty—a "marvellous combination of wit and words, pungency and politeness," as St. Augustine puts it, "with his trick of confessing ignorance and concealing knowledge," unlike the mantic laconism of Sophocles' Teresias.[9] There is a difference in principle between an esotericism stemming from the possibility that the light of the substantive truth about beings might be too much to bear and the possibility that there is no "truth" beyond the issuing of seeming/being out of chance and necessity. As the Image of the Cave suggests, whatever we can learn about nature is of a whatness whose clarity is so blinding that, when it is considered apart from the becomings in which it is ordinarily instantiated, the differences and distinctions that are both the spice and the burden of most people's lives threaten to vanish into the sunlight. Being is not profound, but radiantly superficial, not so much invisible as hyper-visible.

Indeed, if there is an esoteric teaching about the forms, it is not that they do not exist, but that they exist all too thoroughly. What is esoteric about the teaching is not that Plato invented the forms as an edifying fiction to camouflage the truth that Being offers no grounding for morality. The esoteric dimension resides in the fact that Plato may overstate the degree to which the stability of the virtues participates in the stability of the forms. It is not that the truth about Being undermines the forms and civic virtue. It is that the truth about Being—that Being is articulated as forms—may undermine civic virtue by exposing it to a light too brilliant for it to retain its independent identity as a twilight entity in the realm of "correct seeming." It is the forms themselves that may subvert morality by exposing the virtues to a criterion of universality and non-contradiction whose transcendental clarity they cannot come into direct contact with and not be burned up. This is precisely the charge laid by Nietzsche and Heidegger against Plato and his Socrates for destroying the civilization of the tragic age, Greek culture at its Homeric and Heracleitean zenith. If we equate Plato's account of Being with Nietzsche's or Heidegger's, we transform the hallmark of Platonic metaphysics into a purely thaumaturgic, mythopoetic fiction, thereby missing the point both about Platonic metaphysics *and* Nietzsche's and Heidegger's critiques of the forms.

The truth about phusis is not to be found in the sub-visible recesses of the Cave. The Image encapsulates Socrates' argument in Books 5 and 6 that Sophistry itself, including its ontological underpinnings, derives from the human vices that ordinarily characterize most political authority and public opinion. When the philosopher reenters the Cave and first sees things for what they really are—the passions and loyalties that are thought by most people in the Cave to be so important for conferring either happiness or despair—they turn out, as Socrates puts it, to be "silly nothings," not movingly tragic destinies (515d). They involve one in behavior that is more ludicrous than profoundly revealing of any truth about existence. The antidote to their ill effects is not less knowledge, but more. In his critique of poetry in the *Republic*, Socrates reduces the grand rhythms of Homer's *Iliad* to the banal plot of a man who gets angry because his boss stole his girl ("I'll speak without meter; I'm not poetic" [393e]). At least for the purposes of educating the Auxiliaries, he would probably sum up the lessons of Sophocles' tragedy in a similarly dry-eyed manner: (1) Do not beat someone's brains in just because they blocked your path on the highway; (2) Orphans arriving in a strange town should probably do a background check on an older person whom they plan to marry. But there is a serious point to Socrates' seeming imperviousness to the charms of tragic poetry. For Oedipus could have restrained his anger at the man blocking his path, whom he did not know to be Laius. Only if we believe that whenever we experience a strong feeling we are in the insuperable grip of primordial motions that issue from the depths of existence and overpower all merely human injunctions to live in a restrained and clearheaded manner will we treat Oedipus's insane anger at a slight to his honor as a tragic necessity.

For a biblical parallel to the wisdom of blindness, we might think of God's command to Lot's wife not to look upon His destruction of Sodom and Gomorrah. Man must remain in holy awe of God's acts of justice. We must not reduce such an act to an object of curiosity or speculation by turning around to survey it. We must not revel in it, question its severity, see how it is done, or wonder about its inconsistency. (Why does God not punish all sinners so severely and consistently? Did everyone there deserve to die—for example, the children?) In short, one must not subject God's actions to the search for a consistent, noncontradictory eidos, as does Socrates in the *Euthyphro* and in the reformed theology of the *Republic*. Here, too, blindness is wisdom—a pious sense of the limits to human knowing.

In Book 4 of the *Republic,* we are reminded that every political order tries to evoke this awe in its subjects as regards the dark underside of its authority. It is indecent to try to film Gary Gilmore's execution, as most people felt at reports of journalists hovering in helicopters trying to get a closer look. An execution must seem sober, serious, and impersonal. To revel in it makes it seem like the murderous passion it is meant to punish, and makes the city's whole authority seem like just another contender for mastery, a brigand whose crimes are on such a large scale that, as the Sophist Thrasymachus puts it, he can frighten or cajole his victims into pronouncing his actions just (343e–344c). It is not surprising, therefore, that in fashioning a rhetoric to win public support for their view, opponents of capital punishment make one of their most telling points when they routinely equate legal execution with "killing" by the state.

Tragedy was one way the Greeks attempted to instill this sense of awe, not by proclaiming a single omnipotent deity as in the Bible, but by evoking a sense of human limits, destiny, and necessity. As Benardete has observed, the dawning of philosophy, by contrast, is conveyed by the story of Gyges in Herodotus, where looking directly at the naked beauty of nature leads Gyges to usurp traditional authority to the length of making himself tyrant and stealing the king's wife.[10] He openly and consciously commits the kind of erotic-political crime that Oedipus unconsciously committed. And he gets off scot (or Lydian) free. Whereas Oedipus was punished because his anger, eros, and pride exceeded the limits appropriate to humans even though he did not set about to kill his father and marry his mother, Gyges' clear-sightedness about the difference between customary, conventional authority and natural satisfaction enabled him to commit his crimes without remorse or penalty. Gyges ignores the traditional advice to obey what the ancestral authorities "say." Instead, he pays attention to what he "sees" when he looks past the conventions—symbolized in the story by the naked queen, stripped of the garb of conventional authority and propriety that forbids access to her by a lowly shepherd like Gyges. As Glaucon implies when he incorporates the tale into his speech in Book 2, Gyges' ability to become tyrant through stealth is an example of the sort of exemption from the usual bad consequences of injustice that the Sophists implied they could provide their customers through the protective skills of rhetoric.

These considerations amplify one of the main themes of our study of tyranny and ambition: how Socrates tries to found political philosophy as an alternative to (1) the ontology of primordialism, which tended, as it was employed by the Sophists, to undermine justice and moderation, and (2) the tragic version of the primordialist ontology that culminated in the defense of virtue as something harsh, unpleasant, and unnatural. For Socrates also relies on the "eyes" of intellection and reflection on nature over the received words of tradition. But while he thus does not accept the tragic equation of wisdom with blindness, neither does he argue that knowledge of nature leads to gratifying the passions and becoming a tyrant. Socratic wisdom is a knowledge that we do not know what we believe we know: a clear-sighted apprehension of limits. In presenting an argument that will enlist spiritedness in the service of justice and decency, Socrates defers to a story that he "heard." That is to say, he defers to authority out of a regard for the political community's need for some fixed principles of morality not constantly subjected to the refutational investigations he was most wont to carry out in his own conversations. At the same time, while it is a story that promotes a kind of blindness, Socrates does not accept it *solely* on authority, but has reflected on it in the light of clear knowledge, thus concluding that it is worthy of "trust"—worthy, so to speak, of a provisional kind of acceptance even if it does not stand up to the most rigorous tests of knowledge. It is thus a prime example of what Socrates eventually terms "correct seeming" or "correct opinion," a middle ground between simple ignorance and true knowledge that is the special element of the political community

(476d–480a). Correct opinion is a blend of as much clarity as the community's convictions can sustain without losing the certainty required by all civic loyalty with as much commitment as is needed without degenerating into mindless patriotism, religious fanaticism, and partisan hatred. But this returns us to the problem with which these reflections began: While the initiates to a philosophical education may be able to live with this delicate balance of truth and convention as the most coherent account that philosophy can render of civic morality, can "these men" whose characters the story of Leontius is meant to exemplify be told that their convictions have such an uncertain basis without becoming "angry" at their philosophical instructors?

A Comparison of Oedipus and Leontius

In order to bring out the full force of this tension from the side of moral conviction before proceeding to examine it from the side of the philosopher-kings, let us pursue the parallel between Leontius and Oedipus a step further. Comparing the blindness of Leontius and Oedipus, we might say that the corpses in the executioner's pit are Socrates' way of depicting the same kinds of illicit passion that lead to Oedipus's downfall. I realize that, on the face of it, this is a peculiar identification to make, since the chief occasion of Oedipus's tragic nadir was his incestuous relationship with his mother. The *Republic* as a whole abstracts from eros, and so we should not expect from it a complete account of the dangers of illicit passion. Nevertheless, I believe an argument can be made that Leontius's longing to look at the corpses might well represent the "tragic" view of the passions altogether as this view is reflected on and clarified by the philosopher who reenters the Cave. From the Socratic perspective, in other words, desire and eros of the tragic variety lead to an indiscriminate miasma of carnal lust, like the mangled and heaped corpses in the executioner's pit. In *Oedipus the Tyrant*, the tragic denouement mingles the elements of violent death and sexual passion in a sort of Dionysian orgy. When we see Iocasta naked, at the moment when her attractiveness as the object of Oedipus's eros is thus most fully revealed, we also see her broken and disfigured by hanging, much indeed like the corpse of an executed criminal. When Oedipus takes her brooches to dash out his eyes, her robe falls open, so that in mutilating himself with the ornaments of his beloved, Oedipus effects a kind of posthumous ravishing of her even as he punishes himself for this very passion (1265–1272). The pit of broken bodies and criminal lusts toward which Leontius is drawn, then, symbolizes the primordial substratum of violence and horror beneath our everyday reliance on a stable and beneficent world. Leontius seems to enjoy dwelling on human fragility and vulnerability. This is the kind of taste that might also be sublimated and uplifted by the Oedipus tragedy. When Oedipus gouges out his eyes with Iocasta's own brooches after gazing on her dead and naked body, Sophocles implies that when eros and the other passions have their way, the solid boundaries of conventional morality—mother and son, husband and wife, king and queen—dissolve and unravel; that eros at bottom is rooted in violence:

> He struck his eyes again and yet again with the brooches. And the bleeding eyeballs gushed and stained his beard—no sluggish oozing drops but a black rain and bloody hail poured down. So it has broken—and not on one head but troubles mixed for husband and wife. (1275–1280)

The passions lead down to Dionysian dismemberment, destruction, and flying apart, much as in the poetic and etymological sources of thumos that we considered in chapter 4. As Oedipus's old life as tyrant, patricide, and regicide goes down, his chastened reemergence as blind wanderer is preceded by a kind of death-in-life, the complete collapse of Apollonian eidos:

> O, O, where am I going? Where is my voice borne on the wind to and fro? . . . Horror of darkness enfolding, resistless, unspeakable visitant sped by an ill wind in haste! (1305–1315)

At the beginning of the play, Oedipus, with his pride in the fact that his authority over Thebes stems chiefly from his cleverness and skill rather than mere hereditary descent, might be taken to exemplify precisely those intellectual virtues of statecraft whose special patron was Apollo. Yet, as Oedipus laments, it is Apollo himself, the Far-Darter, who has sped him from afar to his destruction (1325–1330). As the second to last stanza cited implies, in the tragic version of the primordialist ontology, the destruction of man's pride and confidence in his eidetic reasoning to unriddle his fate and achieve mastery of the polis is necessary precisely in order for the Apollonian dimension of Being—the laws and arts of peaceful government that prevail in everyday life—to reemerge newly invigorated and sustained by its tension with Dionysian becoming. Phusis issues out of chance (Dionysian spontaneity) and through necessity (Apollonian form), returning recurrently to tuchē so as to emerge pregnant with a necessity more awesome. The blood "pours down" and "breaks" as if Oedipus's self-mutilation triggers the birth pangs of a world refreshed. As other myths reveal, Apollo attains his greatness among the gods only after he becomes "Pythian" Apollo, absorbing and continuously surmounting the serpent of the vanquished god of earth, eros, and genesis.[11]

According to the tragedy, our only refuges from this horrible truth at the bottom of everyday life are law and custom themselves. Archetypal figures like the tyrant Oedipus follow their grand passions and ambitions all the way down into the primordial abyss from which they issue.[12] We more ordinary people in the audience learn from this awful spectacle that we should not follow the lead of our own passions, but be grateful for the peace of the established ways and pray to the gods that they last. Law and custom purge passion of its scope and savor, but provide a haven from the awful vengeance that Apollo must recurrently visit upon Dionysos.

A play like *Oedipus the Tyrant* is thus supposed to support morality. But for Socrates, as we learn from his critique of poetry in Books 2 and 3, the tragic identification of the profoundest truth about life with Dionysian chaos leads either to hopelessness about the possibility of ever transcending our destructive passions, of ever assimilating passion to knowledge, or, as a reaction to this hopelessness, the exacerbation of passion, the Sophists' maxim that one should take as much pleasure as one can get. This is the more so if, as both tragedians and Sophists seem to agree, the laws themselves are against what we naturally want to do. They are repressive, perhaps dreadful or majestic, perhaps useful, but they contain no prospect for happiness. Glaucon's speech in Book 2 demanding proof of the naturalness of justice expresses the Sophists' reaction to the primordialist ontology, while Adeimantus's complaints about the more traditional poetic education show how ambivalent those earlier authorities were about the relationship between virtue and natural satisfaction.

To sum up: the Leontius story is a delicate balancing act, crystallizing a number of the tensions we have noted throughout the *Republic*. By telling it, Socrates recognizes the need for a degree of blindness—a degree of mere opinion or prejudice, albeit correct—in political morality. The story has a mild humor with just a touch of pathos. Viewed from the transcendental perspective as it is sketched in the *Republic,* Leontius's immoderate passion for gazing at corpses is more humorous than serious—just as, we might say, Socrates' Aristophanean badinage with Callicles treats the kind of hubris the Athenians display on Melos, and which for Thucydides has a serious if not a tragic provenance, as more ludicrous than tragic. From the Socratic perspective, the violently exciting outcome of the tragedy of Oedipus appeals to and inflames the passions even as it attempts to purge them. This awe-inspiring catharsis is replaced in Socrates' tale by the rather silly tableau of a blustering man with his cloak over his eyes.[13]

Morality and the consequences of violating nomos are thus taken less seriously in the Socratic account than in the tragic one. The mild humor of the Leontius story helps prepare us for the jocose tone of Socrates' proposals for the abolition of the family—effectively dismissing the crime of incest that brought down Oedipus as a mere administrative difficulty, blandly remarking that people can have sex as often as they like as long as there are no unplanned childbirths (461b–c). But the Socratic view of morality is also gentler than the tragic view, without the frightful uncanniness of man's place in the cosmos between the crushing powers of chance and necessity. Indeed, having responded to Adeimantus's desire to see poetry purged of the implication that virtue is not pleasant, Socrates is subsequently dismayed by the harshness of the young man's moral strictures for the optimal city they are fashioning in speech (426b–e, 499e). As Bloom suggests, Adeimantus liked the City of Sows because it provided everyone with a moderate wherewithal within a sober and disciplined community. But once his brother throws open the sluice gates of eros, giving their imaginary citizens the chance to acquire and enjoy without limit, Adeimantus is progressively more keen to impose severe limits on pleasure. By the end of Book 5, Glaucon's erotic and courageous passions begin to be drawn away from their political-pedagogical project toward the dazzling splendors of philosophy. But the more earnest Adeimantus, once Socrates convinces him to part with his attachments to property and family, becomes even more intolerant of subversive influences in the kallipolis than Socrates requires of him in order to complete the reform of poetry. When Adeimantus has to be persuaded not to turn his intolerance against philosophy itself (487b–e), we can already envision the optimal city's downfall at the hands of those sober and moderate Auxiliaries who believe their honor is slighted by the authority over them of this strange philosophic caste.

While Socrates responded to Adeimantus's complaints about the poets by undertaking to show that justice was natural rather than a mere conventional imposition, hence compatible with happiness, Adeimantus becomes more interested in purging poetry of its ambiguities about the naturalness of virtue so as to make moralistic severity the equivalent of human satisfaction. It is to dampen this potential of the just city for an excessive harshness that has all along been inherent in the elevation of thumos as the seat of moral virtue that Socrates puts the failure of moral duty to conquer erotic passion in a partly humorous light. For he is at least as much concerned that thumos will be too zealous in chastening pleasure (especially the immoderate pleasures of philosophizing) as he is that it will not be harsh enough. For Socrates, the political community is threatened not only by Achillean insubordination and Oedipal immoderation, but by those who vent their belligerence in spasms of moral wrath ostensibly on behalf of virtue. Indeed, in the pristine experience of thumos, the two motives are often hard to distinguish. Achilles believed that Agamemnon treated him unjustly and out of keeping with his own high rank when he rebelled against the king of king's authority. Socrates' own prosecutor Meletus maintained at his trial that Socrates alone corrupted the Athenians, and refused to debate the point. Callicles and Socrates agree, as they agree on little else, that the wrath of the Athenian dēmos against leaders whom it believes have betrayed it can be lethal. Thus, after telling the story of Leontius, Socrates immediately goes on to stress that spirit is to be wrathful only when reason is on its side. When reason fails to justify anger, spirit will subside and, if necessary, itself submit to punishment in a "well-bred" manner (440c).

SOME OBSTACLES TO THE HARMONY OF PHILOSOPHY AND CIVIC-SPIRITEDNESS

But will it? Socrates offers no demonstration beyond simply asserting that this must follow from the role they have established for spiritedness in the city and the soul. Thumos is still the ticking time bomb in the political psychology of the *Republic*, as it has been since its introduction in Book 2.[14] There, we recall, Socrates almost gave up exploring the parallel between the soul and the city when faced with the erratic doubleness of thumos, its tendency to veer between doglike loyalty and bestial savagery. The discussion went forward on the assumption that a civic education might be elaborated that could breed a second nature of self-control in the spirited character to modify these extremes. As the exposition of that education and the role of spiritedness in the community draws to completion, we see increasingly how tenuous that assumption has been. Just as the Auxiliaries must be savage only to enemies and never to friends, so within themselves their anger must never go so far, even in the name of morality, that righteous wrath becomes an end in itself rather than a means toward the rule of reason. But this is the most problematic part of the parallel between the soul and the city, and the reason for the breakdown of the optimal community in Book 8. As a result of their education, the Auxiliaries are supposed to be in no doubt that the particular set of conventions they defend has the status of philosophical knowledge. This is the hypothesis Socrates proposed to explore at the outset when, in Book 2, he equated the Auxiliaries' distinction between friends and enemies with philosophy's search for the difference between what is and what is not. This hypothetical identification of convention with reason is what made it possible to explore further whether a certain correct set of political conventions might be in harmony with nature, not against it, as the Sophists maintained all conventional authority must be. But the education received by the Auxiliaries, while it may be an intimation of the orderly cosmos studied by philosophy, is clearly not synonymous with philosophizing or the objects of philosophical speculation.

Five Difficulties with the Noble Lie

The civic education in Books 2 and 3 is, as Socrates describes one of its chief components, a noble lie (414c). In contrast with some interpretations that stress its falsity, implicitly reducing its nobility to a kind of candy-coating, I would stress instead that it is a lie that is nonetheless sustained by the power of the beautiful to a certain degree. Like correct opinion as a whole—or, to take the parallel from Diotima's Ladder, the realm of prudence grounded in Eros's demonic divinations of the bounded extent and limitation of our enlightenment—that education is a middle ground between transcendental being and the depths of ignorance. To take a more familiar tack, it is rhetoric in the classical sense first established by Socrates: a cosmology simplified or exaggerated where necessary so as to ground certain moral convictions necessary for the stability and unity of a particular political community. As Aristotle was to sum up the same approach, it is necessary for the statesman to know only so much about metaphysics and the nature of the soul as is useful for dealing with the problems of governing.[15]

I will discuss a few of the more notable ambiguities of this noble falsehood as they relate to our theme.

(1) The unquestioning identification of one's fellow citizens with those whose friendship one ought reasonably to seek. In the very first pages of the dialogue, Socrates perplexes Polemarchus with the observation that we cannot always assume that those who deserve to be our friends and who therefore deserve good are synonymous with our fellow-citizens, or that those who deserve harm are

synonymous with the enemies of our particular country (334b–e). This problem is "solved" only in the formal sense that the interlocutors agree to proceed on the premise that the distinction thumos makes between friend/citizen and enemy/noncitizen or aberrant citizen corresponds to knowledge of what truly is and is not. As we have seen, much of the ensuing dialogue is a commentary on the untenability of that assumption, or, to put it another way, an exploration of the limits of reason within politics.

(2) The preference in all instances for the common good over one's own. As we have seen, the plausibility of making the honor of the Auxiliaries seem a happier life than that of the Artisans depends very much on Socrates' success in expelling pleasures other than the pedestrian and banausic from the discussion. As soon as eros is reintroduced, the tension between the common good and the good of the individual bursts back onto the scene—exemplified by none other than the rulers themselves, as I will discuss below at greater length.

(3) A belief that the hierarchy of authority in the city is grounded directly in nature and not in a merely conventional distribution of privileges. The Myth of the Metals is a recipe for pure meritocracy unaffected by inherited position, with provisions for appropriate upward and downward mobility for the offspring of the three classes (415a–d). In itself, it is perfectly consistent, a paradigm for the distinction between nature and convention in the Socratic sense. What is "false" about it is Socrates' attempt to graft it onto a particular local community born and bred in one place. Because of their blood ties and autochthony, the ruling order—even granting that they scrupulously observe the rules about upward and downward mobility—could never be drawn from, or judged in accordance with, the universal natural talent pool that the idea of meritocracy entails. For what if the polis next door has people whose virtues better entitle them to be in the ruling class of the optimal politeia than some or any of its current members? Socrates never suggests that the kallipolis would open its doors to a foreign ruler or citizens on meritocratic grounds—on the contrary, he is explicit in advising this city how to defend itself against any external threat to its independence (422a–423b).

On the other hand, what is "beautiful" about Socrates' falsehood is, I venture to suggest, the inspiring notion that a band of civic brothers friendly because of their common ancestry and rearing in a land that has been theirs forever could indeed conjoin with these customary sentimental ties of patriotism and love of country a rational standard of natural meritocracy. The problem is whether such a perfect natural standard of merit is compatible with the nature of any polis, even the best one "according to logos." The "false" dimension of the city's meritocracy is a notable instance of the larger problem that even this best constitution will be subject to stresses between reason and prejudice, to say nothing of the internal and external contradictions to which any political community is subjected by the dangers of internal class strife and external assault. Later on, I will discuss the possibility of a middle ground between the poles of this tension. Absent that possibility, the only way to purge this reform entirely of its false component would be to take it in one of two directions that were explored by Plato's colleagues, and on the basis of their objections to his *Republic*. One route is that taken by Aristotle, where the merit of the "best" constitution is frankly *conceded* to be limited in light of nature's highest standard, but necessary given the limitations of the polis, and sufficient for the requirements of political practice. The other route is that explored in Xenophon's *Cyropaedia,* where the polis vanishes into a cosmopolitan multinational state based on the strict division of labor and reward of demonstrated merit cutting across all ethnic divisions.[16]

(4) The problem of force. Even though Socrates had demonstrated to Polemarchus in the first pages of the *Republic* that a just person would never injure anyone, even a deserving enemy (335d–e), the justice of the optimal community as it unfolds in the *Republic* certainly permits at least two types of injury: a foreign policy of preemptive aggression and internal subversion against neighboring countries, and the enforcement of the upper classes' authority against the lower class of artisans.

The first case points to the practical limitations imposed by the polis on Socrates' educational experiment for imparting to conventional "manliness" a degree of his own more sober "steadfastness." If these Auxiliaries are to defeat other cities in battle or through fomenting civil strife within them, the kind of sobriety that Socrates displayed in retreating in an orderly manner from a battle initiated and led by other people will not be a sufficient criterion for citizen courage. Real martial prowess, initiative, and deception will be necessary, not just the strength of character to withstand danger when it is visited upon one who plays no leading role in such affairs. The best polis is still a polis with external foes. This is why, of the definitions of justice explored and refuted in the opening pages of Book 1, one survives intact in the elaboration of the best city's justice: doing good to friends/citizens and harm to enemies/noncitizens. As a private individual living in Athens, Socrates is arguably a good man, but more in the sense of refraining from unjust acts than in the sense of a spirited commitment to combating the city's enemies and helping those who help it. He was brave in retreating, and he refused to be a party to the execution of Leon of Salamis (*Symposium* 220d–221b, *Apology* 32c–d). But he did not come forward to serve the city militarily or politically. He was never in the forefront of the great causes and partisan political clashes of his day. His name never appears in Thucydides. As a matter of temperament, would such a man be any more likely to lead a perfect city into battle than a flawed one?

Let us take the second case, the enforcement of the upper classes' authority against the lower classes. As is often noted, the measures recommended for the purgation of sloth and self-interest in the best city are often extreme—for instance, allowing the sick to die without treatment or even killing the unfit (410a), or controlling the eugenics of the class hierarchy by abortion and the exposure of unsanctioned offspring (459e, 460d). These passages and others like them have often prompted outrage at Plato's alleged totalitarianism. But the severity of these measures "in speech" is required by the strange hypothesis that the dialogue explores:

that a city could remove *any* contradiction between the good and one's own. Plato was not proposing them as an agenda for actual reform, although we cannot conclude from this that he might not have been in favor of their partial implementation subject to the limitations of the Cave. They should not be taken literally. By the same token, they should not be taken as a Kantian ideal categorically distinct from natural behavior. For Plato, the best city is by definition the most "real," more "real" than the ones we actually experience and observe. The excessiveness of these measures is heuristic, pointing to likely obstacles in the way of achieving this pure synonymity between reason and convention. However, the need for injury and force in order to shape a city into the pattern of the Good is enough to show that, in Plato's understanding, the requirements of even an optimally ordered political community are not entirely harmonious with what reason might lead us to conclude about the just treatment of others when we are not constrained by such exigencies of statecraft—in other words, as Socrates first argues to Polemarchus, that we should never do harm to anyone (335d–e).

The problem of force, then, reopens the fissure that Book 2 sought to close. If the Auxiliaries are too gentle—too close to the philosophical capacity alleged to direct their passion—they may cease to be warriors. But if they perform vigorously the military and police duties that even a well-ordered community requires to protect itself from external threat and internal disaffection or indiscipline, they may be too savage for the rule of reason. At the same time, it is very much to be doubted whether the philosopher's absorption in the immoderate pursuit of the beautiful and good will leave him the time or the disposition to provide these tough guard-dogs with the forceful and energetic kind of leadership they are likeliest to respect. Socrates is tough only in speech.

(5) The contradictory character of the philosopher-king. Because there remains a tension between what is required by the justice of the optimal city and what the philosopher's own unconstrained speculation might lead him to believe about how to live, the "jobs" of philosopher and king in the *Republic* are never merged into one. To be sure, they are not double in the contradictory Heracleitean sense of "opposites." But, like thumos itself, they are not quite single either. Socrates maintains that the two ways of life need not conflict, and that "genuinely and adequately philosophizing" is the way of life that also provides the best character and knowledge for ruling (472c–e, 484b–487a). Philosophy does not contradict ruling, in other words, because the effects of philosophizing on the philosopher's character entail the traits that best suit a ruler, should the philosopher happen to choose to rule if a city should happen to ask him. But we are left with the paradox that the person best suited to exercise the art of ruling is not fully satisfied in his own nature by doing so, and, indeed, as Glaucon's response to the image that Socrates fashions for his own philosophical initiation suggests, might well prefer to devote himself exclusively to the pleasures of thinking rather than sacrifice some of this empyrean happiness to the dimmer realm of statesmanship (519d–520a).

For Plato, the pleasures of philosophizing and the pleasures of governing are not, at bottom, synonymous. Thus, although I agree with those who argue that the philosopher's own soul is arguably enriched by the opportunity to rule with the many interesting problems of theory and practice it presents, it still seems to me that these opportunities are not sufficient to establish the desirability of ruling—especially given the time they might take away from thinking—unless one adds, as Socrates suggests in the Image of the Cave, a certain sense of philanthropy motivating a duty to go back "down."[17] At the very least, the double job of philosopher-king violates the strict division of labor ("one nature, one job") that was to guide the elaboration of the parallel between a well-arranged individual soul and a well-arranged city. The tension at the very apex of the best city's hierarchy between the responsibility of governing and the naturally most satisfying way of life for an individual shows how tenuous the hypothesis equating civic paideia with knowledge has been all along.

In coming to the famous proposition that philosophers should rule, we have occasion to reflect on the whole problematic relationship between wisdom and civic authority that we have seen arise in a variety of ways in the *Gorgias, Symposium,* and *Republic.* As we have observed, Socrates is forceful, but only in speeches. Yet he makes it clear that, although rhetoric and persuasion are always preferable to punishment, sometimes a ruler will have to combine speeches with actual punishments (*Gorgias* 480a.6–d, *Republic* 465a–b, 471a–b, 590d–591b). The ruler cannot practice statecraft by weaving a spell of words alone, and to this extent, the statesman is not simply assimilable to the rhetorician, but has a distinct psychology and art that employ rhetoric in combination with more direct forms of coercion and punishment. But Socrates himself is so far from being this kind of person that he declined both to participate in the group sent to arrest Leon of Salamis and to act or speak forcefully to try to reverse Leon's conviction. As both Callicles and Alcibiades complain, Socrates can be a man of force in speeches. But he is not a man of force in deeds. He lacks partisan zeal. Moreover, even his forcefulness in speech is restricted to private conversations. Prior to his enforced appearance at his trial, Socrates had never in his long life addressed the Athenian citizenry. Even in his private conversations, moreover, Socrates sometimes pauses to obtain his interlocutors' agreement before carrying his refutation of them through to its conclusion (*Gorgias* 457c–458b).

Although he recognizes that not all citizens are amenable to assenting voluntarily to reasonable arguments, Socrates prefers voluntary assent in his conversations and only launches into a negative refutation when such assent is not possible. Understanding the need for force in politics, but not capable of exercising force himself, Socrates could never literally "practice politics" in Athens (as he claims to do in the *Gorgias*) in the way that he governs the small circle of his interlocutors and intimates, guided by his art of erotics and his skill as a midwife of the soul. Together they batten on the phenomenological richness of life in the greatest polis by using its problems and its human types as occasions for philosophical investigations into the good life, forming a kind of philosophical sub-polis based on philanthrophy alongside the democratic empire based (as Thucydides says) on fear, honor, and interest.[18]

In order for the wise to rule, they would need a belligerent ally or supplement, summed up in the *Republic's* proposition that thumos serve reason as the enforcer of justice. But we must bear in mind that it is not clear that someone like Socrates would be capable of ruling even in his own philosophically guided city. It does not follow from the fact that this city may be governed according to reason that the person best equipped to discover what is reasonable is the one best equipped to govern it. Although the Auxiliaries who form the bulk of its citizenry are educated never to turn their aggressiveness against their own city, they are punitive on behalf of the city's justice and aggressive in defending it from foreign threats, even to the extent of the preemptive fomenting of subversion in other cities. Socrates, who establishes for Polemarchus that a just man never does harm, would arguably not be able to carry out—perhaps not even order others to carry out—the punitive measures entrusted to the Auxiliaries of his own hypothetical polis. He would not likely function as a distinguished or daring military commander. How, then, could he expect such honor-loving men to obey one such as himself? The upshot is that they will not. The Auxiliaries overthrow the best regime because its ruling hierarchy is too repressive of their passion for honor (*Republic* 546a, 547b–550b). Thumos declares war on philosophic eros.

The ambivalent relationship between the two components of the job description "philosopher-king" leads us once again to wonder, as we have at a number of junctures in this study, whether philosophy and civic virtue are intrinsically related objects of the soul's fulfilment, or sharply divergent pursuits. Earlier in my discussion of the *Republic,* I noted that Socrates' identification in Book 4 of the governing virtue of the city and soul with wisdom was at best a place-holder, since no attempt was made to explain the origins or content of that wisdom apart from a kind of general orderliness or calculation. As the *Republic* unfolds, this aporia in the argument grows into a very large hole. The kind of specifically political wisdom, phronēsis or politikē, exercised by the Guardians over the Auxiliaries and Artisans is never properly distinguished from the Auxiliaries' education in correct opinion and elaborated in its own right—as distinct from the philosophic life per se, which only emerges in Book 5 after the completion of the civic education. Even though in the formal presentation of the parallel between the soul and the city the virtue of wisdom has supposedly been explained and set into place in the tripartite hierarchy by the time Book 4 ends, beginning in Book 5 we learn that the Guardians, as philosophers, are driven by a desire for the wisdom they manifestly lack. Indeed, a shorthand definition of the philosophic life would be that these people know better than anyone else that they lack wisdom, since they continually run up against the limits of their knowledge in every given phenomenon they investigate. So, as early as Book 4, the virtue of wisdom has been bricked into the civic hierarchy of the kallipolis, not only before we have really been told what it is, but indeed before we learn that the condition for the Guardians' pursuit of philosophy is their awareness of *lacking* this virtue.

The more we probe the apparently seamless identification between the Guardians, sketched in Books 2 to 4 as the possessors of wise statesmanship among the classes of the city, and the philosophers introduced toward the end of Book 5, the thornier and more knotted the relationship becomes. Because of the suppression of eros in the consideration of civic virtue beginning all the way back in Book 2, it is difficult to see how the erotic philosophers introduced in Book 5 might pursue their desire for wisdom in conjunction with their strictly political capacities as rulers. On the other hand, when eros does reemerge late in Book 5, it is not clear how this philosophic passion is supposed to translate into the wisdom for governance that the Guardians are supposed to have possessed all along. The identification of the Guardians' activity with wisdom is institutionalized within the pseudo-history of the best regime's evolution, and pretty much left at that. As we observed earlier, the Image of the Ship of State simply posits an analogy between the pilot's actual knowledge of the stars and the presumptive knowledge that a wise Guardian of the city would exercise in ruling it.

Socrates' contention that the philosopher-king holds one job is consistent with the guiding premise established in Book 2 that virtue is analogous to technē. It papers over for the sake of the formal continuation of the argument what is in many ways a contradictory set of activities—on the one hand, the civic Guardian of grave mien, who knows how to govern and does so; on the other, the needy lover of wisdom, profligate in his addiction to uncertainty, unable to accept any opinion without skeptical scrutiny. As Hyland has argued, according to the presentation of philosophy in the *Symposium* and other dialogues, the philosopher-kings of the *Republic* would have to be considered gods rather than human beings.[19] According to Diotima, philosophy's search for wisdom and avoidance of ignorance places it in a middle realm between the mortal and the divine. If the philosopher-kings (as Guardians) actually do possess wisdom, as opposed merely to longing for it as does the needy philosopher of the *Symposium* (and Book 5 of the *Republic*), then they have arguably transcended the mortal sphere altogether and moved onto a divine "hyperouranian" plane.

Of course, from a Platonic perspective, it is always possible in principle that a human being could at length, through pursuing wisdom, actually achieve it, or a sufficient measure of it to rise above the hunger that Socrates exhibits as a lover of knowledge. Although it is extraordinarily unlikely, given the impediments that our passions and prejudices, or physical limitations posed by illness or fatigue, place on this upward ascent, it is not impossible. Were it so, philosophy would have to be considered as existentially absurd. Man would be the "great stupidity," as Nietzsche writes, fated to ask questions for which neither we nor the world are so constituted as to be capable of yielding answers. In the Platonic cosmos, a wise individual could emerge, and could conceivably coincide with royal status. Obviously, these occurrences would be so rare as to make the *Republic* impracticable as a standard for political reform here and now. But the deeper problem is whether the philosopher-king is desirable even theoretically, given the portrait of Socratic philosophizing that emerged in chapter 3. For, on the evidence of the *Symposium* and even the *Republic* itself, where philosophy is presented as a profligate eros for wisdom, either the philosopher-king would be too Socratic to be a stable king or too certain of the art of ruling to be a philosopher in the Socratic sense. The single job of philosopher-king seems to split into two alternatives: a ruler like Socrates who subjects everything to scrutiny—including, therefore, the correct opinion guiding the very city he rules—or a ruler possessed of an apodictic art of statecraft that would give little leeway to Socrates' philosophical erotics.

One response to the tensions between wisdom and statecraft can be construed from the *Laws,* where "preludes" introduce a certain philosophic flexibility into the citizens' understanding of correct opinion. Another response can be found in the *Statesman,* where the archetypal monarch rules with apodictic certainty because his royal art derives directly from the ontological supremacy of Oneness over change and becoming. He is not merely a lover of wisdom, but wise. Indeed, this monarch is in every respect a counter-paradigm to the primordialist ontology and its exacerbation of tyranny as a life of natural impulse and force. He rules according to knowledge (epistēmē) rather than laws, guided by noetic insight into the stable reality that supervenes over change and motion. He is above the laws because law is but an imperfect approximation of his knowledge (*Statesman* 300c–e, 307e–309d).

Might we then flesh out the philosopher-king of the *Republic* by recourse to the royal art of ruling presented in the *Statesman*? Not necessarily, because the monarch of the *Statesman* is the teaching of the Eleatic Stranger, not of Socrates. This noetic monarchy is a reflection of the Parmenidean ontology, which opposes the Heracleitean ontology by insisting that being is One, motionless and eternal. The Parmenidean monarch is like a disembodied principle of pure intellection, bereft of eros or any other passion. The difficulty with looking to the Eleatic Stranger's account of monarchy as a way of clarifying the characteristics of the philosopher-king in the *Republic* is that, although the philosopher-kings do at times appear to share in the divine stability and calm certainty of the Parmenidean monarch, it is not possible to conjoin this "hyperouranian" monarch with the *Socratic* account of how wisdom is acquired. Socratic political philosophy reflects the difference between Platonic and Parmenidean philosophy altogether. Whereas Parmenides stressed the pure stability of the One and the superior claim of reason over all motives affected by motion and becoming, Socrates attempts to show that the route to the stability of the One must account for the variability of desire and experience, symbolized by his initiation by Diotima into the mysteries. While Parmenides taught that nous rules, in Socrates' account of virtue in the *Symposium,* nous rules the soul by enlisting the aid of "demonic" Eros in suppressing the aberrances of the other desires by fulfilling its own deepest longing for completion. By arguing for the participation of becoming in true being, the Platonic Socrates attempts to reconcile the Heracleitean ontology to the Parmenidean ontology in a synthesis that does justice to both. The route to political "oneness" must be by way of an education that allows the passions to fulfill themselves in a constructive and satisfying manner.

Hence, in the *Republic,* as we have seen, wisdom is pursued neither though an attunement to Heracleitean flux, nor through a direct intuition of Parmenidean Oneness, but through an education that heals the doubleness of thumos and, later, a philosophic education that guides eros toward its satisfaction. But for the very reason that Socratic philosophizing seeks the One though what becomes, through what "participates" in being, there is no easy resolution within the terms of the *Republic* of the tension inherent in the description "philosopher-king," which most improbably conjoins the "hyperouranian" monarch with the barefoot satyr. Given the manifest failure of a human being to emerge so far who both possesses wisdom, even the limited wisdom of ruling (rather than still being in need of it), and is a king, Socrates' philosophical erotics remain the best available alternative for pursuing further knowledge of how to live and how to govern. The coincidence of wisdom and power is an unlikelihood of utopian dimensions, not only because of the slight chance that a wise man could be born into or chosen for monarchy, but because philosophizing may not yield the requisite wisdom.

The Questionable Parallel between Soul and City

These are some of the obstacles to the full reconciliation of wisdom, statesman-ship, and civic-spiritedness in the just city. As our investigation nears its end, how-ever, let us bear in mind the possibility of a middle ground. Throughout this study, I have suggested that Socratic philosophizing holds to both unity and division, eros and analysis. Only by thinking through the possible unity of the city will we be able to clarify its contradictions in the fullest manner. Moreover, as I observed at the end of chapter 4, if the tension between philosophy and civic education is utterly irreconcilable (as opposed to posing serious difficulties), it would render the entire hypothesis of the *Republic* not merely heuristic, but absurd. Absurdity is a Nietzschean stance toward the cosmos—"a vicious circle made God"—with only an accidental resemblance to Socratic irony. Given everything we have con-sidered so far, it would be quite un-Socratic to conclude from the stresses and ambivalences between philosophy and statesmanship that they are absolutely con-tradictory activities.

Accordingly, the following question remains open in the *Republic.* Granted that the education of the Auxiliaries does not match that of their philosophic rulers, is there a continuum between the two educations or a tension, and if a tension, how severe? In Book 2 the Auxiliaries were said to be "philosophic" in the sense that the particular conventions they defend have the universal validity of being accord-ing to nature. But Socrates quickly introduced a third class of those especially suited for philosophy, and this splitting up of the citizen body, while seeming innocuous at first, steadily develops, as we have seen, into a tension, such that by the beginning of Book 6, Socrates is arguing that it is not the just citizen as such who is happy, but the individual philosopher whose passion for knowledge absorbs the passions that ordinarily result in injustice toward others (485d–e). The tension between the Guardians and the Auxiliaries is prefigured by Leontius's covering his eyes as he castigates their curiosity. His inner struggle on behalf of calculation (logismos)—on behalf of what is supposed to be knowledge—requires a salutary ignorance, just as the arrangements of the best community require some beautiful lies to narrow the gap between the political order and the cosmos.

We can see the problem in a politically more forthright manner if we return to the city side of the parallel between the city and the soul, as Socrates frequently reminds us to do. Within the soul of a single individual, it is plausible that calculation might rule over desire, given that we accept the diminished status that Socrates assigns to passion in Books 2 and 4 (its reduction from eros to epithumia). Given that the desires are degrading and witless "diseases" of impulse, a person might well want to arrange his or her inner emotional economy so as to keep a sense of restraint in the driver's seat. The problem is that, when we proceed to the city side of the parallel, the reconciliation of the Auxiliaries to the rule of the Guardians does not take place within one personality who might arguably make this accommodation of passion to reason for his or her own good. Instead, it is an externally ordered relation between two separate classes, both of whose natures incline them to perceive their own good in different ways. This subordination of one class to another takes place by means of educating one class to obey the other, not by means of one person's wish to order his or her own life in the most advantageous manner.

There is a further problem. Spirit is only one of three elements within the soul of an individual who, if properly educated, can be expected to subordinate spirit to some sort of sensible restraint. But the spirited class in the city is made up entirely of people whose personalities are characterized by the *predominance* of this aggressive passion. The education of the Auxiliaries must therefore convey to them the reasonableness of their own subordination to the rule of reason when their psychological makeup prevents reason from being their own chief motivation— or, arguably, even an important motivation—for action. Their education has to inculcate a deference to reason in people who by definition cannot defer to reason on reasonable grounds. Moreover, while on the one hand they are supposed to be loyal to reason on reasonable grounds—as opposed to blind patriotism, partisan zeal, or hatred—their own vigilance on behalf of the supposedly natural conventions of the "city in speech" requires a large measure of unquestioning obedience and a capacity for outrage. While being told to be gentle, they are still expected to be capable of force.

These considerations bring us to what has been identified as one of the main logical quandaries of the *Republic*.[20] The two lower classes of the best community are each characterized by a predominantly nonrational trait, which is why they need to be ruled and moderated by the wise. Yet the individual soul is supposed to be able to achieve this harmony within itself. So why cannot the individuals making up each class achieve this harmony without being ruled by another class? There are at least three possible answers.

(1) Only the philosophical character can fully achieve the proper ordering of the soul. He is the only truly just and happy person. As Aristotle puts it in his critique of the *Republic,* this philosopher assimilates all virtues, including citizen virtues, to himself. Thus, although it is called a city, the optimal politeia of the *Republic* is really the household of one person.[21]

(2) The three parts of the soul are not absolute distinctions that correspond absolutely to the three classes of the city. Rather, they are modulations along a continuum of human traits whose three main tendencies are heightened by Socrates for heuristic purposes. In this view, a member of the Auxiliary class, although more spirited than reasonable, is still sufficiently reasonable that, reinforced by the right kind of education, he will participate to some degree in the philosopher's direct insights into nature—not enough actually to philosophize, or to philosophize fully, but enough to ground his self-control in the nature of the cosmos and so win the battle against desire and fanaticism. Moreover, as we observed in chapter 4, Socrates implies that reason itself has a spirited dimension not distinguishable from reason to the highly schematized degree required by the tripartite division of city and soul that was agreed upon in order to launch the discussion. This is the case both in the pragmatic sense implied in Book 4 that a ruler has to have the guts and spirit to back up reason's commands, and in the subtler sense I raised in chapter 3 that Socratic reasoning itself has an aggressive, refutational dimension as well as a holistic one. I suggested at the outset of this discussion of the *Republic* that the education of thumos to "see" represents Socrates' attempt to impart to the civic-spirited some of the "force" of his own skepticism so that they might resist the tug of the passions. In following that particular logos, we should always bear in mind the totality of eros and analysis—of Diotima and the Gadfly—from which that premise has been abstracted.

(3) The Auxiliaries are not capable of achieving inner harmony among the three states of each individual's soul. Consequently, as a class within the city, they will not be able to bear the rule of reason because their root pride and aggressiveness will eventually lead them to chafe against the restrictions of this unwarlike upper order, and to feel that their own honor is being slighted.

Possibilities 1 and 2 are not, in my view, incompatible. There are textual grounds for thinking that Socrates regarded all three possibilities as arguable. But in Book 8 he makes it clear that, while the third possibility might not always or quickly happen, it definitely will happen at some point in the evolution of even the best political ordering. It may be possible, at least in speech, to explore a political ordering that patterns the community on the transcendental good. But, set into the swirls and eddies of chance, contingency, and decay, of civil strife, ambition, and jealous honor, even this eidetic city is likely at some point to be sucked back into the primordial undertow of passion as the honor-seekers throw off the restraints of the wise (546a–547a).

THE CRITIQUE OF TYRANNY: RETURN TO THE PROBLEM
OF CALLICLES

In reviewing and concluding these studies, let us begin by returning to our start-ing point: the problem of Callicles. As I have argued, Callicles' eros for Demos and the dēmos is emblematic of the problem of whether and to what degree human nature with its longings for transcendence can be satisfied within a specific order-ing of the political community. In considering the *Gorgias,* we saw that the pri-mordialist ontology, although congenial to Callicles' attraction to the means for political mastery, cannot furnish him with an account of the ends for which his eros longs. The *Symposium* aims to provide this account, and thus helps illuminate Socrates' claim to Callicles that he alone undertakes the proper art of ruling. In Diotima's speech, political eminence is presented as the second-best object of eros—an approximation of the consummate dignity and repose that reside in the object of philosophical longing. In the *Republic,* however, political eros is dimin-ished and driven into the background, while the combative, self-defensive side of passion is highlighted and elevated by Socrates into one of the three parts of the soul. But in making this argument, Socrates reduces desire to pedestrian needs, treating it strictly as epithumia rather than eros. It is only by reducing eros to pedestrian hedonism that Socrates can so rapidly and plausibly establish the dis-tinctness and superiority of thumos. As long as desires are only for food, drink, or sex abstracted from their respective kinds of goodness, there is not too much trou-ble establishing the superior dignity, satisfaction, and reasonableness of self-con-trol. But if desire were treated, as it is in the *Symposium,* as the adjunct of an eros for union with the beautiful, Socrates would not find it so easy to override Glau-con's suggestion that thumos might be not be a "different nature" from epithumia. For if desire were directed by eros toward the soul's union with the beautiful, then thumos might well serve eros—including political eros—rather than the arid type of "calculation" that Socrates sketches as the lynchpin of the *Republic's* political psychology. Instead, the transcendent satisfaction that, in the *Symposium,* politi-cal fame approximates is, in the *Republic,* drained out of political life altogether and kept exclusively on the level of philosophy. Once he has reduced the scope of political life to a prisonlike cave of ignorant prejudice and painful confusion, Soc-rates allows eros to return to the foreground, but only as a motivation for wisdom. Thus, the problem of Callicles is dealt with in two ways by the other dialogues. In the *Symposium,* Socrates shows through his recounting of Diotima's teaching how the erotic longings of politically ambitious men like Callicles arguably point to philosophy by way of the civic association. In the *Republic,* however, the politi-cal part of the erotic continuum is given a cold shower, and the Calliclean type of personality is educated to be the grave and gracious guardian of philosophic morality. Such erotic longings as remain will be satisfied by philosophy or not at all. But even when political ambition has been divested of its erotic longing for transcendence and reduced to thumotic self-control and public-spiritedness, the problem of Callicles continues to haunt the *Republic*. For ambition chafes under the restrictions imposed on it by the rule of philosophy. The city is undone by the rebellion of the very part of the soul that was to have made reason politically efficacious.

And here is perhaps the supreme irony: It is Socrates himself—who regards the kallipolis as the pattern of a city "worthy of the philosophic nature" (497b), and whom we understandably regard as a candidate for philosopher-king in such a city—who is in effect its grave-digger. For, by training the Auxiliaries to elevate honor over pleasure, Socrates fashions the timocracy that will overthrow the aristocracy of philosophic Guardians. Similarly, we recall that Callicles' rebellious and truculent refusal to be persuaded to order his life according to the good was exacerbated by Socrates' arousal of his most combative instincts in the attempt to redirect his energies from the pursuit of pleasure to the strength of self-command. In this light, we can view the outcome of the "city in speech" in pragmatic political terms as an ironic recapitulation "writ large" of Socrates' encounter with the ambitious Callicles. It shows us the limited hopes he has of actually ruling the city, either directly or through the mediation of the civic-spirited.

The relation of the *Gorgias* to the *Republic,* then, is not one of progress and supersession, but of circularity. Socrates' proposals for the education of thumos represent only one path within Platonic political philosophy as a whole for answering the question of whether the soul's longing for transcendence might be satisfied through a particular political community. Diotima's Ladder represents a continuing dialectical foil for the procedure of the *Republic,* since according to it, eros is not the enemy of the good that needs to be expelled, but on the contrary the surest route to it. As the *Republic* heads toward the rebellion of the Auxiliaries in Book 8, we are provoked to reconsider whether virtue bereft of erotic pleasure is, after all, a likely inducement to serve the common good. At bottom, the Platonic way of asking about the good of the soul in relation to the political community revolves continually around both eros and thumos, pleasure and honor—abstracting one from the other so as to investigate the potentialities of each. The fall of the city in speech at the hands of the honor-seekers is Plato's way of returning us to his original evocation of the problem: Can someone like Callicles be satisfied?

The Return of Eros

The elaboration of the optimal city began with Socrates' attempt to prove that a just life was happy and satisfying "in the soul," regardless of the consequences of obeying the law. But by Book 4, it is difficult to maintain that the citizen as such is leading an intrinsically satisfying life, or at any rate a happy one. The Auxiliaries' satisfaction is the sense of honor that comes from upholding the constitution and the rule of reason. As Adeimantus and the others begin to object by Book 4, it is difficult to call these avatars of self-control happy, stripped as they are of family, property, and every other ordinary human satisfaction (419a). By Book 5, however, the need for the rule of philosophy obscures this problem by displacing the centrality of civic virtue per se with a new way of posing the question of the soul's satisfaction. Socrates finally fulfills the mission set for him by Glaucon and Adeimantus through their speeches at the beginning of Book 2. He does argue that a certain way of life is by nature both happiest and not prone to injustice. But it is the life of the philosopher, not the just and law-abiding citizen whose life Glaucon originally contrasted with that of the successfully unjust man. Moreover, the philosopher's justice does not stem from the thumotic self-mastery that they set forth in Books 2, 3, and 4 as the psychology of a well-educated citizen, but, on the contrary, from a self-abandonment to the pleasure of learning so complete that it leaves no energy for pleonexia.

This shift is particularly clearly illustrated when, in discussing the soul of the philosopher at the end of Book 5, Socrates reverses the premises he established earlier when presenting the soul in relation to the requirements of civic virtue alone. In Book 4, we recall, he insisted that the soul cannot achieve unity through any one of its actions. He denied that the desires promise any such unified erotic fulfilment, banishing them to a realm of witless impulse with eros lurking in the lowest "form" of the irrational. In Book 5, by contrast, Socrates uses fulsomely erotic language to evoke the soul's pursuit of knowledge. An "erotic man," he now tells Glaucon, loves everything that is beautiful, delightful, and worthy of attention (474d–475c). In order to stimulate Glaucon's imagination with the open vistas of philosophizing, Socrates allows himself a speculative wantonness that he had strictly forbidden earlier. Whereas earlier he denied that even mundane pleasures like eating and drinking were concerned with the goodness of their respective objects, in illustrating by analogy the philosopher's sampling of delights, he now claims that a person is not a good eater if he does not want the most delightful food available.

Much like Diotima, Socrates now depicts the longing for as many of the beautiful objects of desire as possible as an intimation of philosophic desire's longing for unity with true being—"the whole eidos"(475b). Like Diotima, he says that the erotic man who thirsts for "all" pleasure, rather than a merely partial happiness, must come to see that only philosophizing offers the prospect of consummate satisfaction. However, in contrast with Diotima, Socrates does not attempt to link civic virtue with philosophic pleasure as a continuous ascent. For Diotima, civic virtue participates in the prudence grounded in the erotic longing most fully experienced by philosophy. But Socrates draws a firmer line between the philosopher's grasp of the beautiful itself and the ignorance of the nonphilosophers. And whereas in Diotima's Ladder the lovers of honor are seamlessly subordinated to the philosophers, Socrates is frank about the political tension inherent in his own sharper distinction between adequate and inadequate knowledge. For, as he remarks to Glaucon about those who, like the Auxiliaries, merely opine rather than truly know, "What if [this man] gets harsh with us and disputes the truth of what we say? Will we have some way to soothe and gently persuade him, while hiding from him that he's not healthy?"(476e). The suggestion, immediately ensuing, of a middle ground of "correct opinion" between knowledge and ignorance is Socrates' way of trying to soothe the thumotic guard dogs past this shift in the argument that casts their whole education in shadows. "Correct opinion" sums up doctrinally the need that has all along been implicit to impart to the education of the Auxiliaries a status that will preserve its integrity while acknowledging its inescapable deficiencies in comparison to the philosopher's open-ended, full-time pursuit of the truth. To tell citizens that the convictions they cherish as the source of their self-respect are deluded is, after all, quite likely to make them angry.

The Image of the Sun with which Socrates sketches a philosophic education appeals above all to "seeing"—to an open-ended, unrestricted gazing upon the spectacle of "the whole eidos," including the interest in foreign gods that brought Socrates down to the Piraeus in the first place. But as we saw with the story of Leontius, the decent citizen exists in an element of blindness. In Socrates' own account of civic virtue—as opposed to the teaching about eros that he originally received from Diotima—it is doubtful whether the longing for erotic wholeness can be addressed on the level of civic life. As we recall from chapter 3, the seeress opened Socrates' eyes to the amazing phenomenon of political honor and urged him to pay attention to it so that he could reflect on it. In the *Republic*, I would suggest, we encounter some of the conclusions Socrates reached after Diotima did him the benefit of convincing him to look. How Socrates' reflections on political honor differ from the teaching about eros that Diotima employed to open his eyes to this phenomenon is summed up by Socrates' own Image of the Sun, the closest approximation of Diotima's Ladder in the *Republic* (508a–509c). The use of the sun with its warming powers of growth and fruition as an analogy in the visible realm for how all beings are summoned toward completion by the good is, like Diotima's speech, an erotic account of knowing. But it conspicuously omits all political and moral phenomena. Whereas Diotima knits together the eros for knowledge of the good with the noble longing for civic fame, Socrates banishes politics from the sunny realm of his epistemology to the dim recesses of the Cave.

We should qualify this, however, by adding that it is only in comparison with the splendors of philosophy evoked in this poetic way that politics looks so tawdry, and that Socrates heightens these splendors through his use of images because his main purpose in those passages is to convert Glaucon into one of his philosophic friends. After he has been initiated into the pleasures of philosophizing, Glaucon could return to a somewhat more balanced assessment of political virtue in comparison with philosophic virtue of the kind that we certainly find in other dialogues. Moreover, whatever the provenance of the Images of Philosophy in Books 6 and 7, the discussion *continues* to preserve the doctrine of "correct opinion" set out in Book 5, which establishes a twilight middle ground for citizen virtue between complete ignorance (darkness) and philosophic knowledge (the sun). Although the presentation of the philosophic soul in Books 5, 6, and 7 is a shift from the presentation of the politically virtuous soul in Books 2, 3, and 4, both stages of the discussion are preserved intact. Because of this middle ground for civic virtue, the *Republic* does not float off entirely after Book 5 into the empyrean realms of first philosophy or the private friendships of Socrates' inner circle. Correct opinion saves the phenomenon of civic justice, enabling Socrates to proceed to try to resolve the original question of whether the just life is preferable to the unjust life.

Correct Opinion as the Middle Ground between Philosophy and Civic Virtue

"Correct opinion," doctrinally formulated midway through the dialogue as the status of the knowledge with which the Auxiliaries are inculcated, is the hinge between the civic and philosophic educations (476a–480a, cf. 429c). Because correct opinion participates in genuine knowledge, the satisfaction of civic honor can be clearly distinguished from the superior satisfaction of philosophy without thereby simply being negated. Socrates can treat the meaning of civic-spiritedness as largely a settled matter by Book 4 and proceed to resolve the initiating question of whether the just life is preferable to the unjust life. The formal results of the discussion up to this point can thus be summarized as follows: if the difficulties we have noted with correct opinion do not cause the civic education to break down under the simmering "doubleness" of thumos, this education can be assumed to have dealt with the potential of the warlike part of the soul for tyranny. Indeed, it is the doctrine of correct opinion grounding the status of civic virtue that enables Socrates and the others to perform the ascent from primordial to transcendental limned in the Image of the Cave itself. After the logos leads them up toward philosophical transcendence in the middle books (Books 6 and 7), Socrates and his interlocutors do their duty according to the Image of the Cave and go back down to the "in- between" of correctly ordered politics in Books 8 and 9. In this respect, the tawdry status to which the Images of the Sun and Cave metaphorically reduce politics is in some measure reversed when the Images are reintegrated with the dialectical ascent from which they emerge and whose components they crystallize. For the ascent would not have been possible except by way of the search for clarity about the true nature of justice "in the soul." Whatever may be the difficulties with reforming political life in the direction of the good studied by philosophy, at a minimum it would seem as if philosophizing in the Socratic sense is not a way of life that one can reach by leaping over political and moral concerns. As we observed in chapter 3, the investigation of civic virtue is the subject matter of philosophical erotics.

In going back down to their original, more pragmatic concern with finding the best way of ordering the city, Socrates and his companions do, however, return to the discussion of the best way of life with an altered sense of its basic elements — just as the Image of the Cave tells us would happen to someone who returned to everyday life after glimpsing the light at the top (515d–516b). For, in the meantime, the just life as a life of law-abidingness has been assimilated to the philosophic life. By Book 9, therefore, the philosophic life is explicitly used as the foil for exposing the deficiencies of the tyrant's life, formally resolving the debate initiated by Glaucon's comparison of just and unjust lives in Book 2. While Socrates began by attempting to demonstrate that justice makes for an intrinsically happier life than tyranny, he ends up demonstrating that philosophy, which entails justice, makes for an intrinsically happier life than tyranny.

Glaucon introduced the feverish pleasures of eros into the hypothetical city, and he and Socrates agreed that until eros was present, they could not fully study the unjust life or the contrasting life of justice. But the significance of eros was immediately driven underground by Socrates' abstraction of thumos from the rest of the passions and its elevation as the basis of civic-spiritedness. Book 9 formally takes up this long-neglected erotic aspect of Socrates' mission in the dialogue to defend justice and criticize injustice. The famous critique of tyranny in Book 9 is a more elaborate version of the arguments Socrates employs with Callicles in the *Gorgias*: the tyrant's life of unrestrained eros is really a life of pain—chaotic, degrading, leading to a constant fear of competitors. By contrast, the philosopher's pleasures are calmly ordered, do not depend on exploiting others, and are hence more pure and free of pain (*Republic* 579a–c, 582a–583a). In a way, therefore, Book 9 offers a resolution of the impasse to which Socrates and Callicles are brought in their encounter. Only when he has reintroduced the theme of eros in the *Republic* after initially suppressing it is Socrates equipped to make a full response to the Calliclean type of personality, which is, in its spontaneous emergence, as fundamentally motivated by pleasure as it is by honor or anger.

And eros is the tougher call. For honor can be more readily satisfied within an austere republican aristocracy like the Auxiliaries than can pleasure. The thumotic man's angry resentment of competitors or superiors can be co-opted to a rigorous defense of communal equality and decency within the citizen body. In effect, he can revenge himself for the pain he causes himself by successfully resisting pleasures on behalf of the civic code by punishing those who step out of line or aim too high. Thumos is the passion best suited for conversion to the defense of justice, and justice is the one virtue that unambiguously relates us to other people and minimizes our selfish detachment from the community. But erotic longing requires personal satisfaction, even if this satisfaction is achieved through the performance of deeds that benefit others. Even in Diotima's hopeful rendition of political eros as naturally inclined to just and moderate statesmanship, the man who longs for fame through serving the common good must have an individual concrete experience of personal pleasure and fruition—the "offspring" of present and future glory. Both eros and thumos have natural proclivities to serving the common good that education and persuasion can fortify. But thumos is more directly oriented toward zeal on behalf of a common code, while eros spontaneously tends more to tyranny with its promise of supreme personal pleasure and mastery. For Socrates, the greatest danger proceeding from an excess of thumos is that it will become too zealous a guardian of the common good, while the greatest danger from excessive eros is a kind of rule that is, in effect, an anticonstitution, swallowing up any notion of the common good whatsoever (563e, 565d–e).

Socrates is considerably better equipped in Book 9 of the *Republic* to refute tyranny than he is in the *Gorgias*. Let us briefly recall the career of eros in the dialogues we have considered. Socrates implied to Callicles that his argument about the best way to live was grounded in his own life. In contrast with the confusion betokened by the different objects of Callicles' longing having the same name, Socrates' love is a whole clearly articulated by a rank ordering of parts—philosophy and politics. In the *Symposium*, the feminized "Madame Philosophy" who Socrates claims to Callicles directs his speeches emerges full-blown as the seeress Diotima with her beautifully sober praise of love. The *Republic* attempts to account for the more belligerent side of political ambition that Diotima softens—or of which she is perhaps insufficiently aware—in contrast with the skeptic Socrates. Having presented an account of the thumotic soul in which its honor-seeking kind of satisfaction is arguably best satisfied by a moderate politeia, Socrates can then revive philosophy in all its splendor through the reinterpretation of the soul on an openly erotic basis. Philosophy thus emerges in Book 9 ready to refute the tyrannical longings typified by Callicles' love of the dēmos, having been established by the preceding investigation both as the governor of pride and ambition in the political community *and* as the most erotically satisfying way of life for an individual.

But there are, I suggest, at least three problems with this way of defending justice and critiquing tyranny. Would Callicles not have to be a philosopher, or at least philosophically inclined, in order to assent to this demonstration of philosophy's superiority? Even granting that philosophizing somehow does confer more of the kind of delight that most people benightedly seek through limitless sexual intercourse and other excesses (a rather big if), the hedonistic superiority of philosophy in a way simply begs the question of what to do if you are a tyrant who does not feel himself fit, as it were, to aspire to such heights. Does the proof of tyranny's inferior pleasure leave the tyrant or would-be tyrant who cannot philosophize free to go on as before? This is one of the difficulties, I think, with deriving justice from a kind of philosophic immoderation that, on Socrates' view of human nature, will typify a very few exceptional people, and trying to make this exceptional vocation stand for moral decency in general as opposed to the extremes of tyrannical self-indulgence. As an illustration of the self-serving uses to which it might be put, we might recall Alcibiades' ambivalent profession of his inferiority to Socrates in the *Symposium*. It is doubtless sincere in part. But by placing the exemplar of virtue on a level far removed from himself, it suspiciously insulates him from giving up his enormous political ambitions.

Then there is the problem of whether even a person who does have the potential to philosophize is equally open at every stage of life to the Socratic argument for abjuring tyrannical temptations. Glaucon, who is not yet committed to his path in life, may be more readily bedazzled by the prospect of "turning around" to look at the light than someone like Callicles, who has already burned some of his bridges.

Finally, there is the problem of the citizen who does not want to exploit the city, but whose ambition to serve is such that he demands a leading role in its affairs. This type of leader is not a tyrant in the sense of the monster of hedonistic depravity criticized in Book 9. At the same time, such a ruler can clearly pose a threat to the equality of the other citizens and their opportunity to participate in government. If he does not want to philosophize, yet is not a monster of pleasures, and is also not content with the honor of equals such as that enjoyed by the Auxiliaries, where does he fit in?

Posing the debate over the best life as a contest between philosophy and tyranny seems to exclude the whole realm of nontyrannical inegalitarian statesmanship. The realm of the greatest political achievements and honor in response to the most serious issues of internal justice and stability or external relations—the realm of Pericles, Lincoln, or Churchill—must, on the argument of Book 9 for defending justice against the tyrannical extremes of injustice, either sink to the level of the tyrant's depravity or disappear into the empyrean bliss of the philosopher. This is the problem Aristotle identifies when he criticizes Socrates for failing to distinguish phronēsis (the practical wisdom of a statesman) from sophia (the wisdom sought by speculative philosophy and metaphysics).[22] As we return to the Cave, then, we must return to the problem of Callicles. For, assuming that Socrates might convince such a man that he should avoid the depraved self-indulgence of the tyrant as he is offered up for judgment in Book 9, has Socrates left any alternative for someone who is convinced to this extent of the need for moderation but who still prefers a life of political action to one of contemplation?

Altogether, then, the relationship between the philosopher and the citizen remains highly problematic in the Platonic exploration of whether and to what extent reason might govern. For both the claim that philosophers should rule and the claim that philosophic pleasure is superior to tyrannical pleasure, while on one level vindicating Socrates's self-defense in the *Apology* as the ally of virtue, on another level undermines the status of all nonphilosophic statesmanship and the virtues of non-philosophic citizens. Even in the optimal "utopian" situation of the *Republic*, as we have seen, the relationship between the philosopher and the citizen is fraught with difficulties. The rebellion of the Auxiliaries against their philosophic Guardians in Book 8 appears to suggest that their education does not "take" over the long run. Although the education of the Auxiliaries begins as a proto-philosophic one in Book 2 (inasmuch as it includes a theology based on eidos), in the course of the optimal regime's pseudo-historical evolution "in speech," it emerges that the natures of the Auxiliaries and of the philosophers are too different from each other for a single kind of education to make them friends. The "doubleness" of thumos, which paideia was first introduced in Book 2 in order to heal, bursts the constraints of the civic education.

Given the real life of Athens in which Socrates conducts his conversations, with its tumultuous and sometimes lethal political rivalries, we can sense from Socrates' ironical assertion in the *Gorgias* that he alone truly "rules" in the city how great the practical objections are to one such as himself exercising authority. Certainly Socrates has some success in making philosophic friends from among his fellow citizens. Some of these people have more influence in political affairs than Socrates himself, and to the extent that they befriend him, they do provide intermediaries between him and the dēmos. Socrates was certainly not a total failure in winning these intermediaries—the vote of the jury at his trial was close (a change of thirty votes would have acquitted him [*Apology* 36a]).

But even Socrates' philosophic friends, as we have seen, retain reservations or disagreements that they do not express, while some of the more overtly political actors are not persuaded at all. Hence, for example, while the Sophist Thrasymachus is tamed and won over by Socrates, his sidekick Cleitophon is simply silent after his single brief attempt at an argument with Socrates' proxy Polemarchus (*Republic* 340a–b). Just as the taciturn Meletus does not accept Socrates' basic premise that the city's laws and conventions are open to doubt and reflection, so does the taciturn Cleitophon see no need to distinguish between what rulers believe to be advantageous and what knowledge would reveal to be truly to their advantage. The action of the dialogues repeatedly reminds us that Socrates' acquisition of philosophic friends is not necessarily tantamount to the acquisition of political friends, or making inroads among the larger citizenry, and that even his philosophic friends have lapses into demotic behavior.

Callicles will talk with Socrates for a time, but then, like Meletus and Cleitophon, he refuses to converse. He is a halfway house between the philosophic and the demotic. What makes him such an alluring figure in the Platonic dialogues is that his eros spontaneously emerges as both political and transpolitical. On the face of it, he presents an equally compelling case for the natural openness of human beings to high political ambition and to a longing for knowledge as opposed to mere opinion. Callicles needs philosophy because he wants to live the good life according to nature rather than convention, even though he does not believe the good life that philosophy discovers to be philosophy itself. At the same time, his eros for political mastery entails a need for honor and virtue both in himself as a lover and in his choice of a beloved—including, most interestingly, the political community he wants both to possess and to revere. As we observed earlier, in his great speech, it is Callicles who comes forward as the philosopher and who brings philosophy (as opposed to rhetoric) into the open for the first time in the *Gorgias*. It is he who, in contrast with Socrates' moralizing, speaks openly of nature, the philosophers' concern. Disdaining appeals to common opinion, he offers to set the "mob orator" Socrates on the right track by instructing him in the difference between the noble and just by nature and the noble and just by convention (*Gorgias* 482c–483a). Doubtless this is all said with some bravado—pre-empting a competitor's claim to the high ground is a tried and true rhetorical technique. But it also stems from a genuine need on Callicles' part to find someone capable of understanding this distinction. He wants to convert Socrates to a dedication to the advent of the natural master, a curious reverse parallel to Socrates' search for devotees of philosophy. A thoughtful and conflicted citizen like Callicles may need Socrates even more than Socrates needs him as a subject for investigation, and this neediness helps to illustrate how Socrates can be philanthropic through refutation.

The cumulative outcome of Socrates' encounter with Callicles is that erotic yearnings for political satisfaction such as Callicles evinces may open up trans-political yearnings of the sort that only philosophy can satisfy, yearnings that cannot be satisfied even partially on a political level. The question this outcome leaves unanswered is: What is a man like Callicles to do if, convinced that political mastery will prove to be gall and bitter wormwood, a disappointment, if not downright dangerous due to the fickleness of Demos, the wanton beloved, he nevertheless cannot or does not wish to philosophize either?

In spite of Callicles' ambitions for a political career, from the evidence we possess he "disappears" after his performance in the *Gorgias*. More than one explanation is possible for this disappearance, not only from recorded history, but from the internal world of the dialogues, where other characters like Glaucon and Alcibiades do recur. He may disappear because, on reflection, he is persuaded by Socrates to renounce his ambitions for political mastery and philosophize—hence, as Dodds suggests, he may actually be a telescoped version of Plato's own biography.[23] On the other hand, he may disappear because Socrates has ruined him for politics by undermining his confidence and his joy in the prospects of political pre-eminence without succeeding in enlisting him in the philosophic life—especially since, because of the peculiar constraints of the *Gorgias*, Socrates is not able to offer Callicles a really tempting picture of philosophy's erotic satisfactions.

The third possibility is that Callicles becomes like the kind of moderate citizen, working modestly for a more virtuous politics wherever possible but eschewing grand ambitions, that Socrates prescribes in the course of their dialogue. In this case, it is only natural that he would not have attracted history's attention in the same way as the glorious but ruinous career of Alcibiades. Decent citizens are indistinct; the Auxiliaries in the *Republic* are difficult to picture as individuals, rather like what Tolstoy says about happy families. Callicles' disappearance into moderate but anonymous citizenship might illustrate how philosophy could govern the ambitious proximally and at a remove from actual political power through a philosophic culture, transmitted over the generations, that attracts the "best natures" Socrates describes in Book 5 of the *Republic*—people who are otherwise attracted to the life of an Alcibiades (494c–495b). While no attempt was made during classical antiquity to implement literally the rule of philosophy (the claims of the mad Caligula being the exception that proves the rule), this philosophic culture did become important through the schools. Statesmen like Scipio Africanus and Marcus Brutus did understand themselves, in effect, as virtuous Auxiliaries serving the higher idea of philosophy—a subservience no doubt made easier for them to bear by the fact that they did not serve any actual philosopher-kings.

In suggesting that Plato leaves the status of nonphilosophic statesmanship in serious doubt, I do not mean to suggest that he despairs of the prospect altogether. On the contrary, any such prospect is likely to be strengthened, rather than weakened, by subjecting it to a suitably Socratic skepticism about the adequacy of our knowledge of virtue. Before one can tenably hypothesize a harmony among the parts of the soul and the parts of the city, one must persevere in thinking through their contradictions. I have tried to show in this and earlier chapters that, although the paideia linking citizen and philosopher in Socratic statecraft emerges battered from the severe dialectical rigors to which Socrates himself subjects the hypothesis, it nevertheless does survive, or at least is never wholly refuted. Let me conclude with a brief overview suggesting what gold may have been culled from the dross of doubt and negation.

In its fundamental and most straightforward meaning, "politics" concerns what human beings share in common, expressed in their civic association. In this sense, Socrates can be said to be the only person who "practices politics" because he of all Athenians is exclusively preoccupied with what is truly most common to all human beings—their place in the cosmos. We have summed up the Platonic basis for the pursuit of an epistēmē of statesmanship with the argument that "soul comes first" in the cosmos (*Laws* 892). Technē is an intimation of the orderliness and harmony that characterize the cosmos, not an anthropocentric tool for human mastery. The Platonic Socrates' critique of the primordialist ontology offers the prospect of a formal solution to the problem of the philosopher's relationship to the city exemplified by the *Clouds*. In Aristophanes' presentation of Socrates, he is outstandingly moderate, oblivious to pain and pleasure. But his science is of a kind that puts him across a gulf from politics and morality. In the Platonic dialogues, by contrast, it emerges that only the cosmologist par excellence can offer a grounding for the knowledge needed to promote civic virtue.

To be sure, this is not what we ordinarily mean by political affairs. The civic association is ordinarily concerned with harsher and blunter necessities of war and peace, wealth and poverty, crime and punishment. Only in a very attenuated sense can political life be said to deal with issues of cosmic significance, and even then the connection would ordinarily be through a form of religious worship sanctioned or patronized by the regime. At bottom, then, only if the political community needs some kind of window on the wider world, some kind of direct link to what is universally true, and only if this connection is best supplied by philosophy (rather than, say, through the traditional worship of the gods), can it make sense to say that philosophers should rule, or even advise statesmen. The Platonic dialogues explore this hypothesis. They lead us to reflect on the possibility that we cannot know what good laws are—and therefore cannot deal with issues of war and peace and internal controversy—without knowing what the virtues of the soul are, and we cannot know what these virtues are without reflecting on the place of human life in the cosmos. Socrates argues repeatedly that we need to clarify the eidos of a virtue before we can decide whether a given instance of behavior illustrates the virtue or not—as opposed to simply observing what people do when they claim to be exercising such a virtue and concluding that the virtue must consist of all these (sometimes quite contradictory) instances (*Phaedo* 99e–100d, *Euthyphro* 5d, 6d–e). Insofar as the city turns out to need laws and policies based on knowledge rather than custom or convention, while the philosopher may not need the city, the city may indeed need the philosopher.

Even though the optimal politeia—the city patterned directly on the good such that every tension between the good of the individual and the common good is eradicated—may neither be possible nor in every sense desirable, when we step back from the *Republic* and consider Platonic political philosophy as a whole, there are still grounds for hoping that civic life can be improved in the direction of reason. Since the *Republic* is something of a cold shower for the aetiology of political honor outlined in Diotima's Ladder, let us remember that neither dialogue need be taken as privileged. Just as the *Republic* provides a skeptical corrective to Diotima's Ladder with its altogether tougher appraisal of the motives for civic honor and the passions that undermine virtue, so we should return to the *Symposium* to complement the rather strict divide between virtue and pleasure to which the *Republic* leads us in order to arrive at a more balanced cumulative assessment.

As I argued in chapter 3, the core of Socrates' claim to practice politics and to undertake the art of rule resides in the philosophical erotics revealed by the *Symposium*. For Socratic eros is a form of pleasure—hence in a way egoistic and self-perfecting—that is at the same time philanthropic. The benefit to others is not, moreover, a mere second-order consequence of the pleasure, the outward appearance of moderation in a man who is inwardly immoderately devoted to philosophy. Instead, the philanthropic action is bound up with the very essence of the pleasure. In this way, as I suggested, philosophical erotics are the inner core of the "Stoic" position that Socrates argues most consistently in the *Apology*: that he is selflessly devoted to the discussion of virtue and so serves the city better than anyone else. Philosophical erotics also, I now want to argue, mitigate the strikingly "Stoic" account of political psychology that Socrates offers in Book 4 of the *Republic,* leading to an apparent bifurcation between civic virtue and pleasure.

I have suggested that one of Socrates' purposes in the *Republic* in radicalizing the pleasure to be obtained from philosophizing by draining it from civic virtue is to win over the young Glaucon as one of his philosophic friends. Politics is reduced to a cave of ignorance and pain the better that philosophy might be depicted by contrast as a dazzling personal ascent to the young man. I went on to argue that the progress of Glaucon's own philosophic initiation will restore a more balanced relationship between civic and philosophic virtue. For when we look back at the whole progress of the dialogue, it is the original search for natural justice that enabled them to enact the dialectical ascent from primordial to transcendental that the Image of the Cave encapsulates. In proceeding to discuss the defective constitutions and the deficiencies of tyranny in Books 8 and 9, they go back down toward the political reflections from which that ascent initially emerged. But, having ascended, they return equipped with enough light to distinguish the real elements of political morality from the mixture of being and shadow with which they began in their initial groping for justice. Indeed, to amplify an earlier textual observation, when Socrates first broaches the discussion of defective regimes at the end of Book 4 (before he is compelled by the young men to return to the topic of erotic relations in the best regime), he uses metaphors that anticipate the Image of the Cave yet to be introduced in Book 7—they have now "come to a place" where they can see justice and injustice more clearly "from a lookout as it were" (444a, 445b–c). The ascent from civic virtue to philosophic transcendence and back to civic virtue preserves political philosophy as a necessary propaedeutic for reflection. When we reintegrate the value of political philosophy in the *Republic* as the beginning of the ascent to transcendence with the philosophical erotics of the *Symposium*, "practicing politics" emerges altogether as good, both for the ascent to philosophizing and as the primary way in which Socrates cultivates his friends.

Thus, the question of what kind of middle ground is occupied by civic virtue returns us to the nature of philosophical erotics. We saw in chapter 3 that erotic satisfaction for Socrates is indivisibly political philosophy. This is so because the questions with which Socrates probes his interlocutors to pangs of fruitful self-reflection emerge from wondering about the meaning of civic virtue, friendship, and the art of ruling. Socrates practices politics and the art of ruling in order to gratify his pleasure at benefiting his friends.

The *Republic* tells us that the correct opinion of a well-educated citizenry is a middle ground between wisdom and ignorance. We recall that Diotima depicted eros—including the eros for political honor—as a middle realm, a great demon knitting together man and the gods. In the *Symposium,* the philosophical and political reaches of this in-between are closely connected. Eros rises to philosophizing by way of the political longing for immortality. By the same token, philosophizing is the surest source of the prudence that statesmen need to govern their cities with moderation and justice. In the *Republic,* however, the middle ground where civic virtue dwells is more wan and evanescent than the second rung of Diotima's Ladder. This is because the *Republic's* analytical account of the soul, and the division of labor within the soul and the city, tend to drive the soul's components of desire, spirit, and wisdom further apart and demarcate them more strictly. Whereas Diotima's Ladder firmly grounds civic excellence in the longing for transcendence, in the *Republic* civic excellence sometimes seems in danger of vanishing between the pleasures of philosophizing and the habituation of the Auxiliaries to do their duty. There is more of a disjunction between philosophical self-perfection and moral self-mastery. The *Republic* does not include civic virtue as being among the pure pleasures of soul in the unambiguous, unqualified way that Aristotle, for instance, does in the *Nicomachean Ethics*.[24]

Still, just as in chapter 3 we referred to the *Republic* to qualify the holistic account of the soul offered by Diotima, now we should recall that holistic unity in order to qualify the hardness of Socrates' distinctions in the *Republic* between pleasure and duty. Whereas the purpose of Diotima's speech was to think through the unity that underlies the soul's distinctions, the purpose of the *Republic* is to think through the distinctions that render problematic any permanent harmony between the good and a particular ordering of the political community. But the philosophical erotics of the *Symposium,* issuing in friendship devoted to the understanding of virtue, are implicit in the argument of the *Republic* as well. The *Symposium* elaborates eros as a positive doctrine that the agonistic action of the dialogue—especially after the entrance of Alcibiades—undercuts and qualifies. The *Republic* does the reverse. The analytical account of the soul (established with the principle of one man, one job) suppresses the erotic continuum linking its parts, thereby throwing into much sharper relief the tensions between civic justice and philosophic pleasure. But the conversational quest for justice in the *Republic* is itself a progressive ascent toward transcendence, an ascent fueled by the eros and courage of Glaucon that reconnects the elements of the soul broken down by analysis. The ascent is crystallized in the Images of Philosophy in Books 6 and 7. The Images of the Sun, Divided Line, and Cave delineate what Diotima's Ladder synthesizes: the ontological, epistemological, and political dimensions respectively of the soul's search for fulfilment through union with the beautiful and the good. But Glaucon's conversion to the splendors of philosophy in Books 6 and 7 only comes after, and by way of, his initial longing for a natural basis for justice "all alone in the soul." It is his own erotic longing for the natural basis of civic virtue that links the separate dimensions of the three images together. Moreover, in wooing Glaucon with the pleasures of philosophizing, Socrates demonstrates the same rhetorical skills grounded in philosophical erotics that he displays in the *Symposium.* Just as, there, he fashioned the speech of Diotima in order to win Agathon's friendship, here he devises the three Images in order to woo Glaucon to a friendship devoted to the good. As we observed in chapter 3 in considering Diotima's three parallels between eros and the whole, in both the *Symposium* and *Republic,* eros is the "demon" linking the human and the divine, grounding correct opinion as the intuitive first grasp of the soul's continuous ascent to knowledge and happiness (*Symposium* 202e–203a).

Putting together the two routes to transcendence offered by the *Republic* and *Symposium* then, we find that they converge in eros. For although the soul must be thought through in both its unity and differentiation, its unity is the primary ground. As Hegel observes,[25] whereas modern philosophy establishes the primacy of Subjective being over Immediate being—establishes, in other words, the striving for mastery that Plato traces to thumos as the ground of whatever Immediacy is created through cumulative historical action—for Plato, analysis and division are entailed by the Immediate being that always already summons all beings toward their respective completions. At bottom, philosophical erotics are demonstrated as clearly and convincingly in the *Republic* as in the *Symposium.* The logos

of the *Republic* leads the soul up from "the Piraeus"—up from the shadowy constituent elements of the city in commerce and familial relations—through the
nature of civic excellence toward the light of true being. It then leads the soul back
down to see the nature of politics newly clarified. The soul's need for wholeness
is a recurrent and uncompletable ascent from civic life toward wisdom. Virtue is
neither a tragic battle against unfathomable necessity, nor is it the triumph of the
lone natural individual over fraudulent convention. It is, as Diotima teaches, a
wondrous necessity that emerges within the in-between of the human concerns
with honor and pleasure that constitute the political community. "Eros wants the
good to be one's own forever."

NOTES

1. Thomas Hobbes, *Leviathan,* ed. C. B. Macpherson (Baltimore: Penguin Books,
1971), 161.
2. See the excellent article by Skemp on how the psychology of thumos epitomized by
Leontius in Book 4, and especially by Leontius's failure to master his desires, prefigures
the rebellion of the Auxiliaries in Book 8. J. B. Skemp, "Causes of Decadence in Plato's
Republic," *Government and Opposition* 17 (Winter 1982): 80–93.
3. On the tenuous character of the best regime in the *Republic* in general, see Diskin
Clay, "Reading the *Republic,"* in *Platonic Readings/Platonic Writings,* ed. Charles L. Griswold, Jr. (New York: Routledge, 1988).
4. As Allan Bloom observes, there appears to be no "form" of the city in the argument
of the *Republic.* Allan Bloom, "Response to Hall," *Political Theory* 5, no.3 (1977):
115–118.
5. Jacob Klein, *A Commentary on Plato's Meno* (Chapel Hill: University of North Carolina Press, 1965), 115–118.
6. Alexandre Kojève, "Tyranny and Wisdom," in *On Tyranny* by Leo Strauss (London: Collier-Macmillan, 1963), 144–162.
7. Stanley Rosen, "Heidegger's Interpretation of Plato," *Journal of Existentialism*
(Summer 1967) : 477–504.
8. Sophocles, *Oedipus the King,* in *Sophocles 1,* ed. and trans. David Grene and
Richard Lattimore (Chicago: University of Chicago Press, 1973).
9. Augustine *City of God* 7.3.
10. Seth Benardete, *Herodotean Inquiries* (The Hague: Martinus Nijhoff, 1969), 11–16.
11. On the deepening of Apollo by the Dionysian, see Eliade, *Religious Ideas,* 267–274.
According to Scully, the cult center of Apollo at Delphi embodies this relationship. Vincent Scully, *Architecture: The Natural and the Man-made* (New York: St. Martin's Press,
1991), 57–63.
12. As Euben notes, at the beginning of the play, Oedipus thinks he is the child of tuchē
or fortune, independent of nomos or convention. J.P. Euben, *The Tragedy of Political Theory* (Princeton: Princeton University Press, 1990), 98, n.8.
13. On the *Republic's* greater affinity with comedy than with tragedy, consider Euben,
Tragedy, 241 and Arlene Saxonhouse, "Comedy in the Callipolis," *American Political Science Review* 72, no. 3 (September 1978):888–890.

14. As Skemp observes, after Book 4 "we forget Leontius" until the rebellion of the Auxiliaries in Book 8. Skemp, "Causes of Decadence," 91.

15. Aristotle *Nicomachean Ethics* 1102a.20–26.

16. See W. R. Newell, "Superlative Virtue and the Problem of Monarchy in Aristotle's *Politics*," *Western Political Quarterly* (March 1987): 159–178; Newell, "Tyranny and the Science of Ruling," 108–130; and Newell, "Machiavelli and Xenophon," 889–906.

17. See Edward Andrew, "Descent to the Cave," *Review of Politics*, 45, no. 4(1983): 510–535. See also Dale Hall, "The *Republic* and the Limits of Politics," *Political Theory* 5(1977); Bloom, "Response to Hall;" and Bloom, *Republic*, 407–408. As regards the *Republic*, I incline more to Bloom's view than to that of Andrew or Hall. But I am also arguing that, for Plato, philosophic happiness in general is unintelligible apart from the philosopher's concern with civic virtue, at least to the extent that the debate about its meaning forms the core of his philosophical friendships. As I have argued, this is the only sense we can make of Socrates' claim that, although politically powerless, he actually does "rule" here and now in Athens.

18. Thucydides *The Peloponnesian War* 1.75–77.

19. Drew Hyland, "Plato's Three Waves and the Question of Utopia," *Interpretation* 18, no.1 (Fall 1990):103–107.

20. See B. Williams, "The Analogy of the City and Soul in Plato's *Republic*," *Phronesis* supp. vol. 1 (1973): 196–206; J. R. S. Wilson, "The argument of *Republic* IV," *Philosophical Quarterly* vol.26, no. 103 (April 1976); J. L. Stocks, "Plato and the Tripartite Soul," *Mind* 24 (1915); F. A. Wilford, "The Status of Reason in Plato's Psychology," *Phronesis* 4 (1959).

21. Aristotle *Politics* 1261a.10–22. See also J. Cooper, "The Psychology of Justice in Plato," *American Philosophical Quarterly*, 14, no. 2 (April 1977): 151–157; and Newell, "Superlative Virtue," 159–178.

22. Aristotle *Nicomachean Ethics* 1141a.10–1141b.5; 1143b–1145a.10.

23. Dodds, *Gorgias*, 14, 267.

24. Aristotle *Nicomachean Ethics* 1117b.30–35.

25. G. W. F. Hegel, *Phenomenology of Spirit*, trans. A. V. Miller (Oxford: Oxford University Press, 1979), 10.

Conclusion

Socratic Statesmanship

Throughout this book, I have mostly dealt with what might be termed the positive Socratic prescription for civic virtue and some of its inner tensions and ironies. By way of concluding this study, I would also like to dwell more specifically on the place in the political community of the philosopher himself, both as citizen and thinker. In modern times, Hegel and Nietzsche have rekindled interest in "the problem of Socrates"—that is to say, whether and to what degree philosophic rationality is compatible with, or on the contrary is corrosive of, the closed moral horizon of any people or community.[1] Even granting that Socrates might be able to tell the non-philosophic citizens how to live (and it is far from self-evident that he possesses this wisdom), is it clear that he himself can live this way? How are we to reconcile the education of the Auxiliaries in certain fixed opinions about the virtues with Socrates' defiant claim at his trial that "the unexamined life is not worth living" (*Apology* 38a)? Is any stable view of virtue compatible with philosophic skepticism? On the other hand, it would seem impossible to commit oneself to any specific civic association or code of justice if, like Socrates, one is always in doubt about what to believe. As Hegel observed, the *Apology* is a tragedy because both sides are right.[2]

Having tried to elaborate the Platonic understanding of eros in the *Gorgias, Symposium,* and *Republic,* let me conclude this study by summarizing what I think, on the evidence of those dialogues, are some of the main issues that arise from this tension between philosophy and civic virtue. Both of what I have termed the two paths to transcendence—love and honor, rooted respectively in eros and thumos— have a problematic relationship both with philosophy and with the requirements of a well-ordered political association. As I have shown, each constitutes a very different kind of path to the good. In Diotima's speech in the *Symposium,* eros rises continuously from civic virtue to wisdom. In the *Republic,* by contrast, the relationship of eros and thumos to both civic virtue and philosophy is more complicated. Thumos is indubitably the basis for civic virtue in the soul, but only dubiously a path to philosophy, while eros is indubitably excluded as a basis for civic virtue and reintroduced solely as the route to philosophy.

185

It may be that, contrary to Diotima's Ladder, wisdom and civic virtue are not intrinsically related objects of the soul's longing, or at least not seamlessly related. As we have seen, there are grounds for thinking this to be Socrates' considered view, as opposed to the more optimistic view of their relationship that he ascribes to Diotima. According to the *Symposium,* as I have argued, it may have been Diotima who first convinced Socrates to pay attention to the love of honor, which she grounds in eros, and in this respect, Socrates' initiation by her into the rites of eros symbolizes his "turn" from natural science to political science. As if in keeping with this initiation, in his first encounter with Alcibiades, Socrates reasons as if an eros for world fame and power could lead the ambitious young man continuously to a more philosophic self-awareness, entailing more thoughtful statecraft along the way (*Alcibiades 1* 105a–c).[3] But in the long run Socrates does not succeed in moderating Alcibiades. Indeed, he may only have fueled Alcibiades' ambitions for tyranny without these ambitions acting as a spark for philosophical reflection— and, in so doing, increased the distrust of the Athenians for Socrates himself, whom they knew to be one of Alcibiades' associates. Partly as a consequence of how things turned out with Alcibiades, I have suggested, Socrates takes a more sober view of the relation of eros to virtue, so that in the *Gorgias* and *Republic* we find him focusing more on the spirited side of the soul as the basis for an austere politics of communal moderation, reserving eros for the delights of philosophy alone and discouraging an erotic intoxication with political fame and glory. Thus, it is questionable within the cumulative arguments of the *Republic,* and even the *Symposium* itself, whether Diotima's teaching that philosophic eros entails, in a smooth ascent, an eros for civic virtue stands up to scrutiny.

If the relationship between philosophic eros and civic virtue is a shaky one, the relationship of thumos to civic virtue is also problematic. Although (as I argued in chapters 4 and 5) Socrates believes thumos to be a more reliable basis than eros for civic virtue in the soul, it is still questionable whether the need of thumos for a closed educational horizon to tame its Achillean belligerence and zeal is compatible with philosophy's ongoing skepticism toward any fixed moral conventions. As Socrates argues in the *Republic,* a certain kind of paideia *may* prove capable of reconciling civic virtue and philosophy. But one cannot presuppose any such harmony—as Socrates warns us, the argument will be a long one full of myths (376d). The famous parallel between the city and the soul introduced in Book 2 of the *Republic* is supposed to reconcile thumos with philosophy, making civic-spiritedness serve reason in both a soundly ordered individual and a soundly-ordered community. But the rest of the *Republic* comprises an extended reflection upon whether this reconciliation is tenable either in the individual or the city. As we saw, the education of the Auxiliaries does indeed impart to them certain quasi-philosophic tastes and character traits. But the problem of thumos remains a ticking time bomb within the unfolding of the kallipolis, exploding with the revolt of the Auxiliaries and the collapse of the best regime.

The dialogue form keeps the ambiguous relationship between philosophy and civic authority an open question by making Socrates himself a character in the discussions. "The problem of Socrates" centers on the fact that he was executed for philosophizing, and all the Platonic dialogues circle around this awful event. Although the *Apology of Socrates* concerns the last events in Socrates' life, by most assessments it is among the first works Plato wrote. In other words, the gateway to the Platonic world is the massive and appalling fact that a philosopher was tried and executed by his fellow citizens, and not by a particularly repressive society, but indeed by the most open-minded of Greek city-states, one that prided itself on combining democracy and empire with learning. In reading the Platonic dialogues, we are always being asked to wonder why this trial took place, and what Socrates did that got him into such trouble. How can we reconcile the apparent admiration and loyalty of his friends with a hostility on the part of the larger population strong enough to sustain an indictment on a capital offense? How could Socrates' life-long concern with virtue have been considered seditious and corrupting? As we consider the likelihood of Socrates' hypothesis that philosophy might govern civic virtue, we must also bear in mind the profound controversy surrounding Socrates' own fitness as a citizen.

In the *Apology,* Socrates begins by recalling the depiction of himself in Aristophanes' play the *Clouds* (18b–19d). In that play, Socrates is depicted in broad strokes as a representative "Sophist," precisely the kind of person from whom the Platonic Socrates is constantly and radically distinguished. The Aristophanean Socrates believes that rigorous knowledge is possible only from the study of the physical universe (for example, astronomy and geography) and mathematics. His way of relating himself to the moral and political concerns of his fellow citizens is to teach techniques of deceptive rhetoric for pay. He can make the weaker argument the stronger (exactly as the real Socrates was eventually charged with doing), and he attracts the debt-ridden Strepsiades with the prospect of arming him with techniques for defeating his creditors in court.

In the *Apology,* Plato's Socrates appears to recall the *Clouds* in order to tell his accusers: If you plan to convict, please convict me for what I actually am, not for how I am lampooned in this play. The story of the Delphic Quest purports to show that, in contrast with Aristophanes' portrait, Socrates does indeed share with his fellow citizens the concerns about justice and morality presided over by the gods. He now seeks rigorous knowledge of these human concerns, not the natural sciences. By attempting to displace Aristophanes' portrait of him with his own self-presentation as being engaged on a mission on behalf of the Oracle to seek clear knowledge of virtue, Socrates was apparently building up to what he hoped would be a dialogue with Meletus, his chief accuser, that would refute the indictment.

This dialogue, however, is a striking failure. Meletus refuses to admit any ambiguities or doubts in his purblind assertion that Socrates alone corrupts the Athenians (25a, 26e). Subsequently, as if giving up on any possibility of reaching a common ground with Meletus for discussing the indictment, Socrates presents himself in a more aggressive, uncompromising light. He is no longer the servant of the Oracle joined with his fellow Athenians in awe of Apollo, but a gadfly who goads and stings them into reflection about virtue (30e). However, the two self-presentations are not entirely at odds. Socrates' service of the Oracle consists of testing its extraordinary praise of himself. Moreover, while the Oracle had gone no further than to claim that "no one is wiser" (21a) than Socrates (meaning to say that everyone else could conceivably be just as wise or just as ignorant), in Socrates' own reformulation of the Oracle's pronouncement (21b) he is "wisest"—a larger claim that already lets us hear the gadfly's buzz within the holy precincts of Apollo's temple. Socrates tests the Oracle's praise of his wisdom by subjecting it to a skeptical examination in contrast with the claims to wisdom of others. It is almost as if, when God told Noah that He had chosen to spare him from the flood because he was the most righteous man living, Noah had replied: We'll see about that. The upshot is that, in comparison with the claims to wisdom of other authoritative figures (such as poets, politicians, and artisans), the Oracle's praise of Socrates' wisdom is confirmed. But Socrates confirms the Oracle by reacting to it initially with complete doubt, and in the process of attempting to confirm this doubt, he deflates the reputations of the political community's conventional moral authorities (including the "seers," among whom would presumably be numbered the Oracle's own priestess [22c]). On these grounds, Socratic piety might well be identified with sedition. Take away the reverent housing of the Delphic Quest, and you find the Gadfly, an annoyingly critical creature of a different species from the horse he torments.

But Socrates' peculiar skepticism-within-piety, and even his openly contrarian self-presentation as the Gadfly, could be exculpatory *if* Socrates is correct about the central contention of his self-defense: that he does indeed benefit his city and educate it to virtue by subjecting its beliefs to relentless skepticism. For if this were so, it might be the city's own morality and piety, not Socrates' way of life, that stand in need of correction, including reforms of theology and education such as the *Republic* hypothesizes. Does Socrates' unvarnished claim toward the end of his defense that the "unexamined life is not worth living" establish that his philosophic activity does indeed contribute to the Athenians' virtue, as opposed to undermining it? This is the question we must ultimately bear in mind when pondering the *Gorgias, Symposium,* and *Republic.* At least on the face of it, Plato's answer is clear. In the *Republic,* Socrates, in defending philosophers against the charge entertained by Adeimantus that they are vicious and useless to the city, says the city itself is the biggest Sophist, leading the best natures astray and corrupting them into preferring power, wealth, and prestige to virtue (492b–c, 493a–c). The Platonic Socrates accepts none of the responsibility for Athens' corruption. Not only does he not exacerbate the corrupting influence of the city, he alone stands against it. He alone "practices politics," as he puts it in the *Gorgias* (521d). He cares exclusively for virtue to the sacrifice of all his other interests (*Apology* 31b–c). Indeed, there can be no relief from the city's ills unless philosophers rule (*Republic* 473d).

In turning to the *Gorgias, Symposium,* and *Republic,* we saw how Socrates engages some of his fellow citizens in the kind of speculative dialogue about virtue and the good life against which Meletus sets his face. Meletus is an enemy. But Socrates' interlocutors in the dialogues usually already entertain doubts about how they and their fellow citizens should be living. Hence they are open to discussion and friendly to Socrates as someone who might clarify their perplexity. Another question that arose from considering these three dialogues was whether Socrates is indeed able to find a bridge among these prospective civic leaders between philosophy as a life of ceaseless self-examination and the closed horizon necessary for civic commitment and action. Does he succeed in enlisting any of his fellow Athenians in his claim to want to reform rhetoric and make it serve a statesmanship based on justice and moderation? Do his efforts to engage his friends and interlocutors in reflection on virtue plausibly succeed in benefiting them while not only not detracting from their civic attachments, but positively improving the character of political life? What sense, again, are we to make of Socrates' strange assertion in the *Gorgias* that he alone "practices politics" in Athens? Here is where the positive doctrine of civic virtue grounded in eros and "the problem of Socrates" come together, mediated by the study of the soul.

The aim of this book has been to explore these questions by focusing on the crucial middle realm of psychology. Socrates claims to provide a kind of therapy for the soul, educating its passions of eros and thumos toward their proper fulfilment so as to make his interlocutors more virtuous and happy. As I have argued, this claim is the trait that most clearly and radically distinguishes the Platonic Socrates from the Socrates of the *Clouds.* Where the Socrates of the *Clouds* is blind to the passions of the nonphilosophic, blind to the moralistic rage of Strepsiades that eventually does him in, Plato presents Socrates as a psychologist of unsurpassed finesse, a diagnostician par excellence of anger, erotic longings, and troubled love life. Plato's transformation of the ascetic natural scientist in the *Clouds,* hanging in a basket and looking down upon mere human concerns with bleak and constipated contempt, into the man who begins his dialogue with Callicles by diagnosing Callicles' love life, and who puts himself in the role of both inseminator and midwife for the pangs of self-doubt he awakens in the pregnant souls of young men like Glaucon and Theaetetus—all this is an astonishing reversal. As I argued in chapter 3, eros is the hidden heart of Socratic skepticism, the Dionysian secret behind the Stoic carapace of the *Apology,* the unexpected link between the centrality of civic virtue to philosophy and the deflation of every settled opinion provoked by philosophy.

The problem remains, however, whether an eros for philosophy of the kind I have just summarized can also govern the thumotic part of the soul that forms the psychological basis for civic virtue in a well-governed polity. This is the question I took up thematically in chapters 4 and 5. Broadly stated, there is a difference between the philosophical longing for an understanding of virtue and the practical art of governing the virtuous, a difference glossed over but not eradicated by the paradoxical job description of "philosopher-king" in the *Republic*. Whereas the *Symposium* links eros and thumos in a seamless subordination of civic virtue to the longing for wisdom, the *Republic* strains their alliance to the breaking point, while insisting on their reconciliation nevertheless. The consistent theme, as I have tried to show, is the Platonic Socrates' exploration of eros as a hypothetical link between philosophy and civic virtue. The dialogues themselves call the hypothesis constantly into question, whether through Socrates' irony about his own claims or through the dissatisfactions of his interlocutors and his failure to convince them. Callicles and Alcibiades are willing to converse, but they eventually reach a point where, like Meletus, they will not be drawn into further dialogue. Thus, even in leisurely conversations about virtue, to say nothing of the pressing exigencies of political practice, Socrates' proposed alliance between philosophy and civic-spiritedness is fragile and dubious, as is his own capacity to govern men of action like these even conversationally. It remains an open question whether Socrates is substantially more successful in the dialogues at establishing this link between philosophy and statesmanship than he is in his trial, where the absence of this link is made lethally apparent by his conviction. As I have argued at some length, rhetoric and education emerge as especially important candidates for an intermediary between unconstrained philosophical speculation, on the one hand, and a rigorous civic morality, on the other.

For reasons such as these, in exploring the possibility of a Socratic cure for tyrannical eros, I have always stressed (to return to a remark from the introduction to this book) that it is at best a possibility. The difficulties explored by the dialogues of knowing for certain what this treatment would be, and of persuading the patient to undergo it, are Plato's way of pointing to the larger issue of the troubled relationship between philosophy and politics altogether. For us to take Socrates seriously as an effective diagnostician and therapist of tyrannical eros, we would have to take seriously the prospect of Socrates as a statesman, or at least an advisor to statesmen. And yet, the dialogues we have considered constantly call into question Socrates' ability even to persuade interlocutors relatively well disposed to him like Callicles and Alcibiades in private conversation to abandon their pursuit of political mastery. At bottom, Plato invites us to consider the Socratic cure as a way of thinking through the ironies and complexities of the uneasy relationship between philosophical reflection and political authority.

The passionate longing for preeminence and victory may prove to be less susceptible to philosophical therapy than is immediately evident from Socrates' statements or even from what the intended beneficiaries of this therapy such as Callicles and Alcibiades profess to believe. At a certain point, Callicles and Alcibiades stop listening. As I suggested in chapter 3, even Alcibiades' most fulsome praise of Socrates' superiority to himself is in part a self-serving stratagem for avoiding actually acting on Socrates' advice about how to change his life. That Callicles and Alcibiades stop listening much further along in their exchanges with Socrates than does his prosecutor Meletus, who shuts up after a few minutes, is a measure of how successful Socratic persuasion can be under circumstances more favorable than a public trial on a capital offense. But it is also a measure of how far this persuasiveness would have to travel before it would actually stop someone from pursuing their political ambitions.

Of course, the ability to persuade someone already inflamed with tyrannical ambitions to give them up is a lot to demand of any philosophy. It is an extreme case. As I have argued, the civic education Socrates sketches in Books 2 and 3 of the *Republic* responds to his failure with the proto-tyrants Callicles and Alcibiades by exploring how to forestall the extreme case from arising. By suggesting how someone might be educated from earliest age so as to absorb a taste for harmony and order, Socratic paideia explores the prospect of nipping tyrannical eros in the bud. As we saw in chapters 4 and 5, however, the same problems that emerge from the proposition that Socrates can cure the would-be tyrant also emerge from the proposition that philosophy must rule the city in order to put such a civic education in place. By purging the citizen class of the best regime of the ungoverned erotic longings that characterize tyranny, Socrates arguably goes some way toward curing tyranny by forestalling the psychological aberration that impels it. But the passion of spiritedness that characterizes the citizen purged of eros presents its own set of equally formidable obstacles to the rule of reason over the soul.

The civic paideia of the Auxiliaries is presented as a path to and a preparation for philosophizing, inasmuch as the divine "forms" of their civic theology (*Republic* 380d) constitute an adumbration of the forms eventually revealed as ordering the cosmos. Initially, the Auxiliaries are not categorically distinguished from the Guardians, and when the Guardians first emerge as a special subgroup of the Auxiliaries toward the end of Book 3, their education is at first depicted as an extension of the education in cosmic harmony set forth earlier, not as an alternative to it (412d–e). It can hardly be otherwise at this early stage in the discussion, since the best regime is premised on the hypothesis that thumos can philosophize. But because the Auxiliaries are at length inclined to resist the rule of reason—inclined by the very passion of thumos that forms the basis for their civic zeal—in having Socrates trace the stages of this education, Plato subjects it to a suitably Socratic skepticism. The *Republic* as a whole invites us to consider the limitations of the identification of an education in civic virtue with wisdom. The relationship between philosophy and civic virtue turns out to be neither a smooth nor a continuous ascent. The civic education of the *Republic* repeatedly provokes us to ask whether (as Diotima teaches) philosophy and civic virtue are intrinsically connected (albeit ranked) objects of the soul's longing for completion, or whether instead a life of civic virtue and a life of philosophizing might be fundamentally different and even in conflict.

The education of the Auxiliaries hinges on the proposition that the acquisition of civic virtue through the inculcation of "correct opinion" can be satisfying and fulfilling in the same manner as philosophical reflection, or at least in some degree. This is already implied when, in introducing the theme of paideia in Book 2,

Socrates identifies thumos with a philosophical capacity to "see" the difference between being and nonbeing (376a–b). But as that education unfolds, we grow progressively aware of the tensions between the open-ended skepticism of Socratic philosophizing and the fixed beliefs necessary for the Auxiliaries if they are to perform their duty as protectors of the community and enforcers of the Guardians' authority. Based on everything we can observe about Socrates as a character in the Platonic dialogues, were he to find himself living in the optimal regime that he and his interlocutors elaborate in the *Republic,* he would be just as likely to confront and criticize the beliefs of the Auxiliaries as he does those of the Athenians. Indeed, as I suggested in chapter 4, the "analytical" theory of the soul that Socrates presents in the *Republic* as the grounding for the education of the Auxiliaries flatly contradicts the "holistic" psychology that Socrates sets forth in the *Symposium* and, when turning from civic virtue to philosophy, in the *Republic* itself. In other words, even as the elaboration of the best regime unfolds, Socrates begins to dissent from his own hypothesis for a psychology to ground the education of its citizens.

By trying to think through the tension between, on the one hand, Socrates' identification of philosophy with open-ended questioning and, on the other, the claim implicit in the Auxiliaries' education to have settled the meaning of the good life in a fixed and authoritative form, we find a path to the underlying question of whether the Platonic Socrates really does emerge as a good citizen from the dialogues. It is Plato himself who provides us with the evidence for unfolding "the problem of Socrates" in a way that will not brook easy solutions. It is Socrates more than anyone else who forces his fellow citizens to confront their most cherished convictions and prejudices, and to this extent erodes the bonds of nomos — of authoritative laws, customs, and mores — that unite the political community.

As I have tried to show, particularly in chapters 3 and 5, for Socrates, political philosophy provides the subject matter for an erotic ascent to transpolitical contemplation, and as such is the indispensable propaedeutic for the theoretical life. It is in this sense that Socrates can claim to "rule" Athens. Making his interlocutors think about the meaning of the political good is the best route to making them think about the good per se. Thus, as I argue, Socrates practices politics by cultivating friendships devoted to philosophy rooted in the shared investigation of virtue. He is philanthropic because he is aggressive on behalf of love. What I term Socrates' philosophical erotics unite the proto-Stoic Socrates of the *Apology* (manning his post for virtue) with the barefoot seducer of the *Symposium.* But we cannot presuppose that the rarefied politics of this Socratic circle of friends is necessarily in harmony with the actual requirements of statesmanship and civic commitment. Philosophical friends are not necessarily the same as political friends or friendly citizens. Philosophical friends share bonds of affection that arise from the common good of their shared investigation of virtue, an investigation on which no conventional limitations can be placed. Civic friends, on the other hand, share bonds of affection that arise from their sharing a common sense of decency and loyalty to the laws and customs of their country. Insofar as Socrates acquires friends by prompting them to question all political orthodoxy, he loosens the hold of these conventional beliefs on the citizens, and to this extent undermines the basis of their special friendship as members of a political association.

As we saw in chapters 4 and 5, Socrates well understands that even in his own optimal polity, the citizens will likely become "angry" when it dawns on them that the education that makes them civic friends is viewed by their own philosophic rulers as possessing the status of mere opinion rather than truth. Whereas the Socrates of the *Clouds* is unprepared for Strepsiades' angry rejection of his education in the distinction between nature and convention on behalf of outraged morality, the Platonic Socrates has the psychological sensitivity to see it coming. It transpires that, for a variety of reasons, thumos cannot "see," or if so, only dimly. If even the Auxiliaries of the best regime are likely to grow angry at philosophy's undermining of their convictions, how much more likely it is that citizens like Meletus or Cleitophon will grow angry as they grasp that the friendship of Socrates' intimates stems from the common good of investigating, and thereby undermining, the basis for loyalty and affection among citizens. For these reasons, we need to look long and hard at the ostensible Platonic claim that Socrates, far from exacerbating the inclination toward tyranny of intimates like Alcibiades and Critias as is implied by the *Clouds,* was the only person in Athens who stood firmly against those tyrannical inclinations. For behind the ostensible claim is the more complicated possibility that, precisely by placing philosophy far above tyranny as the best way of life, Socrates may indeed have contributed to the appeal of tyranny in contrast to ordinary nonphilosophic civic virtue.

It is not self-evident, in other words, that people like Callicles and Alcibiades were simply benefited by their exposure to Socrates. Since they were temperamentally incapable of living the philosophic life with its rigors of ceaseless self-examination, their exposure to Socratic skepticism may have further corroded their attachment to the conventional virtues. Philosophy may be, as Socrates argues in Book 9 of the *Republic,* erotically more satisfying than tyrannical pleasures. But if civic virtue is not harmonious with the pleasures of philosophizing, then there is no reason necessarily to suppose that civic virtue is erotically more satisfying than tyranny. If the highest happiness does not entail civic virtue, why should those citizens whose primary avocation is not philosophy prefer a life of austere citizen virtue to the pleasures of tyranny? If one cannot ascend to the highest happiness of philosophy, why not settle for tyranny, according to the *Republic* itself the second-best erotic satisfaction? Socrates' accusers might have been right that Socrates harmed those around him.

These are some of the obstacles to the positive Socratic prescription for the reform of civic virtue that emerge from a considered assessment of the *Gorgias, Symposium,* and *Republic.* Formidable as they may be, however, I have also tried to show that paideia survives this internal critique. The possibility of a civic education that in some manner unites the concerns of civic commitment with those of unprejudiced philosophical reflection remains at least an open question throughout the dialogues considered in this book, if not a hard and fast prescription. The reason for its survival has not only to do with the need of human beings for a politics guided by knowledge rather than untutored passion, convention, or prejudice—the fundamental Socratic assertion that virtue is knowledge—but with what I have tried to establish is the inner character of Socratic philosophizing itself. Socratic skepticism applies to skepticism itself. If we are indeed called upon to examine everything, we cannot exempt doubt. If we fail to doubt doubt, no thought, including skepticism, is possible, for there can be no link between the knower and the known; the world is *maya*, form is illusion. As I argue in chapter 3, love and reverence are as necessary to Socratic philosophizing as are doubt and refutation, and ontologically more fundamental. Not only in the soul of the citizen, but in the soul of the philosopher, eros entails thumos. The analytical account of the soul is only intelligible on the basis of the holistic account.

Accordingly, while we should beware of taking Socrates' positive claims as an educator and psychotherapist too literally or optimistically, we should also resist an unself-conscious Augustinianism that deflates from the outset the very possibility of erotic wholeness through a natural love of the beautiful, which grounds prudence and good citizenship. Irony must be ironic about itself; it must not forsake the edifying surface for the abysmal depth, or degenerate from open-mindedness into cynicism. It is unlikely that Plato would have written thirty-five dialogues to serve no purpose other than to demonstrate the impossibility of philosophically guided civic virtue and a love of the noble that might plausibly reconcile statesmanship with the desire for wisdom. In looking at this hypothesis for a harmonious relationship between philosophy and civic virtue, I have tried to show how Plato calls it constantly and radically into question. But I also try to show how Plato rescues the hypothesis so that it remains at least plausible, and perhaps even strengthened in its plausibility by being subjected to such a severe internal critique. Ultimately, Plato directs us to eros over refutation, to wholeness over skepticism, and to gentleness over aggression. The Gadfly can be derived from the Delphic Quest, inasmuch as skepticism is a necessary moment in the search for clarity. But the reverence and wonder before the whole that the Quest symbolizes cannot be derived from the Gadfly. Skepticism cannot ground itself, but must be stirred in us by an eros for the wholeness that we sense we lack.

NOTES

1. See, for example, G.W.F. Hegel, *Hegel on Tragedy,* ed. Anne and Henry Paolucci (New York: Doubleday/Anchor Books, 1962), 346–350, 358–362; and Nietzsche, *Twilight of the Idols,* 473–479.

2. Observing that Socrates was tried for impiety and for alienating his young followers from their families ("corrupting the youth"), Hegel comments that his claim to be guided by a demonic sign really was subversive: "[S]ince established religion was identified with

public life so closely that it constituted a part of public law, the introduction of a new god who formed self-consciousness into a principle and occasioned disobedience, was necessarily a crime. We may dispute with the Athenians about this, but we must allow that they are consistent." As for familial piety, it was "the substantial key-note of the Athenian state. Socrates thus attacked and destroyed Athenian life in two fundamental points; the Athenians felt and became conscious of it. Is it then to be wondered at that Socrates was found guilty? We might say that it had to be so" (Hegel, *Tragedy,* 388–389).

3. Socrates begins by confessing his erotic passion for Alcibiades (104c), but quickly goes on to intrigue the young man about himself, by telling Alcibiades what Socrates has divined about him from afar—his matchless ambition for fame among all human beings (104d–105c).

Bibliography

PLATO: EDITIONS, TRANSLATIONS, AND COMMENTARIES:

Four Texts on Socrates. Translated with notes by Thomas G. West and Grace Starry West. Ithaca: Cornell University Press, 1984.

Gorgias. Translated by W. C. Helmbold. New York: Bobbs-Merrill, 1952.

Gorgias. A revised text with introduction and commentary by E. R. Dodds. Oxford: Oxford University Press, 1979.

The Laws of Plato. Translated with notes and an interpretive essay by Thomas L. Pangle. New York: Basic Books, 1980.

Platonis Opera. Edited by J. Burnet. 5 vols. Oxford: Clarendon Press, 1902.

Plato's Theaetetus. Translated and with commentary by Seth Benardete. Chicago: University of Chicago Press, 1986.

The Republic of Plato. With critical notes, commentary, and appendices by James Adam. 2 vols. Cambridge: Cambridge University Press, 1920.

The Republic of Plato. Translated with notes and an interpretive essay by Allan Bloom. New York: Basic Books, 1968.

The Statesman. Translated with introductory essays by J. B. Skemp. London: Routledge, 1961.

Symposium. Translated with introduction and notes by Alexander Nehemas and Paul Woodruff. Indianapolis: Hackett, 1989.

The Symposium of Plato. Edited with introduction, critical notes, and commentary by R.G. Bury. Cambridge: W. Heffer and Sons, 1932.

OTHER PRIMARY AND SECONDARY LITERATURE:

Al Farabi. "Plato's Laws." In *Medieval Political Philosophy,* edited by Ralph Lerner and Muhsin Mahdi. Ithaca: Cornell University Press, 1972.

Andrew, Edward. "Descent to the Cave." *Review of Politics* 45, no. 4 (1983).

Artistophanes. *The Clouds*. In *Four Texts on Socrates,* translated by Thomas G. West and Grace Starry West. Ithaca: Cornell University Press, 1984.

Aristotle. *Nicomachean Ethics*. Translated by H. Rackham. London: Loeb Classical Library, 1977.

———. *Politics*. Translated by H. Rackham. London: Loeb Classical Library, 1967.

Augustine, Saint. *The City of God*. Translated by Gerald G. Walsh. New York: Image Books. 1958.

Benardete, Seth. *Herodotean Inquiries*. The Hague: Martinus Nijhoff, 1969.

———. *The Rhetoric of Morality and Philosophy*. Chicago: University of Chicago Press, 1991.

———. *Socrates' Second Sailing*. Chicago: University of Chicago Press, 1984.

Bloom, Allan. "Response to Hall." *Political Theory* 5, no. 3 (1977).

Bremmer, Jan. *The Early Greek Concept of the Soul*. Princeton: Princeton University Press, 1987.

Clay, Diskin. "Reading the *Republic*." *Platonic Writings/Platonic Readings*. Edited by Charles L. Griswold, Jr. New York: Routledge, 1988.

Cole, Thomas A. "The Relativism of Protagoras." In *Yale Classical Studies*. Vol. 22, edited by Adam Parry. Cambridge: Cambridge University Press, 1972.

Cooper, John. "The *Gorgias* and Irwin's Socrates." *Review of Metaphysics* 35 (March 1982).

———. "The Psychology of Justice in Plato." *American Philosophical Quarterly* 14, no. 2 (April 1977).

Craig, Leon. *The War Lover: A Study of Plato's "Republic."* Toronto: University of Toronto Press, 1994.

Cross, R. C., and A. D. Woozley. *Plato's "Republic": A Philosophical Commentary*. New York: St. Martin's Press, 1966.

Dodds, E. R. *The Greeks and the Irrational*. Berkeley: University of California Press, 1984.

Eliade, Mircea. *A History of Religious Ideas*. Vol. 1. Chicago: University of Chicago Press, 1978.

Euben, J. Peter. *The Tragedy of Political Theory*. Princeton: Princeton University Press, 1990.

Foucault, Michel. *The Use of Pleasure*. Translated by Robert Hurley. New York: Vintage Books, 1986.

Freeman, Kathleen. *Ancilla to the Pre-Socratic Philosophers*. Oxford: Basil Blackwell, 1948.

Friedlander, Paul. *Plato: An Introduction*. Princeton: New Jersey: Princeton University Press, 1973.

Gadamer, Hans-Georg. *Dialogue and Dialectic*. Translated by P. Christopher Smith. New Haven: Yale University Press, 1980.

Gould, John. *The Development of Plato's Ethics*. New York: Russell and Russell, 1972.

Grant, George P. *Technology and Empire*. Toronto: House of Anansi, 1969.

Griswold, Charles L. "*Politikē Epistēmē* in Plato's *Statesman*." In *Essays in Ancient Greek Philosophy*. Vol. 3, edited by John Anton and Anthony Preuss. Albany: State University of New York Press, 1989.

———. *Self-knowledge in Plato's "Phaedrus."* New Haven: Yale University Press, 1986.

Grube, G. M. A. *Plato's Thought*. London: Methuen, 1935.

Guthrie, W. K. C. *The Greek Philosophers*. New York: Harper Torchbooks, 1975.

———. *History of Greek Philosophy*. Vol. 1. Cambridge: Cambridge University Press, 1969.

———. *The Sophists*. Cambridge: Cambridge University Press, 1983.

Hall, Dale. "The *Republic* and the Limits of Politics." *Political Theory* 5 (1977).
Hall, Robert. "Psyche as Differentiated Unity in the Philosophy of Plato." *Phronesis* 8 (1963).
Halperin, David. *One Hundred Years of Homosexuality.* New York: Routledge, 1990.
Hegel, G. W. F. *Hegel on Tragedy.* Edited by Anne and Henry Paolucci. New York: Doubleday/Anchor Books, 1962.
————. *Phenomenology of Spirit.* Translated by A. V. Miller. Oxford: Oxford University Press, 1979.
Heidegger, Martin. *Early Greek Thinking.* Translated by David F. Krell. Chicago: Harper and Row, 1984.
Herodotus. *The History of Herodotus.* Translated by David Grene. Chicago: University of Chicago Press, 1988.
Hesiod. *The Homeric Hymns and Homerica.* Translated by H. G. Evelyn-White. Cambridge: Loeb Classical Library, 1977.
Higuera, Henry. "Persuasion and the Citizenry in Ancient Democracy: A Platonic Perspective." Paper presented at the annual meeting of the Proceedings of the Southern Political Science Association, November 1989.
Hobbes, Thomas. *Leviathan.* Edited by C. B. Macpherson. Baltimore: Penguin Books, 1971.
Homer. *The Iliad of Homer.* Translated by Richmond Lattimore. Chicago: University of Chicago Press, 1973.
————. *The Odyssey of Homer.* Translated by Richmond Lattimore. New York: Harper and Row, 1968.
Hyland, Drew. "Plato's Three Waves and the Question of Utopia." *Interpretation* 18, no. 1 (Fall 1990).
————. *The Virtue of Philosophy.* Athens: Ohio University Press, 1981.
Irwin, Terrence. *Plato's Moral Theory.* Oxford: Clarendon Press, 1977.
Jaeger, Werner. *Paideia.* Vol. 1. Translated by Gilbert Highet. New York: Oxford University Press, 1965.
Kant, Immanuel. *The Critique of Practical Reason.* Translated by Lewis White Beck. Indianapolis: Bobbs-Merrill, 1956.
Klein, Jacob. *A Commentary on Plato's "Meno."* Chapel Hill: University of North Carolina Press, 1965.
Klosko, George. *The Development of Plato's Political Theory.* London: Methuen, 1986.
————. "The Insufficiency of Reason in Plato's *Gorgias*." *Western Political Quarterly* 36 (1983).
Kojève, Alexandre. "Tyranny and Wisdom." In *On Tyranny,* by Leo Strauss. London: Collier-Macmillan, 1963.
Kosman, A. "Platonic Love." *Phronesis.* Supp. vol. 2. Edited by W. H. Werkmeister. (1976).
Kraut, Richard. "Egoism, Love and Political Office in Plato." *Philosophical Review* 82, no. 3 (1973).
————. *Socrates and the State.* Princeton: Princeton University Press, 1984.
Nanikhian, George. "The First Socratic Paradox." *Journal of the History of Philosophy* (1973).
Nelson, Lowry, Jr. "Alcibiades' Intrusion in Plato's *Symposium*." *Sewanee Review* 94 (1986).

Newell, W. R. "Machiavelli and Xenophon on Princely Rule: A Double-Edged Encounter." *Journal of Politics* 50 (February 1988).

———. "Superlative Virtue and the Problem of Monarchy in Aristotle's *Politics.*" *Western Political Quarterly* (March 1987).

———. "Tyranny and the Science of Ruling in Xenophon's *Education of Cyrus.*" *Journal of Politics* 45 (February 1983).

Nicholls, Mary P. *Socrates and the Political Community: An Ancient Debate.* Albany: State University of New York Press, 1983.

Nietzsche, Friedrich. *The Twilight of the Idols.* In *The Portable Nietzsche,* edited and translated by Walter Kaufmann. New York: Viking Press, 1974.

Nussbaum, Martha. *The Fragility of Goodness.* Cambridge: Cambridge University Press, 1983.

Pangle, Thomas L. Introduction to *Studies in Platonic Political Philosophy,* by Leo Strauss. Chicago: University of Chicago Press, 1983.

———. "The Political Psychology of Religion in Plato's *Laws.*" *American Political Science Review* 70, no. 4 (December 1976).

Plutarch. *Plutarch's Lives.* Translated by John Dryden. New York: Modern Library, 1964.

Ricoeur, Paul. *Fallible Man.* Translated by Charles Kelbley. Chicago: Henry Regnery, 1965.

Rosen, Stanley. "Heidegger's Interpretation of Plato." *Journal of Existentialism* (Summer 1967).

———. *Hermeneutics as Politics.* New York: Oxford University Press, 1989.

———. *Plato's Symposium.* New Haven: Yale University Press, 1968.

———. *The Quarrel between Philosophy and Poetry.* New York: Routledge, 1993.

Sachs, David. "A Fallacy in Plato's *Republic.*" In *Plato II,* edited by G. Vlastos. Indiana: University of Notre Dame Press, 1978.

Santas, Gerasimos. "Plato on Goodness and Rationality." *Revue internationale de philosophie* 40 (1986).

Saxonhouse, Arlene. "Comedy in the Callipolis." *American Political Science Review* 72, no. 3 (September 1978).

Scully, Vincent. *Architecture: The Natural and the Man-made.* New York: St. Martin's Press, 1991.

Shorey, Paul. *What Plato Said.* Chicago: University of Chicago Press, 1968.

Skemp, J. B. "Causes of Decadence in Plato's *Republic.*" *Government and Opposition* 17 (Winter 1982).

Sophocles. *Oedipus the King.* Translated by David Grene. In *Sophocles I,* edited by David Grene and Richard Lattimore. Chicago: University of Chicago Press, 1973.

Stocks, J. L. "Plato and the Tripartite Soul." *Mind* 24 (1915).

Strauss, Leo. *On Tyranny.* Ithaca: Cornell University Press, 1968.

———. "Plato's *Apology of Socrates and Crito.*" In *Studies in Platonic Political Philosophy,* edited by Thomas Pangle. Chicago: University of Chicago Press, 1983.

———. *What is Political Philosophy?* Westport, Conn.: Greenwood Press, 1973.

Tait, Marcus B. "Spirit, Gentleness and the Philosophic Nature." *TAPA* 80 (1949).

Thucydides. *The Peloponnesian War.* Edited by John H. Finley, Jr. New York: Modern Library, 1951.

Vlastos, G. "The Individual as Object of Love in Plato." *Platonic Studies.* Princeton: Princeton University Press, 1981.

————. "The Theory of Social Justice in the *Polis* in Plato's *Republic.*" In *Interpretations of Plato,* edited by H. F. North. Leiden: E. J. Brill, 1977.

Wilford, F. A. "The Status of Reason in Plato's Psychology." *Phronesis* 4(1959).

Williams, B. "The Analogy of the City and Soul in Plato's Republic." *Phronesis.* Suppl. vol. 1 (1973).

Wilson, J. R. S. "The Argument of *Republic* IV." *The Philosophical Quarterly* 26, no. 103 (April 1976).

Xenophon. *Cyropaedia.* 2 vols. Translated by Walter Miller. London: Loeb Classical Library, 1968.

————. *Memorabilia, Oeconomicus, Symposium, Apology.* Translated by E. J. Marchant and O. J. Todd. London: Loeb Classical Library, 1968.

Zeigler, Gregory. "Plato's *Gorgias* and Psychological Egoism." *Personalist* 60(1979).

Zuckert, Catherine, ed. *Understanding the Political Spirit.* New Haven: Yale University Press, 1988.

Index

About the Author

Waller R. Newell is professor of political science and philosophy at Carleton University in Ottawa, Canada. He was educated at the University of Toronto and Yale University. He is the author of numerous books and articles on classical, Renaissance, and modern European political philosophy and literature, including *What Is A Man? 3,000 Years of Wisdom on the Art of Manly Virtue,* and co-author of *Bankrupt Education: The Decline of Liberal Education in Canada.* He has been a Fellow of the Woodrow Wilson International Center for Scholars in Washington, D.C., a Fellow of the National Humanities Center in Research Triangle Park, North Carolina, and a John Adams Fellow at the Institute of United States Studies at the University of London. He has also held a National Endowment for the Humanities Fellowship for University Teachers and a Social Sciences and Humanities Research Council of Canada Postdoctoral Fellowship.

KING ALFRED'S COLLEGE
LIBRARY